PROJECTIONS OF EDUCATION STATISTICS TO 2004

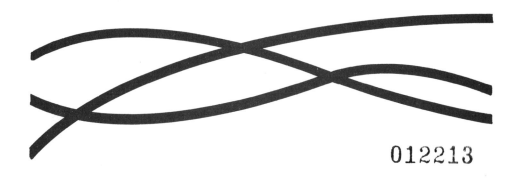

Debra E. Gerald
William J. Hussar

National Center for Education Statistics

U.S. Department of Education
Richard W. Riley
Secretary

Office of Educational Research and Improvement
Sharon P. Robinson
Assistant Secretary

National Center for Education Statistics
Emerson J. Elliott
Commissioner

National Center for Education Statistics

"The purpose of the Center shall be to collect, analyze, and disseminate statistics and other data related to education in the United States and in other nations."—Section 406(b) of the General Education Provisions Act, as amended (20 U.S.C. 1221e–1).

October 1993

For sale by the U.S. Government Printing Office
Superintendent of Documents, Mail Stop: SSOP, Washington, DC 20402-9328
ISBN 0-16-042091-1

Foreword

This edition of *Projections of Education Statistics to 2004* is the 23rd report in a series begun in 1964. This report provides revisions of projections shown in *Projections of Education Statistics to 2003* and includes statistics on elementary and secondary schools and institutions of higher education at the national level. Included are projections for enrollment, graduates, classroom teachers, and expenditures to the year 2004.

The projections presented in this report reflect the 1990 census. The revised population projections developed by the Bureau of the Census reflect the incorporation of the 1992 estimates and latest assumptions for the fertility rate, net immigration, and mortality rate.

The report also contains a methodology section describing models and assumptions used to develop the national projections. The projections are based on an age-specific enrollment rate model, exponential smoothing models, and econometric models. The enrollment model uses population estimates and projections from the Bureau of the Census.

The exponential smoothing models are based on the mathematical projection of past data patterns into the future. The econometric models use projections of exogenous variables from DRI/McGraw-Hill, an economic forecasting service. Therefore, assumptions regarding the population and the economy are the key assumptions underlying the projections of education statistics.

Most of the projections include three alternatives, based on different assumptions about growth paths. Although the first alternative set of projections (middle alternative) in each table is deemed to represent the most likely projections, the low and high alternatives provide a reasonable range of outcomes.

In the forecast summary, key demographic and economic assumptions appear in chart 1 and selected education statistics are shown in figure 1. A summary of the projections is available in a pocket-sized folder, *Pocket Projections 2004*.

Roger A. Herriot, Associate Commissioner for
Statistical Standards and Methodology
September 1993

Acknowledgments

Projections of Education Statistics to 2004 was produced by the National Center for Education Statistics in the Statistical Standards and Methodology Division under the general direction of Roger A. Herriot, Associate Commissioner, and Theodore H. Drews, Chief, Projections and Special Programs Branch. The report was prepared by Debra E. Gerald, Mathematical Statistician, and William J. Hussar, Financial Economist.

Debra E. Gerald was responsible for the overall production of the report and prepared the projections of the following: elementary and secondary enrollment (chapter 1); higher education enrollment (chapter 2); high school graduates (chapter 3); earned degrees conferred (chapter 4); and classroom teachers (chapter 5). In addition, she prepared the appendixes explaining the methodologies used to develop these projections and the data sources. William J. Hussar prepared the projections of expenditures of public elementary and secondary schools, including public school teacher salaries (chapter 6) and expenditures of institutions of higher education (chapter 7). Also, he prepared the appendixes explaining the methodologies used to obtain these projections, selected portions of the data sources, and glossary. Preparation of selected statistical tables was done by Tai A. Phan.

The technical review was done by Robert S. Burton of the National Center for Education Statistics. Valuable assistance was also provided by the following reviewers: Carol Fuller of the National Institute of Independent Colleges and Universities; Daniel Hecker of the Bureau of Labor Statistics; Vance Grant of the Office of the Deputy Assistant Secretary for Operations, Office of Educational Research and Improvement; and John H. Burkett, William J. Fowler, Kristin B. Keough, John P. Sietsema, and William C. Sonnenberg of the National Center for Education Statistics.

The cover was designed by Philip Carr, Office of the Deputy Assistant Secretary for Operations, Office of Educational Research and Improvement.

Forecast Summary

Chart 1.—Summary of forecast assumptions

Variable	Middle alternative	Low alternative	High alternative
Demographic Assumptions			
Population	Projections are consistent with the Census Bureau middle series estimates, which assume a fertility rate of 2.15 births per woman by the year 2050, a net immigration of 880,000 per year, and a further reduction in the mortality rate.	Same as middle alternative	Same as middle alternative
18-24 year-old population	Average annual decline of 0.9% to 1997; average annual growth rate of 1.7% through 2004.	Same as middle alternative	Same as middle alternative
25-29 year-old population	Average annual decline of 1.2%	Same as middle alternative	Same as middle alternative
30-34 year-old population	Average annual decline of 1.2%	Same as middle alternative	Same as middle alternative
35-44 year-old population	Average annual growth rate of 0.7%	Same as middle alternative	Same as middle alternative
Public Elementary Enrollment	Average annual growth rate of 0.9%	Same as middle alternative	Same as middle alternative
Public Secondary Enrollment	Average annual growth rate of 1.8%	Same as middle alternative	Same as middle alternative
Undergraduate Enrollment	Average annual growth rate of 0.8%	Average annual growth rate of 0.4%	Average annual growth rate of 1.2%
Graduate Enrollment	Average annual growth rate of 0.2%	Average annual decline of 0.1%	Average annual growth rate of 0.7%
First-professional Enrollment	Average annual decline of 0.1%	Average annual decline of 0.4%	Average annual growth rate of 0.6%
Full-time-equivalent Enrollment	Average annual growth rate of 0.8%	Average annual growth rate of 0.4%	Average annual growth rate of 1.2%
Economic Assumptions			
Disposable Income per Capita in Constant Dollars	Annual percent changes range between 0.7% and 1.4% with an annual compound growth rate of 0.9%.	Annual percent changes range between −1.3% and 1.2% with an annual compound growth rate of 0.6%.	Annual percent changes range between 0.7% and 3.9% with an annual compound growth rate of 1.3%.
Education Revenue Receipts from State Sources per Capita in Constant Dollars	Annual percent changes range between 0.7% and 4.4% with an annual compound growth rate of 1.6%.	Annual percent changes range between 0.0% and 2.4% with an annual compound growth rate of 1.0%.	Annual percent changes range between 0.8% and 5.4% with an annual compound growth rate of 2.1%.
Inflation Rate	Inflation rate ranges between 2.9% and 4.0%.	Inflation rate ranges between 4.0% and 5.2%.	Inflation rate ranges between 2.5% and 3.7%.
Personal Taxes and Nontax Receipts to State and Local Governments per Capita in Constant Dollars	Annual percent changes range between 1.3% and 5.3% with an annual compound growth rate of 2.6%.	Annual percent changes range between 1.5% and 4.1% with an annual compound growth rate of 2.4%.	Annual percent changes range between 1.5% and 8.7% with an annual compound growth rate of 3.1%.
Indirect Business Taxes and Tax Accruals (Excluding Property Taxes) to State and Local Governments per Capita in Constant Dollars	Annual percent changes range between −0.1% and 3.0% with an annual compound growth rate of 0.8%.	Annual percent changes range between −1.2% and 2.7% with an annual compound growth rate of 0.5%.	Annual percent changes range between 0.0% and 3.9% with an annual compound growth rate of 1.2%.
Unemployment Rate (Ages 16 to 19)	Remains between 19.2% and 20.2%.	Same as middle alternative	Same as middle alternative

Figure 1
Percent change in selected education statistics:
1978-79 to 1991-92 and 1991-92 to 2003-2004

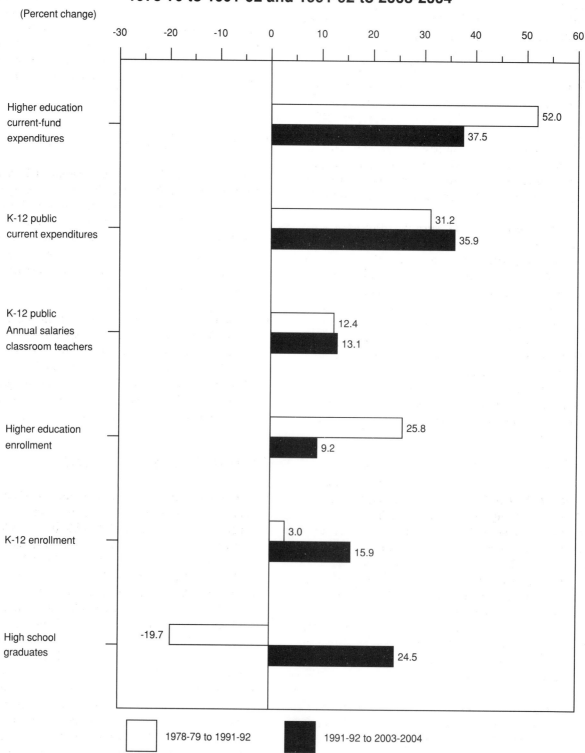

NOTE: Data for 1991-92 expenditures are estimated using past data. All financial statistics are in constant dollars.

Highlights

Enrollment

- **Total public and private elementary and secondary enrollment is projected to increase to 55.7 million over the projection period.** From 1979 to 1984, total enrollment in public and private elementary and secondary schools decreased from 46.7 million to 44.9 million, a decrease of 4 percent. After 1984, total enrollment reversed its decline and increased to an estimated 48.0 million in 1992, an increase of 7 percent from 1984. Total enrollment is projected to continue to increase to 51.8 million by 1996, surpassing the peak level of 51.3 million attained in 1971. Total enrollment is projected to increase further to 55.7 million by the year 2004, an increase of 16 percent from 1992 (table 1).

- **Over the projection period, enrollment in grades K–8 and grades 9–12 will continue to increase.** Between 1979 and 1984, enrollment in grades K–8 fell from 31.7 million to 31.2 million, a decrease of 2 percent. Then, this number increased to 35.2 million in 1992, an increase of 13 percent from 1984. Enrollment in grades K–8 is projected to increase to 39.7 million by the year 2004, an increase of 13 percent from 1992. Enrollment in grades 9–12 decreased from 14.9 million in 1979 to 12.5 million in 1990, a decrease of 16 percent. It then increased to 12.9 million in 1992. By the year 2004, enrollment in grades 9–12 is projected to continue to rise to 16.0 million, an increase of 24 percent from 1992 (table 1).

- **Enrollment in institutions of higher education is projected to increase from an estimated 14.6 million in 1992 to 15.9 million by the year 2004.** Between 1979 and 1983, higher education enrollment increased from 11.6 million to 12.5 million, an increase of 8 percent. In 1984 and 1985, higher education enrollment dropped to 12.2 million. Then, it increased from 12.5 million in 1986 to an estimated 14.6 million in 1992, an increase of 16 percent from 1986. Higher education enrollment is projected to increase to 15.9 million by the year 2004, an increase of 9 percent from 1992. Under the low and high alternatives, higher education enrollment is projected to range between 15.1 million and 16.7 million by the year 2004 (table 3).

- **Women are expected to continue to be the majority of college students over the projection period.** Enrollment of women increased from 5.9 million in 1979 to an estimated 7.9 million in 1992, an increase of 34 percent. Under the middle alternative, this number is projected to increase to 8.7 million by the year 2004, an increase of 10 percent from 1992. Under the low and high alternatives, enrollment of women is projected to range between 8.3 million and 9.1 million by the year 2004. From 1979 to 1990, enrollment of men has fluctuated between 5.6 million and 6.3 million. In 1992, it was estimated at 6.7 million. Under the middle alternative, this number is projected to increase to 7.2 million by the year 2004, an increase of 8 percent from 1992. Under the low and high alternatives, enrollment of men is expected to range between 6.8 million and 7.6 million by the year 2004 (table 3).

High School Graduates

- **The number of high school graduates is projected to increase by 2003–2004.** The number of high school graduates from public and private high schools decreased from 3.1 million in 1978–79 to 2.6 million in 1985–86. It then rose to 2.8 million in 1987–88. Next, it decreased to 2.5 million in 1991–92. Over the projection period, the number of graduates is projected to rise to 3.1 million by 2003–2004 (table 26).

- **Graduates of both public and private high schools are projected to increase by 2003–2004.** The number of public high school graduates is projected to increase from 2.2 million in 1991–92 to 2.8 million by 2003–2004. The number of private high school graduates, which were estimated at 256,000 in 1991–92, is projected to be 319,000 by 2003–2004 (table 26).

Earned Degrees Conferred

- **Over the projection period, the number of bachelor's degrees is projected to fluctuate within a narrow range before rising to 1.3 million by 2003–2004.** Between 1978–79 and 1991–92, the number of bachelor's degrees increased from 921,000 to about 1,120,000. Under the middle alternative, this number is expected to fluctuate and increase to 1,278,000 by 2003–2004. Under the low and high alternatives, bachelor's degrees are projected to range between 1,208,000 and 1,354,000. The number of bachelor's degrees awarded to men declined from 477,000 in 1978–79 to 470,000 in 1980–81. Then, this number increased most years to about 518,000 in 1991–92. Under the middle alternative, this number is expected to fluctuate over most of the projection period and then increase to 598,000 by 2003–2004. Under the low and high alternatives, bachelor's degrees awarded to men are expected to range between 552,000 and 635,000. The number of bachelor's degrees awarded to women increased from 444,000 in 1978–79 to about 602,000 in 1991–92. Under the middle alternative, this number is expected to increase over the projection period to 680,000 by 2003–2004. Under the low and high alternatives, bachelor's degrees awarded to women are projected to range between 656,000 and 719,000 by 2003–2004 (table 28).

- **The number of doctor's degrees awarded to women is projected to increase over the projection period.** The number of doctor's degrees increased from 32,700 in 1978–79 to about 40,100 in 1991–92. Under the middle alternative, doctor's degrees are expected to increase to 41,400 by 2003–2004. Under the low and high alternatives, the number of doctor's degrees is projected to range between 39,900 and 47,300. Under the middle alternative, the number of doctor's degrees awarded to men is projected to decrease gradually from 25,200 in 1991–92 to 21,200 in 2003–2004. Under the low and high alternatives, doctor's degrees awarded to men are projected to range between 19,800 and 27,000. Under the middle alternative, the number of doctor's degrees awarded to women is expected to increase from 14,900 to 20,200 over the projection period. Under the low and high alternatives, doctor's degrees awarded to women are projected to range between 20,100 and 20,300 (table 30).

Classroom Teachers

- **The number of classroom teachers is projected to rise over the projection period.** Between 1979 and 1981, classroom teachers in public and private elementary and secondary schools decreased from 2.46 million to 2.44 million. Then, this number increased to about 2.81 million in 1992. Under the middle alternative, this number is expected to increase to 3.30 million by the year 2004. Under the low and high alternatives, the number of classroom teachers is expected to range between 3.22 million and 3.42 million by the year 2004 (table 32).

- **Both elementary and secondary teachers are projected to increase over the projection period.** Elementary classroom teachers increased from 1.38 million in 1979 to about 1.74 million in 1992. Under the middle alternative, this number is projected to increase to 1.95 million by the year 2004. Under the low and high alternatives, elementary teachers are projected to range between 1.90 million and 2.04 million by the year 2004. Secondary classroom teachers decreased from 1.08 million in 1979 to 1.04 million in 1981. Then this number increased to about 1.08 million in 1992. Under the middle alternative, secondary classroom teachers will increase to 1.35 million by the year 2004. Under the low and high alternatives, secondary teachers are projected to range between 1.32 million and 1.39 million by the year 2004 (table 32).

- **Under the middle alternative, the pupil-teacher ratios in elementary and secondary schools are projected to rise and then fall over the projection period.** Since 1979, the pupil-teacher ratio in elementary schools has decreased from 20.5 to 18.4 in 1989. Then, the ratio increased to about 18.5 in 1992. Under the middle alternative, this ratio is projected to continue to increase to 19.0 in 1994, and then decline to 18.4 by the year 2004. Under the low and high alternatives, this ratio is expected to range between 17.6 and 18.9 by the year 2004. For secondary schools, the pupil-teacher ratio decreased from 17.0 in 1979 to 14.3 in 1990. Then, it increased to an estimated 14.8 in 1992. Under the middle alternative, this ratio will increase to 15.0 in 1993, fluctuate, and then decrease to 14.7 by 2004. Under the low and high alternatives, the pupil-teacher ratio in secondary schools is projected to range between 14.3 and 15.0 (table 33).

Expenditures

- **Current expenditures for public elementary and secondary schools are forecast to continue increasing through 2003–2004.** Current expenditures are estimated to have increased 31 percent in constant dollars, between 1978–79 and 1990–91. (1990–91 is the last year for which there are actual data.) With the increasing enrollments projected for this period, this trend of increasing current expenditures is expected to continue. Under the middle alternative, a 37-percent increase is projected for the period from 1990–91 to 2003–2004. Under the low alternative, current expenditures are projected to increase by 29 percent; under the high alternative, current expenditures are projected to increase by 44 percent (table 34).

- **Increases in current expenditures per pupil are also forecast to continue increasing for the period 1990–91 to 2003–2004.** The period from 1978–79 until 1990–91 saw current expenditures per pupil in average daily attendance (ADA) increase an estimated 33 percent in constant dollars. Under the middle alternative, current expenditures per pupil are forecast to increase another 15 percent between 1990–91 and 2003–2004. Under the low and high alternatives, the increase in current expenditures is projected to range between 9 and 21 percent. Current expenditures per pupil are forecast to increase less rapidly than total current expenditures due to the increase projected for the number of pupils (table 34).

- **Further increases in teacher salaries are forecast.** After a period of declining salaries (teacher salaries in constant dollars fell 7 percent from 1978–79 to 1980–81), teacher salaries rose constantly from 1981–82 to 1989–90. During that time, teacher salaries in constant dollars grew an estimated 21 percent. With the present slowdown in the economy, teacher salaries are estimated to have increased less than 1 percent in real terms from 1989–90 to 1992–93. As the current trend of increasing enrollments continues and as the economy begins to grow again, it is forecast that teacher salaries will also begin increasing. Teacher salaries are projected to increase 12 percent between 1992–93 and 2003–2004 under the middle alternative. An 8-percent increase is projected under the low alternative and a 16-percent increase is projected under the high alternative (table 36).

• **Current-fund expenditures are projected to increase in both public and private institutions**. Current-fund expenditures in institutions of higher education rose 47 in constant dollars percent from 1978–79 to 1990–91. (1990–91 is the last year for which there are available data.) During that time, current-fund expenditures rose 41 percent in public institutions and 60 percent in private institutions. A further 42-percent increase is projected for the period from 1990–91 to 2003–2004 under the middle alternative for all expenditures (table 37).

Contents

Technical Appendixes

Chart

Figures

Tables

High School Graduates

Earned Degrees Conferred

Classroom Teachers

Elementary and Secondary Schools

Expenditures

Public Elementary and Secondary Schools

Institutions of Higher Education

Appendix A

Methodological Tables

Enrollment

Earned Degrees Conferred

Public Classroom Teachers

Public Elementary and Secondary School Expenditures

Institutions of Higher Education Expenditures

Appendix B

Supplementary Tables

Introduction

Guide to This Edition

This edition of *Projections of Education Statistics to 2004* provides projections for key education statistics. This edition includes statistics on enrollment, graduates, classroom teachers, and expenditures in elementary and secondary schools and institutions of higher education. The tables, figures, and text contain data on enrollment, teachers, graduates, and expenditures for the past 14 years and projections to the year 2004. These projections reflect estimates and population projections based on the 1990 census. Appendix A describes the methodology and assumptions used to develop the projections. Appendix B contains tables of supplementary data. Data sources are presented in appendix C. Appendix D is a glossary of terms.

Exclusions

Some of the projections contained in previous editions of *Projections of Education Statistics* are not provided in this edition. The Schools and Staffing Survey (SASS) of the National Center for Education Statistics now provides data on teacher attrition and sources of teacher supply. Therefore, the previous practice of using various assumptions to develop projections of the demand for new hiring of classroom teachers has been discontinued, and the SASS data will be used for future analyses of this variable. However, data from SASS are currently available for only one time period and are thus an insufficient basis for projections. This does not affect the projections of total demand for classroom teachers, which are included.

Also excluded from this edition are projections of instructional faculty, higher education enrollment by race/ethnicity, and state projections of public elementary and secondary enrollment and public high school graduates. Projections of instructional faculty require the development of new time series from existing and new NCES data sources, and that development is not yet complete. Projections of higher education enrollment by race/ethnicity are under development. Projections of public school enrollment and public high school graduates by state cannot be included because the 1990 census-based population projections by state, which are necessary to update these projections, are not yet available.

Limitations of Projections

Projections of time series usually differ from the reported data due to errors from many sources. This is because of the inherent nature of the statistical universe from which the basic data are obtained and the properties of projection methodologies, which depend on the validity of many assumptions. Therefore, alternative projections are shown for most statistical series to denote the uncertainty involved in making projections. These alternatives are not statistical confidence limits, but instead represent judgments made by the authors as to reasonable upper and lower bounds. Alternative projections are presented for higher education enrollment, classroom teachers, earned degrees conferred, and expenditures of public elementary and secondary schools and institutions of higher education.

Chapter 1

Elementary and Secondary Enrollment

Between 1992 and the year 2004, enrollment will increase in elementary and secondary schools. The primary reason for the increase is the rising number of annual births since 1977—sometimes referred to as the baby boom echo (figure 2). As a result, increases in the 3- to 5-year-old population are projected through 1996 and increases in the school-age populations are expected over the next 12 years (figures 3, 4, and 5). In 1993 and beyond, increases in the 5- to 13-year-old population, which began in the mid-1980s, are expected to continue the growth in elementary enrollment. The increase in the 14- to 17-year-old population, which started in 1991, will continue the growth in secondary enrollment over the projection period.

Elementary and Secondary Enrollment

Reflecting the decline in the 5- to 17-year-old population, total enrollment in public and private elementary and secondary schools decreased from 46.7 million in 1979 to 44.9 million in 1984, a decrease of 4 percent (table 1 and figure 6). After reaching a low of 44.9 million in 1984, total enrollment reversed its downward trend in response to an increase in the 5- to 17-year-old population and rose to 48.0 million in 1992, an increase of 7 percent from 1984. Total enrollment is projected to continue to increase to 51.8 million in 1996, surpassing the peak level of 51.3 million attained in 1971. Total enrollment is projected to increase further to 55.7 million by the year 2004, an increase of 16 percent from 1992.

Enrollment, by Control of School

Enrollment in public elementary and secondary schools decreased from 41.7 million in 1979 to 39.2 million in 1984, a decrease of 6 percent (figure 7). Since then, enrollment in public schools has increased to an estimated 42.7 million in 1992, an increase of 9 percent from 1984. Enrollment in public schools is projected to increase to 49.5 million by the year 2004, an increase of 16 percent from 1992.

Since the mid-1970s, enrollment in private elementary and secondary schools has fluctuated between 5.0 million and 5.7 million. A sample survey of private schools conducted by NCES in 1992 estimated that 5.4 million students were enrolled in private elementary and secondary schools. Enrollment in private schools is projected to increase to

around 6.2 million by the year 2004, an increase of 15 percent from 1992.

Projections of enrollments in public elementary and secondary schools are based on projected grade retention rates. The retention rates for grades 2 through 10 are all close to 100 percent. Rates for grade 6 to grade 7 and grade 8 to grade 9 are significantly over 100 percent. Traditionally, these are the grades in which large numbers of private elementary students transfer to public secondary schools. The retention rates for grades 11 to 12 are about 90 percent. The grade retention rates are assumed to be constant throughout the projection period.

Projections of private school enrollment were derived using public school enrollment data for 1992. The ratio of private school enrollment to public school enrollment was calculated for grades K–8 and grades 9–12. These ratios were held constant over the projection period and applied to projections of public school enrollment for grades K–8 and 9–12 to yield projections of private school enrollment. This method assumes that the future pattern in the trend of private school enrollment will be the same as that in public school enrollment. However, a number of factors could alter the assumption of constant ratios over the projection period.

Enrollment, by Grade Group

Between 1979 and 1984, enrollment in grades K–8 fell from 31.7 million to 31.2 million, a decrease of 2 percent. Then, this number increased to 35.2 million in 1992, an increase of 13 percent from 1984. Enrollment in grades K–8 is projected to increase to 39.7 million by the year 2004, an increase of 13 percent from 1992. Enrollment in grades 9–12 decreased from 14.9 million in 1979 to 12.5 million in 1990, a decrease of 16 percent. It then increased to 12.9 million in 1992. By the year 2004, enrollment in grades 9–12 is projected to continue to rise to 16.0 million, an increase of 24 percent from 1992. Since enrollment rates for the school-age populations are nearly 100 percent for elementary grades and junior-high grades and close to 90 percent for high school grades, the historical and projected patterns of decline and growth in enrollment in grades K–8 and grades 9–12 reflect changes in the sizes of the 5- to 13-year-old population and the 14- to 17-year-old population.

Enrollment by grade group in public elementary and secondary schools shows trends similar to those of total enrollment. Enrollment in grades K–8 of public schools decreased from 28.0 million in 1979 to 26.9 million in

3

1984, a decrease of 4 percent. It then increased to 30.9 million in 1992. Enrollment in grades K–8 of public schools is projected to increase to 34.9 million by the year 2004, an increase of 13 percent from 1992. Enrollment in grades 9–12 of public schools decreased from 13.6 million in 1979 to 11.3 million in 1990, a decrease of 17 percent. Then, it increased to 11.7 million in 1992. Thereafter, 9–12 enrollment is expected to increase to 14.6 million by the year 2004, an increase of 24 percent from 1992.

Enrollment by grade group in private elementary and secondary schools will show patterns similar to trends in enrollment in public schools over the projection period by virtue of the private school enrollment projection methodology. The methodology assumes that private school enrollment will reflect trends in public school enrollment. Enrollment in grades K–8 of private schools is projected to increase from 4.2 million in 1992 to 4.8 million by the year 2004, an increase of 13 percent. Enrollment in grades 9–12 of private schools is projected to increase from 1.2 million in 1992 to 1.4 million by the year 2004, an increase of 24 percent.

Enrollment, by Organizational Level

Enrollments may also be aggregated by the level of school attended by students. The reported enrollment in elementary schools is smaller than enrollment in kindergarten through grade 8 because it excludes enrollment in grades 7 and 8 in secondary schools. Enrollment in elementary schools decreased from 28.2 million in 1979 to 28.0 million in 1983, a decrease of 1 percent (table 2). This number increased by 15 percent to 32.1 million in 1992. Enrollment in elementary schools is expected to continue to increase to 36.1 million in the year 2002, before declining to 35.9 million by the year 2004, an increase of 12 percent from 1992. Enrollment in secondary schools, including 7th and 8th graders in secondary schools, decreased from 18.4 million in 1979 to 15.3 million in 1990, a decrease of 17 percent. Then, this number increased by 4 percent to 15.9 million in 1992. Enrollment in secondary schools is projected to rise to 19.8 million by the year 2004, an increase of 24 percent from 1992.

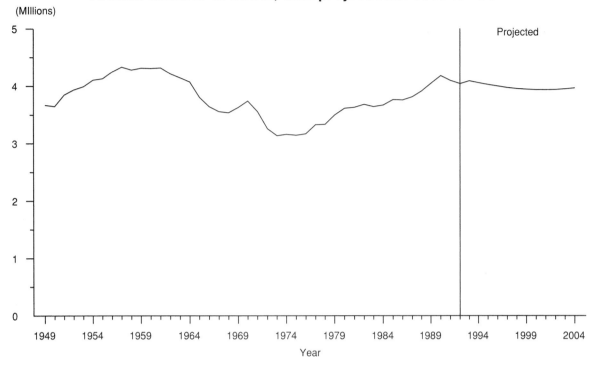

Figure 2
Annual number of births, with projections: 1949 to 2004

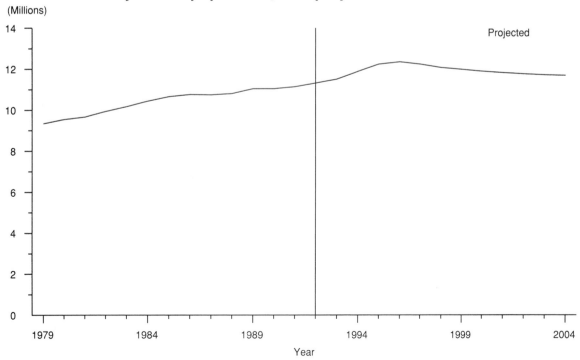

Figure 3
3-to 5-year-old population, with projections: 1979 to 2004

Figure 4
5 to 17-year-old population, with projections: 1979 to 2004

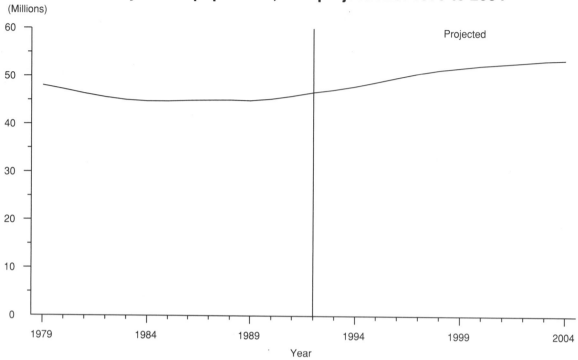

Figure 5
School-age populations, with projections: 1979 to 2004

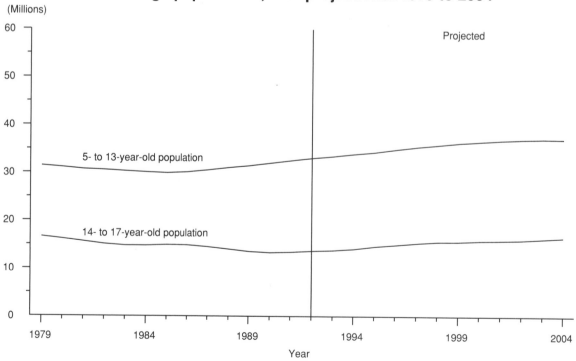

Figure 6
Enrollment in elementary and secondary schools, by grade level,
with projections: Fall 1979 to fall 2004

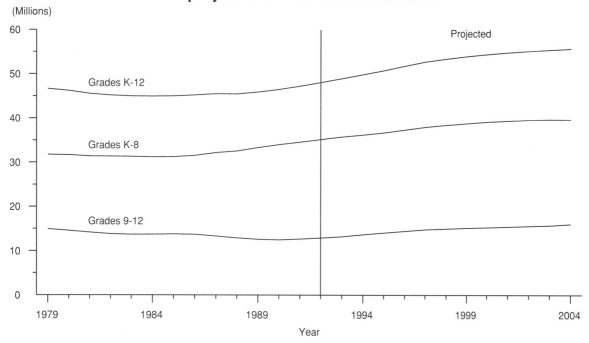

Figure 7
Enrollment in elementary and secondary schools, by control of institution,
with projections: Fall 1979 to fall 2004

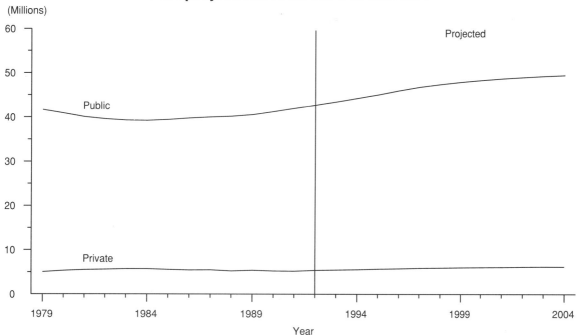

Table 1.—Enrollment in grades K–8[1] and 9–12 of elementary and secondary schools, by control of institution, with projections: 50 States and D.C., fall 1979 to fall 2004

(In thousands)

Year	Total			Public			Private		
	K–12[1]	K–8[1]	9–12	K–12[1]	K–8[1]	9–12	K–12[1]	K–8[1]	9–12
1979	46,651	31,734	14,916	41,651	28,034	13,616	[2]5,000	3,700	1,300
1980	46,208	31,639	14,570	40,877	27,647	13,231	5,331	3,992	1,339
1981	45,544	31,380	14,164	40,044	27,280	12,764	[2]5,500	4,100	1,400
1982	45,166	31,361	13,805	39,566	27,161	12,405	[2]5,600	4,200	1,400
1983	44,967	31,296	13,671	39,252	26,981	12,271	5,715	4,315	1,400
1984	44,908	31,205	13,704	39,208	26,905	12,304	[2]5,700	4,300	1,400
1985	44,979	31,229	13,750	39,422	27,034	12,388	5,557	4,195	1,362
1986	45,205	31,536	13,669	39,753	27,420	12,333	[3]5,452	4,116	1,336
1987	45,488	32,165	13,323	40,008	27,933	12,076	[3]5,479	4,232	1,247
1988	45,430	32,537	12,893	40,189	28,501	11,687	[3]5,241	4,036	1,206
1989	45,898	33,314	12,583	40,543	29,152	11,390	[3]5,355	4,162	1,193
1990	46,448	33,973	12,475	41,217	29,878	11,338	[3]5,232	4,095	1,137
1991	47,199	34,544	12,655	42,000	30,470	11,530	[3]5,199	4,074	1,125
1992	48,045	35,157	12,888	[2]42,670	30,945	11,725	[3]5,375	4,212	1,163
				Projected					
1993	48,925	35,727	13,198	43,454	31,447	12,007	5,471	4,280	1,191
1994	49,819	36,170	13,649	44,254	31,837	12,417	5,565	4,333	1,232
1995	50,709	36,668	14,041	45,049	32,275	12,774	5,660	4,393	1,267
1996	51,762	37,311	14,451	45,988	32,841	13,147	5,774	4,470	1,304
1997	52,714	37,940	14,773	46,835	33,395	13,440	5,879	4,545	1,333
1998	53,382	38,398	14,984	47,430	33,798	13,632	5,952	4,600	1,352
1999	53,942	38,793	15,149	47,927	34,145	13,782	6,015	4,648	1,367
2000	54,412	39,129	15,283	48,345	34,441	13,904	6,067	4,688	1,379
2001	54,816	39,389	15,427	48,705	34,670	14,035	6,111	4,719	1,392
2002	55,162	39,589	15,573	49,014	34,846	14,168	6,148	4,743	1,405
2003	55,459	39,713	15,746	49,280	34,955	14,325	6,179	4,758	1,421
2004	55,706	39,676	16,029	49,506	34,923	14,583	6,200	4,753	1,446

[1] Includes most kindergarten and some nursery school enrollment.

[2] Estimated by NCES.

[3] Estimate.

NOTE: Some data have been revised from previously published figures. Projections are based on data through 1991. Because of rounding, details may not add to totals.

SOURCE: U.S. Department of Education, National Center for Education Statistics, *Statistics of Public Elementary and Secondary Schools*; Common Core of Data surveys; ''Selected Public and Private Elementary and Secondary Education Statistics,'' *NCES Bulletin*, October 23, 1979; ''Private Elementary and Secondary Education, 1983: Enrollment, Teachers, and Schools,'' *NCES Bulletin*, December 1984; 1985 Private School Survey; ''Key Statistics for Private Elementary and Secondary Education: School Year 1988–89,'' *Early Estimates*; ''Key Statistics for Private Elementary and Secondary Education: School Year 1990–91,'' *Early Estimates*; Public and Private Elementary and Secondary Education Statistics: School Year 1991–92,'' *Early Estimates*; and ''Public and Private Elementary and Secondary Education Statistics: School Year 1992-93,'' *Early Estimates*. (This table was prepared May 1993.)

Table 2.—Enrollment in elementary and secondary schools, by organizational level and control of institution, with projections: 50 States and D.C., fall 1979 to fall 2004

(In thousands)

Year	Total			Public			Private		
	K-12[1]	Elementary	Secondary	K-12[1]	Elementary	Secondary	K-12[1]	Elementary	Secondary
1979	46,651	28,247	18,404	41,651	24,547	17,104	[2]5,000	3,700	1,300
1980	46,208	28,188	18,020	40,877	24,196	16,681	5,331	3,992	1,339
1981	45,544	28,137	17,407	40,044	24,037	16,007	[2]5,500	4,100	1,400
1982	45,165	28,016	17,149	39,565	23,816	15,749	[2]5,600	4,200	1,400
1983	44,967	27,950	17,017	39,252	23,635	15,617	5,715	4,315	1,400
1984	44,908	28,042	16,866	39,208	23,742	15,466	[2]5,700	4,300	1,400
1985	44,979	28,330	16,649	39,422	24,135	15,287	5,557	4,195	1,362
1986	45,205	28,613	16,592	39,753	24,497	15,256	[2]5,452	4,116	1,336
1987	45,487	29,447	16,040	40,008	25,215	14,793	[3]5,479	4,232	1,247
1988	45,430	29,776	15,654	40,188	25,740	14,448	[3]5,241	4,036	1,206
1989	45,898	30,570	15,328	40,543	26,408	14,135	[3]5,355	4,162	1,193
1990	46,448	31,145	15,304	41,217	27,050	14,167	[3]5,232	4,095	1,137
1991	47,199	31,638	15,561	42,000	27,564	14,436	[3]5,199	4,074	1,125
1992	48,045	32,110	15,935	[2]42,670	27,898	14,772	[3]5,375	4,212	1,163
Projected									
1993	48,925	32,577	16,348	43,454	28,297	15,157	5,471	4,280	1,191
1994	49,819	32,956	16,863	44,254	28,623	15,631	5,565	4,333	1,232
1995	50,709	33,411	17,298	45,049	29,018	16,031	5,660	4,393	1,267
1996	51,762	34,023	17,739	45,988	29,553	16,435	5,774	4,470	1,304
1997	52,714	34,621	18,092	46,835	30,076	16,759	5,879	4,545	1,333
1998	53,382	35,051	18,331	47,430	30,451	16,979	5,952	4,600	1,352
1999	53,942	35,415	18,527	47,927	30,767	17,160	6,015	4,648	1,367
2000	54,412	35,715	18,697	48,345	31,027	17,318	6,067	4,688	1,379
2001	54,816	35,934	18,882	48,705	31,215	17,490	6,111	4,719	1,392
2002	55,162	36,052	19,110	49,014	31,309	17,705	6,148	4,743	1,405
2003	55,459	36,031	19,428	49,280	31,273	18,007	6,179	4,758	1,421
2004	55,706	35,895	19,810	49,506	31,142	18,364	6,200	4,753	1,446

[1] Includes most kindergarten and some nursery school enrollment.

[2] Estimated by NCES.

[3] Estimate.

NOTE: Some data have been revised from previously published figures. Projections are based on data through 1991. Because of rounding, details may not add to totals.

SOURCE: U.S. Department of Education, National Center for Education Statistics, *Statistics of Public Elementary and Secondary Schools*; Common Core of Data surveys; "Selected Public and Private Elementary and Secondary Education Statistics," *NCES Bulletin*, October 23, 1979; "Private Elementary and Secondary Education, 1983: Enrollment, Teachers, and Schools," *NCES Bulletin*, December 1984; 1985 Private School Survey; "Key Statistics for Private Elementary and Secondary Education: School Year 1988–89," *Early Estimates*; "Key Statistics for Private Elementary and Secondary Education: School Year 1990–91," *Early Estimates*; "Public and Private Elementary and Secondary Education Statistics: School Year 1991–92," *Early Estimates*; and "Public and Private Elementary and Secondary Education Statistics: School Year 1992–93," *Early Estimates*. (This table was prepared May 1993.)

Chapter 2

Higher Education Enrollment

Enrollment in institutions of higher education* is expected to rise between 1992 and the year 2004. The growth is due in part to the rising enrollment rates of most age cohorts. Changes in college-age populations will also affect enrollment levels over the next 12 years (figures 8 and 9). Over the projection period, the 25- to 29-year-old population is projected to decrease by 13 percent, and the 30- to 34-year-old population will also decline by 13 percent. However, during the projection period, the 18- to 24-year-old population will begin to increase beginning in 1998, rising by 12 percent by the end of the projection period. On the other hand, the 35- to 44-year-old population will increase by 9 percent over the projection period despite a slight decrease between 2000 and 2004. The increases in the youngest and oldest populations are expected to offset the loss of students from the 25- to 29-year-old and 30- to 34-year-old populations, thereby contributing to the increases in college enrollment levels in 1993 and beyond.

Higher education enrollment projections were based on projected enrollment rates, by age and sex, which were then applied to population projections by age and sex developed by the Bureau of the Census. The middle series population projections, which assume middle fertility and net immigration, were used. The enrollment rates were projected by taking into account the most recent trends, as well as the effects of economic conditions and demographic changes on the enrollment rates of the younger age cohorts.

Three alternative projections of enrollment in institutions of higher education were developed to indicate the range of possible outcomes. The middle alternative assumes that the enrollment rates of most of the 18- to 24-year-olds will increase over the projection period, while those for older age groups are expected to remain constant at levels consistent with the most recent enrollment rates or increase slightly. In particular, the part-time enrollment rate of 18-year-old men was projected as a function of unemployment rate and disposable income per capita. The part-time enrollment rate of 20-year-old men was projected as a function of disposable income per capita. The part-time enrollment rate of 18-year-old women was projected as a function of disposable income per capita. The low alternative assumes that age-specific enrollment rates will either equal the middle alternative or change at a slower rate, based on past trends. Under the high alternative, the age-specific

enrollment rates are projected to equal the middle alternative or increase at a faster rate, based on past trends for most age groups.

Total Higher Education Enrollment

In 1979, there were 11.6 million students enrolled in institutions of higher education. In the late 1970s and early 1980s, older students, primarily women and part-time students, began to enroll in greater numbers. As a result, college enrollment increased to 12.5 million in 1983. In 1984 and 1985, enrollment declined to 12.2 million. By 1992, it had risen to an estimated 14.6 million, exceeding its previous level attained in 1983 by nearly 2.1 million students (table 3 and figure 10). Under the middle alternative, college enrollment is projected to rise to 15.9 million by the year 2004, an increase of 9 percent from 1992. This will represent an average annual growth rate of 0.7 percent over the projection period, less than the growth rate of 1.8 percent during the 1979–92 period. Moreover, the greatest growth will occur toward the end of the projection period. Between 1992 and 1998, college enrollment is projected to increase at an average annual growth rate of 0.6 percent. Between 1998 and 2004, it will grow at an average annual growth rate of 0.8 percent (figure 11). Although the 18- to 24-year-old population is projected to decline until 1997, a decrease of 4 percent from 1992, this population will increase 12 percent by the year 2004. According to the Bureau of the Census, 58 percent of all college students were 18- to 24-years old in 1991. This increase in the younger population, along with enrollment rates remaining above 1992 levels and the continued increases in the number of older students, is expected to offset the decline in the number of 25- to 34-year-olds enrolled in college.

Under the low alternative, college enrollment is projected to increase from an estimated 14.6 million in 1992 to 15.1 million by the year 2004. This will represent an average annual growth rate of 0.3 percent, for an increase of 4 percent over the projection period. This alternative assumes that enrollment rates will either remain the same as the middle alternative or increase at a slower rate.

Under the high alternative, college enrollment is expected to increase from an estimated 14.6 million in 1992 to 16.7 million by the year 2004. This will represent an average annual growth rate of 1.1 percent, for an increase of 15 percent over the projection period. This level is expected to be maintained during 1993 and beyond if the enrollment rates remain well above their 1992 levels.

---

*This term applies mainly to those institutions that provide study beyond secondary school and that offer programs terminating in an associate, baccalaureate, or higher degree.

For key enrollment statistics, the following tabulations show: (1) the average annual rate of growth (in percent) for 1979–92 and alternative projected rates of change for 1992–2004 and (2) growth rates for 1979–86 and 1986–92 and the middle alternative projected rates of change for 1992–98 and 1998–2004.

Average annual rate of change (in percent)

	1979–92	1992–2004		
		Low	Middle	High
Total	1.8	0.3	0.7	1.1
Men	1.2	0.2	0.7	1.2
Women	2.3	0.4	0.8	1.1
Full-time	1.4	0.5	0.9	1.3
Part-time	2.3	0.1	0.5	0.9
Public	1.8	0.3	0.7	1.2
Private	1.8	0.3	0.7	1.1
4-year	1.6	0.3	0.7	1.2
2-year	2.1	0.3	0.7	1.1
Undergraduate	1.7	0.4	0.8	1.2
Graduate	2.4	-0.1	0.2	0.7
First-professional	1.5	-0.4	-0.1	0.6
Full-time-equivalent	1.6	0.4	0.8	1.2

Average annual rate of change (in percent)
(Middle alternative projections)

	1979–86	1986–92	Projected	
			1992–98	1998–2004
Total	1.1	2.6	0.6	0.8
Men	0.5	2.1	0.4	1.0
Women	1.7	3.0	0.8	0.7
Full-time	0.7	2.3	0.4	1.4
Part-time	1.7	3.0	0.9	0.1
Public	1.0	2.7	0.7	0.8
Private	1.4	2.2	0.5	0.9
4-year	0.9	2.5	0.5	1.0
2-year	1.5	2.7	0.8	0.6
Undergraduate	1.1	2.4	0.7	1.0
Graduate	1.3	3.8	0.5	-0.1
First-professional	0.4	2.8	-0.2	-0.1
Full-time-equivalent	0.9	2.4	0.5	1.1

Enrollment, by Sex of Student

Women played a major role in the increase of enrollment between 1979 and 1992. The enrollment of women in college increased from 5.9 million in 1979 to an estimated 7.9 million in 1992, representing an average annual growth rate of 2.3 percent, for a 34-percent increase over the period (figure 12). Under the middle alternative, enrollment of women is expected to increase to 8.7 million by the year 2004, an increase of 10 percent from 1992. This will represent a growth rate of 0.8 percent per year, considerably less than the growth rate of 2.3 percent for the 1979–92 period. The rate of growth will be higher during the first half of the projection period (1992–98) than during the second half (1998–2004), 0.8 percent per year versus

0.7 percent per year (figure 13). As a share of total college enrollment, women were 54 percent of all college students in 1992 compared with 51 percent in 1979. Women are expected to increase their share slightly to 55 percent of college enrollment in the year 2004. Under the low and high alternatives, enrollment of women is projected to range between 8.3 million and 9.1 million by the year 2004, representing growth rates of 0.4 percent and 1.1 percent, respectively.

Despite fluctuations in enrollment to 1985, the enrollment of men in college has since increased from 5.9 million in 1986 to an estimated 6.7 million in 1992. Over the 1979–92 period, the growth rate of 1.2 percent per year for men was slightly more than half of the rate for women. Under the middle alternative, enrollment of men is expected to increase to 7.2 million by the year 2004, an 8-percent increase from 1992, for an average annual growth rate of 0.7 percent. The growth rate of enrollment of men will be lower in the first half of the projection period than in the second half, 0.4 percent per year versus 1.0 percent per year. Under the low and high alternatives, the number of men enrolled in college is projected to range between 6.8 million and 7.6 million by the year 2004, representing growth rates of 0.2 percent and 1.2 percent, respectively.

Enrollment, by Attendance Status

Full-time enrollment increased from 6.8 million in 1979 to an estimated 8.1 million in 1992 (figure 14). This is an average annual growth rate of 1.4 percent, for an increase of 20 percent over the period. Under the middle alternative, full-time enrollment is expected to increase another 12 percent to 9.1 million by the year 2004, representing an average annual growth rate of 0.9 percent. Over the projection period, the growth rate for the 1992–98 period will be lower than the growth rate for the 1998–2004 period, 0.4 percent per year versus 1.4 percent per year (figure 15). This is probably due to the increased enrollment of 18- to 24-year-olds, who will tend to be enrolled full-time. Under the low and high alternatives, full-time enrollment is projected to range between 8.6 million and 9.6 million by the year 2004.

Part-time enrollment increased from 4.8 million in 1979 to an estimated 6.4 million in 1992. This is an average annual growth rate of 2.3 percent, for an increase of 34 percent over the period. Under the middle alternative, part-time enrollment is expected to increase at an average annual growth rate of 0.5 percent and reach 6.8 million by the year 2004, for an increase of 6 percent over the projection period. Unlike full-time enrollment, the growth rate for part-time enrollment during the 1992–98 period will be more than the growth rate for the 1998–2004 period, 0.9 percent versus 0.1 percent. Under the low and high alternatives, part-time enrollment is projected to range between 6.5 million and 7.1 million, representing growth rates of 0.1 percent and 0.9 percent, respectively.

Enrollment, by Control of Institution

Enrollment in public institutions grew from 9.0 million in 1979 to an estimated 11.4 million in 1992, increasing at an average annual rate of 1.8 percent, for an increase of 26 percent over the period (figure 16). Under the middle alternative, public enrollment is expected to increase to 12.4 million, rising by an average annual growth rate of 0.7 percent, for an increase of 9 percent over the projection period. During the projection period, enrollment in public institutions is projected to increase at an average annual growth rate of 0.7 percent during the 1992–98 period and 0.8 percent during the 1998–2004 period (figure 17). Enrollment in public 4-year institutions is projected to increase from an estimated 6.1 million in 1992 to 6.7 million by the year 2004. Enrollment in public 2-year institutions is expected to increase from 5.2 million in 1992 to 5.7 million by the year 2004.

Under the low and high alternatives, enrollment in public institutions is expected to range between 11.8 million and 13.1 million by the year 2004. For the low alternative, this is a projected average annual growth rate of 0.3 percent over the projection period. For the high alternative, it will be a growth rate of 1.2 percent.

Enrollment in private institutions increased from 2.5 million in 1979 to an estimated 3.2 million in 1992, increasing at an average annual growth rate of 1.8 percent, for an increase of 26 percent over the period. Under the middle alternative, private enrollment is expected to increase to 3.5 million, rising by an average annual growth rate of 0.7 percent, for an increase of 9 percent over the projection period. During the projection period, enrollment in private institutions is projected to increase at an annual growth rate of 0.5 percent during the 1992–98 period and 0.9 percent during the 1998–2004 period. Enrollment in private 4-year institutions is expected to increase from an estimated 2.9 million in 1992 to 3.2 million by the year 2004. Enrollment in private 2-year institutions is projected to increase from an estimated 260,000 in 1992 to 289,000 by the year 2004.

Under the low and high alternatives, enrollment in private institutions is expected to range between 3.3 million and 3.6 million by the year 2004. For the low alternative, this is a projected average annual growth rate of 0.3 percent over the projection period. For the high alternative, it will be a growth rate of 1.1 percent.

Enrollment, by Type of Institution

Enrollment in 4-year institutions increased from 7.4 million in 1979 to an estimated 9.1 million in 1992, increasing at an average annual growth rate of 1.6 percent, for a 23-percent increase over the period (table 4 and figure 18). Under the middle alternative, enrollment in 4-year institutions is expected to rise to 9.9 million by the year 2004, increasing at an average annual growth rate of 0.7 percent, for a 9-percent increase over the projection period. During the projection period, enrollment in 4-year institu-

tions is projected to increase at an annual growth rate of 0.5 percent during the 1992–98 period and 1.0 percent during the 1998–2004 period (figure 19).

Under the low and high alternatives, enrollment in 4-year institutions is expected to range between 9.4 million and 10.4 million by the year 2004. For the low alternative, this is a projected average annual growth rate of 0.3 percent over the projection period. For the high alternative, it will be a growth rate of 1.2 percent.

Enrollment in 2-year institutions rose from 4.2 million in 1979 to an estimated 5.5 million in 1992, increasing at an average annual growth rate of 2.1 percent per year, for a 30-percent increase over the period (table 5). Under the middle alternative, enrollment in 2-year institutions is expected to rise to 6.0 million by the year 2004, increasing at an average annual growth rate of 0.7 percent, for a 9-percent increase over the projection period. During the projection period, enrollment in 2-year institutions is projected to increase at an annual growth rate of 0.8 percent during the 1992–98 period and 0.6 percent during the 1998–2004 period.

Under the low and high alternatives, enrollment in 2-year institutions is expected to range between 5.7 million and 6.3 million by the year 2004. For the low alternative, this is a projected average annual growth rate of 0.3 percent over the projection period. For the high alternative, it will be a growth rate of 1.1 percent.

Enrollment, by Level

Undergraduate enrollment increased from 10.0 million in 1979 to an estimated 12.4 million in 1992, increasing at an average annual growth rate of 1.7 percent, for a 25-percent increase over the period (table 14 and figure 20). Under the middle alternative, undergraduate enrollment is expected to increase to 13.7 million by the year 2004, at a growth rate of 0.8 percent per year, for a 10-percent increase over the projection period. During the projection period, undergraduate enrollment is projected to increase at an annual growth rate of 0.7 percent during the 1992–98 period and 1.0 percent during the 1998–2004 period (figure 21).

Under the low and high alternatives, undergraduate enrollment is expected to range between 13.0 million and 14.4 million by the year 2004. For the low alternative, this is a projected average annual growth rate of 0.4 percent over the projection period. For the high alternative, it will be a growth rate of 1.2 percent.

Graduate enrollment rose from 1.3 million in 1979 to an estimated 1.8 million in 1992, at an average annual growth rate of 2.4 percent, for a 37-percent increase over the period (table 17 and figure 22). Under the middle alternative, graduate enrollment is expected to increase to 1.8 million by the year 2004, increasing at an average annual growth rate of 0.2 percent, for a 2-percent increase over the projection period. During the projection period, graduate enrollment is projected to increase at an annual growth rate of 0.5 percent during the 1992–98 period and decrease at a rate of 0.1 percent during the 1998–2004 period (figure 23).

Under the low and high alternatives, graduate enrollment is expected to range between 1.8 million and 1.9 million by the year 2004. For the low alternative, this is a projected average annual decline of 0.1 percent over the projection period. For the high alternative, it will be a growth rate of 0.7 percent.

First-professional enrollment increased from 263,000 in 1979 to an estimated 318,000 in 1992, an average annual growth rate of 1.5 percent, for a 21-percent increase over the period (table 20 and figure 22). Under the middle alternative, first-professional enrollment is expected to increase to 329,000 in 1994 and decline gradually to 314,000 by the year 2004, declining at an average annual rate of 0.1 percent over the projection period, for a 1-percent decrease from 1992. During the projection period, first-professional enrollment is projected to decline at an average annual rate of 0.2 percent during the 1992–98 period and 0.1 percent during the 1998–2004 period (figure 23).

Under the low and high alternatives, first-professional enrollment is expected to range between 304,000 and 340,000 by the year 2004. For the low alternative, this is a projected average annual decline of 0.4 percent over the projection period. For the high alternative, it will be a growth rate of 0.6 percent.

Full-Time-Equivalent Enrollment

Full-time-equivalent enrollment increased from 8.5 million in 1979 to an estimated 10.5 million in 1992, increasing at an average annual rate of growth of 1.6 percent, for a 23-percent increase over the period (table 23 and figure 24). Under the middle alternative, full-time-equivalent enrollment is expected to increase to 11.5 million by the year 2004, increasing at an average annual growth rate of 0.8 percent, for a 10-percent increase over the projection period. During the projection period, full-time-equivalent enrollment is projected to increase at an annual growth rate of 0.5 percent during the 1992–98 period and 1.1 percent during the 1998–2004 period (figure 25).

The full-time-equivalent of undergraduate enrollment in 4-year institutions, which was an estimated 5.9 million in 1992, will be 6.6 million by the year 2004. The full-time-equivalent of undergraduate enrollment in 2-year institutions, which was an estimated 3.2 million in 1992, will be 3.5 million by the year 2004.

In public institutions, full-time-equivalent enrollment, which was an estimated 7.9 million in 1992, will be 8.7 million by the year 2004. In private institutions, full-time-equivalent enrollment, which was an estimated 2.6 million in 1992, will be 2.8 million by the year 2004.

Under the low and high alternatives, full-time-equivalent enrollment in all institutions is expected to range between 10.9 million and 12.1 million by the year 2004. For the low alternative, this is a projected average annual growth rate of 0.4 percent over the projection period. For the high alternative, it will be a growth rate of 1.2 percent.

Enrollment, by Age

The alternative projections of higher education enrollment by age, sex, and attendance status are shown in table 6 (middle alternative), table 7 (low alternative), and table 8 (high alternative). These projections are based on age-specific enrollment data from the Bureau of the Census and enrollment data from NCES.

Under the middle alternative, the period from 1984 to 2004 will be one of change in the age distribution of college students. The enrollment of students who are 18- to 24-years old increased from 7.1 million in 1984 to an estimated 7.8 million in 1992, an increase of 10 percent (figure 26). This number is expected to increase to 9.1 million by the year 2004, an increase of 17 percent from 1992. As a result, the proportion of students who are 18- to 24-years old, which fell from 57.8 percent in 1984 to 53.6 percent in 1992, is projected to be 57.3 percent by the year 2004.

On the other hand, the enrollment of students who are 25 years old and over increased from 4.9 million in 1984 to an estimated 6.6 million in 1992, an increase of 34 percent. This number is projected to remain around 6.6 million by the year 2004. The projected stability in the enrollment of students 25 years old and over is due, in part, to the declines in the 25- to 29-year-old population and the 30- to 34-year-old population over the projection period. However, the 35- to 44-year-old population will continue to increase for most of the projection period, contributing to the stable enrollment during this period. Over the projection period, the proportion of students 25 years old and over rose from 40.2 percent in 1984 to 45.4 percent in 1992. This proportion is projected to be 41.5 percent by the year 2004.

Under the low and high alternatives, the college enrollment of students 18- to 24-years old is projected to range between 8.4 million and 9.5 million by the year 2004. The college enrollment of students 25 years old and over is expected to range between 6.5 million and 7.0 million by the year 2004.

Figure 8
College-age populations (18-24 years and 25-29 years),
with projections: 1979 to 2004

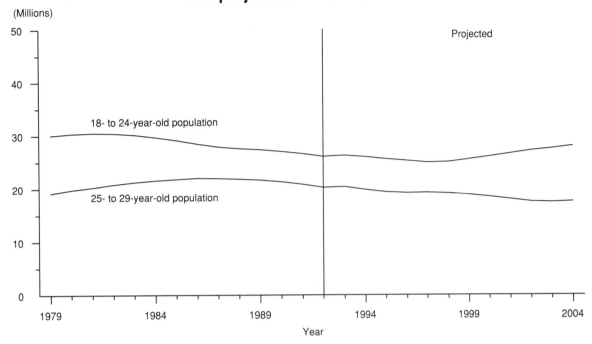

Figure 9
College-age populations (30-34 years and 35-44 years),
with projections: 1979 to 2004

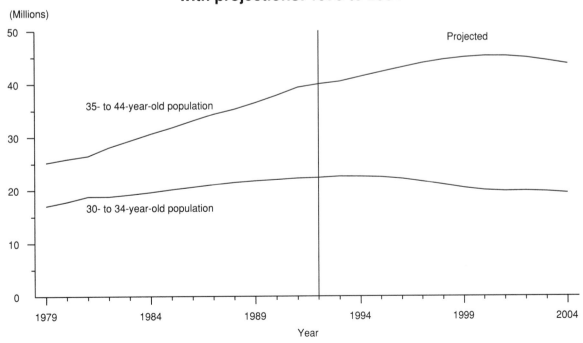

Figure 10
Enrollment in institutions of higher education
with alternative projections: Fall 1979 to fall 2004

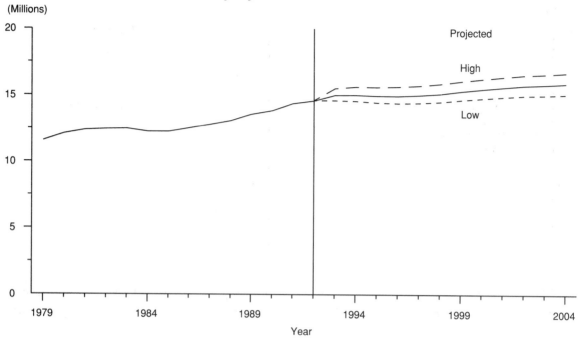

Figure 11
Average annual growth rates for total higher education enrollment

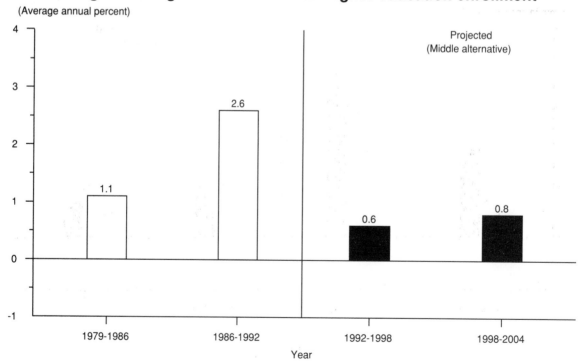

Figure 12
Enrollment in institutions of higher education, by sex, with middle alternative projections: Fall 1979 to fall 2004

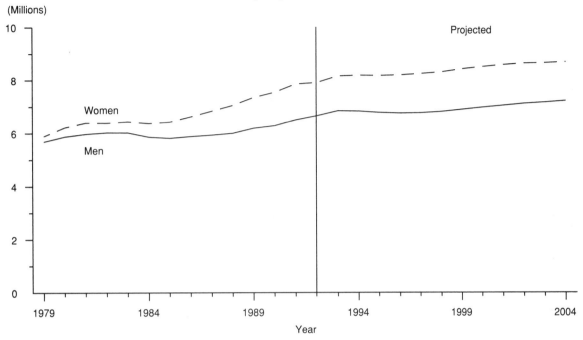

Figure 13
Average annual growth rates for total higher education enrollment, by sex

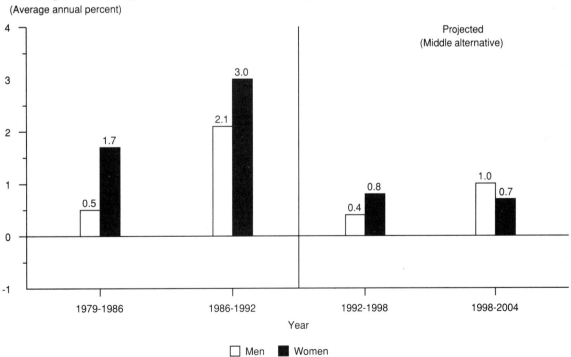

Figure 14
Enrollment in institutions of higher education, by attendance status, with middle alternative projections: Fall 1979 to fall 2004

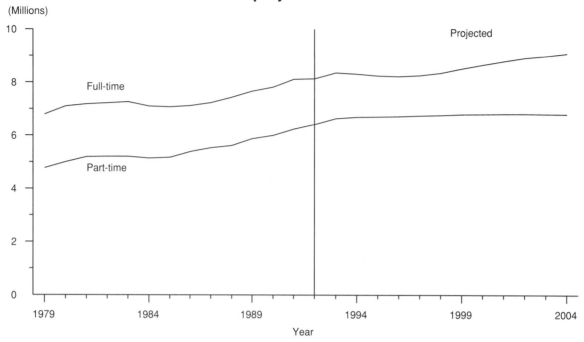

Figure 15
Average annual growth rates for total higher education enrollment, by attendance status

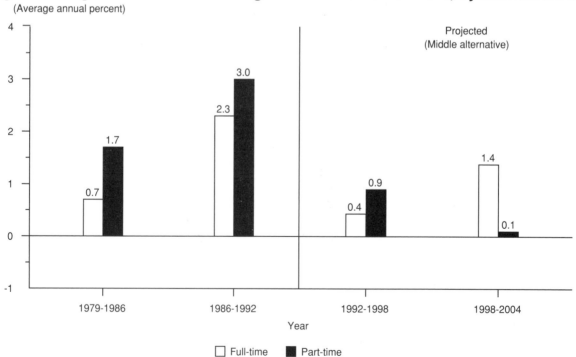

Figure 16
Enrollment in institutions of higher education, by control of institution, with alternative projections: Fall 1979 to fall 2004

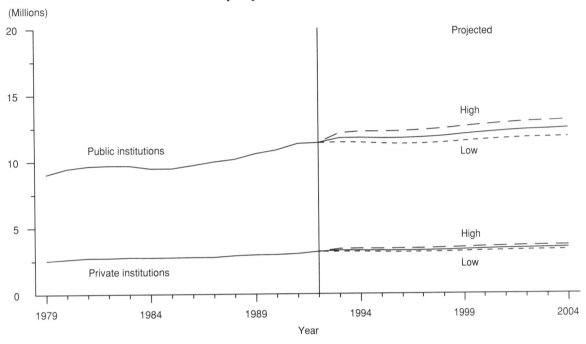

Figure 17
Average annual growth rates for total higher education enrollment, by control of institution

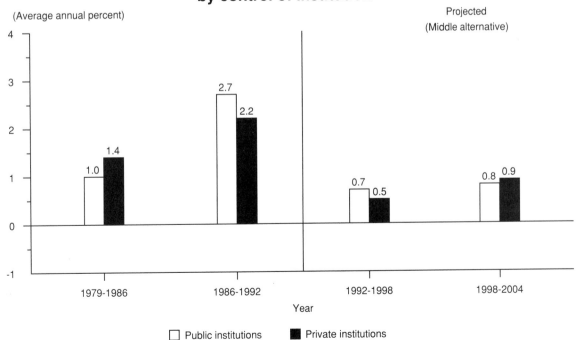

Figure 18
Enrollment in institutions of higher education, by type of institution, with alternative projections: Fall 1979 to fall 2004

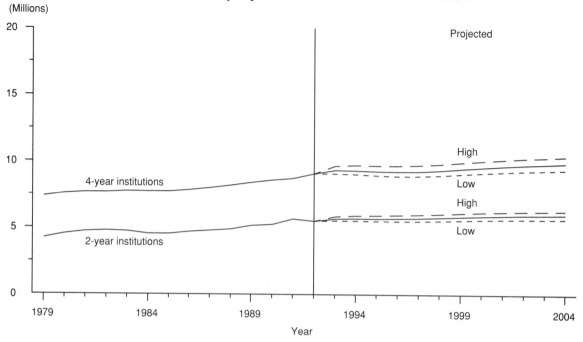

Figure 19
Average annual growth rates for total higher education enrollment by type of institution

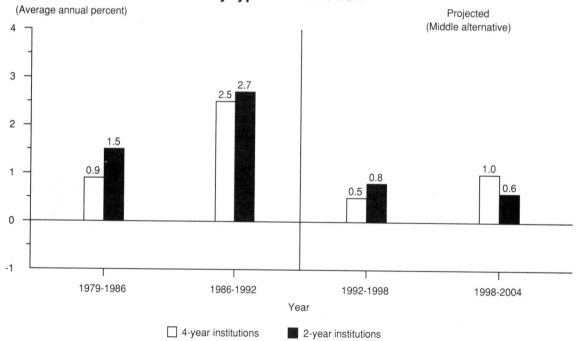

Figure 20
Undergraduate enrollment in institutions of higher education, with alternative projections: Fall 1979 to fall 2004

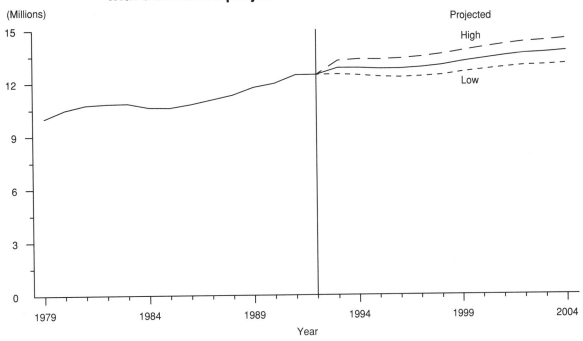

Figure 21
Average annual growth rates for undergraduate enrollment

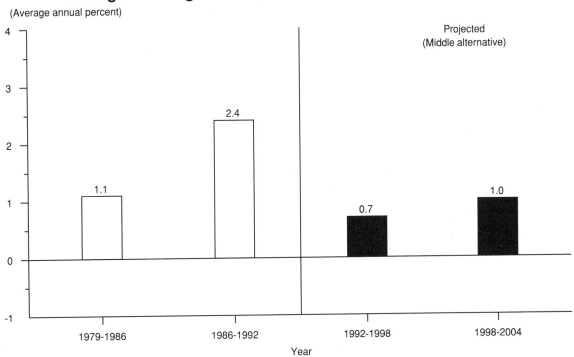

Figure 22

Postbaccalaureate enrollment in institutions of higher education, with alternative projections: Fall 1979 to fall 2004

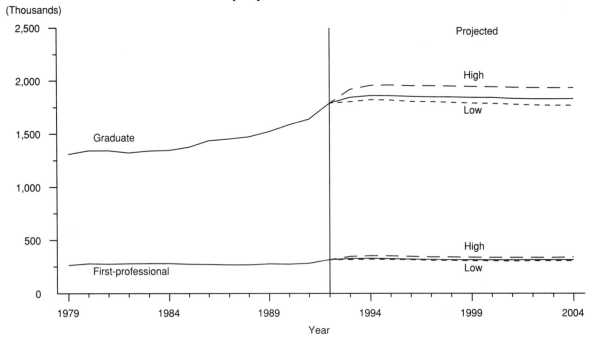

Figure 23

Average annual rates of change for postbaccalaureate enrollment

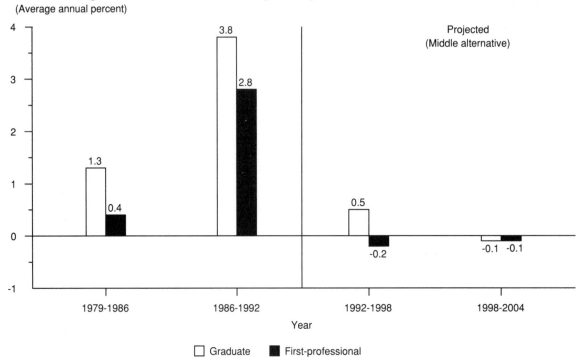

Figure 24
Full-time-equivalent enrollment in institutions of higher education, with alternative projections: Fall 1979 to fall 2004

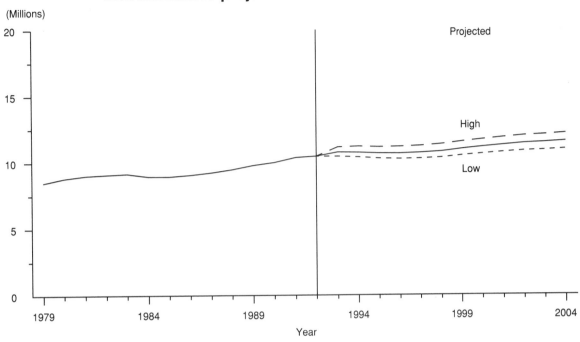

Figure 25
Average annual growth rates for full-time-equivalent enrollment

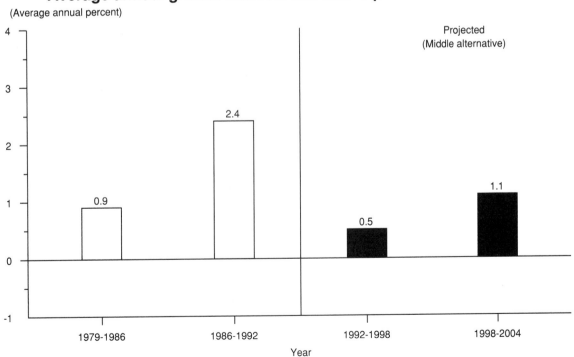

Figure 26
Enrollment in institutions of higher education, by age group
with middle alternative projections: Fall 1984, 1992, and 2004

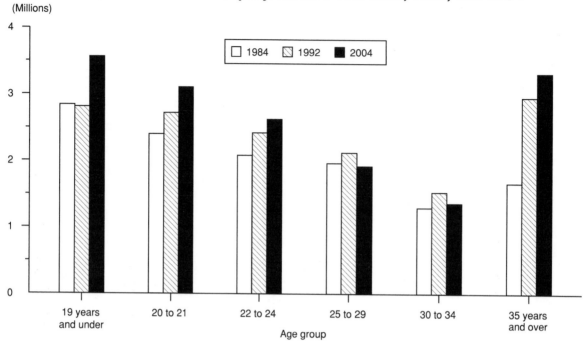

Figure 27
Enrollment of men in institutions of higher education, by age group, with middle alternative projections: Fall 1984, 1992, and 2004

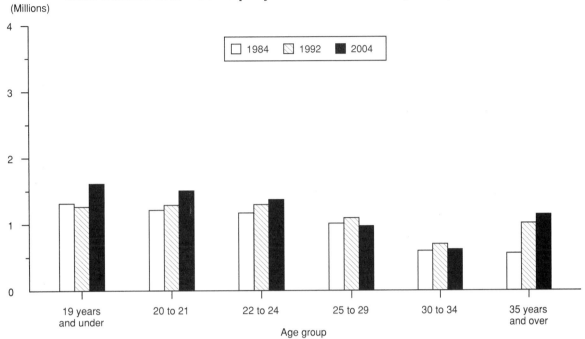

Figure 28
Enrollment of women in institutions of higher education, by age group, with middle alternative projections: Fall 1984, 1992, and 2004

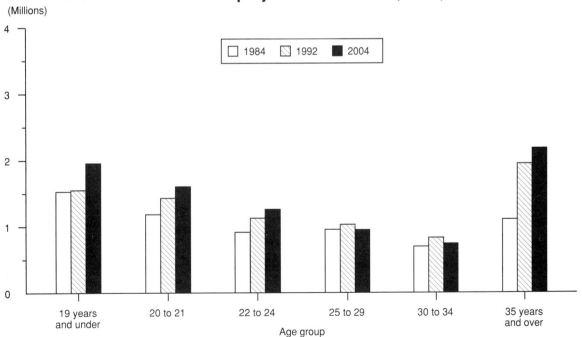

Table 3.—Total enrollment in all institutions of higher education, by sex, attendance status, and control of institution, with alternative projections: 50 States and D.C., fall 1979 to fall 2004

(In thousands)

Year	Total	Sex		Attendance status		Control	
		Men	Women	Full-time	Part-time	Public	Private
1979	11,570	5,683	5,887	6,794	4,776	9,037	2,533
1980	12,097	5,874	6,223	7,098	4,999	9,457	2,640
1981	12,372	5,975	6,397	7,181	5,190	9,647	2,725
1982	12,426	6,031	6,394	7,221	5,205	9,696	2,730
1983	12,465	6,024	6,441	7,261	5,204	9,683	2,782
1984	12,242	5,864	6,378	7,098	5,144	9,477	2,765
1985	12,247	5,818	6,429	7,075	5,172	9,479	2,768
1986	12,504	5,885	6,619	7,120	5,384	9,714	2,790
1987	12,767	5,932	6,835	7,231	5,536	9,973	2,793
1988	13,055	6,002	7,053	7,437	5,619	10,161	2,894
1989	13,539	6,190	7,349	7,661	5,878	10,578	2,961
1990	13,820	6,284	7,535	7,821	5,998	10,845	2,975
1991	14,359	6,502	7,857	8,115	6,244	11,310	3,049
1992 *	14,558	6,654	7,904	8,139	6,419	11,377	3,181
Middle alternative projections							
1993	14,994	6,842	8,152	8,355	6,639	11,722	3,272
1994	15,005	6,831	8,174	8,312	6,693	11,736	3,269
1995	14,946	6,781	8,165	8,242	6,704	11,695	3,251
1996	14,938	6,752	8,186	8,220	6,718	11,696	3,242
1997	14,999	6,765	8,234	8,257	6,742	11,746	3,253
1998	15,111	6,811	8,300	8,346	6,765	11,836	3,275
1999	15,304	6,892	8,412	8,511	6,793	11,986	3,318
2000	15,462	6,970	8,492	8,657	6,805	12,108	3,354
2001	15,607	7,041	8,566	8,795	6,812	12,220	3,387
2002	15,738	7,116	8,622	8,923	6,815	12,318	3,420
2003	15,802	7,161	8,641	8,992	6,810	12,365	3,437
2004	15,892	7,216	8,676	9,087	6,805	12,431	3,461
Low alternative projections							
1993	14,589	6,608	7,981	8,104	6,485	11,408	3,181
1994	14,549	6,602	7,947	8,029	6,520	11,379	3,170
1995	14,448	6,533	7,915	7,938	6,510	11,303	3,145
1996	14,396	6,480	7,916	7,893	6,503	11,268	3,128
1997	14,424	6,479	7,945	7,917	6,507	11,292	3,132
1998	14,500	6,504	7,996	7,987	6,513	11,352	3,148
1999	14,649	6,564	8,085	8,131	6,518	11,468	3,181
2000	14,776	6,620	8,156	8,255	6,521	11,565	3,211
2001	14,887	6,670	8,217	8,370	6,517	11,648	3,239
2002	14,985	6,720	8,265	8,475	6,510	11,722	3,263
2003	15,017	6,745	8,272	8,523	6,494	11,744	3,273
2004	15,083	6,784	8,299	8,604	6,479	11,791	3,292
High alternative projections							
1993	15,493	7,107	8,386	8,673	6,820	12,103	3,390
1994	15,619	7,142	8,477	8,683	6,936	12,206	3,413
1995	15,599	7,124	8,475	8,617	6,982	12,200	3,399
1996	15,634	7,116	8,518	8,625	7,009	12,231	3,403
1997	15,718	7,145	8,573	8,680	7,038	12,301	3,417
1998	15,858	7,207	8,651	8,792	7,066	12,411	3,447
1999	16,054	7,291	8,763	8,963	7,091	12,564	3,490
2000	16,225	7,371	8,854	9,112	7,113	12,696	3,529
2001	16,382	7,449	8,933	9,254	7,128	12,817	3,565
2002	16,525	7,528	8,997	9,383	7,142	12,926	3,599
2003	16,597	7,578	9,019	9,452	7,145	12,980	3,617
2004	16,699	7,638	9,061	9,551	7,148	13,058	3,641

* Projected.

NOTE: Projections are based on data through 1991. Because of rounding, details may not add to totals.

SOURCE: U.S. Department of Education, National Center for Education Statistics, Fall Enrollment in Colleges and Universities surveys and Integrated Postsecondary Education Data System (IPEDS) surveys. (This table was prepared June 1993.)

Table 4.—Total enrollment in 4-year institutions of higher education, by sex, attendance status, and control of institution, with alternative projections: 50 States and D.C., fall 1979 to fall 2004

(In thousands)

Year	Total	Sex		Attendance status		Control	
		Men	Women	Full-time	Part-time	Public	Private
1979	7,353	3,762	3,591	5,202	2,151	4,980	2,373
1980	7,571	3,827	3,743	5,344	2,226	5,129	2,442
1981	7,655	3,852	3,805	5,387	2,270	5,166	2,489
1982	7,654	3,861	3,793	5,381	2,273	5,176	2,478
1983	7,741	3,893	3,849	5,434	2,307	5,223	2,518
1984	7,711	3,847	3,864	5,395	2,317	5,198	2,513
1985	7,716	3,816	3,900	5,385	2,331	5,210	2,506
1986	7,824	3,824	4,000	5,423	2,401	5,300	2,524
1987	7,990	3,859	4,131	5,522	2,468	5,432	2,558
1988	8,180	3,912	4,268	5,693	2,487	5,546	2,634
1989	8,388	3,973	4,414	5,805	2,582	5,694	2,693
1990	8,579	4,052	4,528	5,937	2,642	5,848	2,731
1991	8,707	4,100	4,607	6,041	2,666	5,905	2,802
1992 *	9,060	4,328	4,732	6,177	2,883	6,139	2,921
Middle alternative projections							
1993	9,323	4,452	4,871	6,343	2,980	6,318	3,005
1994	9,310	4,439	4,871	6,302	3,008	6,308	3,002
1995	9,255	4,399	4,856	6,239	3,016	6,270	2,985
1996	9,234	4,374	4,860	6,212	3,022	6,259	2,975
1997	9,259	4,375	4,884	6,228	3,031	6,276	2,983
1998	9,329	4,404	4,925	6,291	3,038	6,326	3,003
1999	9,455	4,456	4,999	6,410	3,045	6,413	3,042
2000	9,563	4,508	5,055	6,519	3,044	6,489	3,074
2001	9,668	4,557	5,111	6,628	3,040	6,563	3,105
2002	9,761	4,608	5,153	6,726	3,035	6,628	3,133
2003	9,816	4,642	5,174	6,786	3,030	6,666	3,150
2004	9,884	4,680	5,204	6,861	3,023	6,712	3,172
Low alternative projections							
1993	9,063	4,293	4,770	6,147	2,916	6,142	2,921
1994	9,023	4,283	4,740	6,084	2,939	6,112	2,911
1995	8,946	4,233	4,713	6,007	2,939	6,059	2,887
1996	8,898	4,190	4,708	5,962	2,936	6,028	2,870
1997	8,909	4,186	4,723	5,971	2,938	6,036	2,873
1998	8,958	4,201	4,757	6,019	2,939	6,071	2,887
1999	9,058	4,240	4,818	6,122	2,936	6,142	2,916
2000	9,149	4,280	4,869	6,215	2,934	6,206	2,943
2001	9,234	4,317	4,917	6,307	2,927	6,265	2,969
2002	9,308	4,353	4,955	6,389	2,919	6,317	2,991
2003	9,342	4,375	4,967	6,433	2,909	6,341	3,001
2004	9,396	4,404	4,992	6,497	2,899	6,378	3,018
High alternative projections							
1993	9,654	4,633	5,021	6,594	3,060	6,538	3,116
1994	9,708	4,645	5,063	6,591	3,117	6,573	3,135
1995	9,673	4,622	5,051	6,532	3,141	6,551	3,122
1996	9,682	4,609	5,073	6,530	3,152	6,558	3,124
1997	9,723	4,623	5,100	6,560	3,163	6,587	3,136
1998	9,811	4,663	5,148	6,640	3,171	6,649	3,162
1999	9,940	4,717	5,223	6,764	3,176	6,739	3,201
2000	10,052	4,768	5,284	6,874	3,178	6,818	3,234
2001	10,166	4,823	5,343	6,987	3,179	6,898	3,268
2002	10,267	4,877	5,390	7,088	3,179	6,967	3,300
2003	10,322	4,912	5,410	7,146	3,176	7,006	3,316
2004	10,397	4,953	5,444	7,225	3,172	7,058	3,339

* Projected.

NOTE: Projections are based on data through 1991. Because of rounding, details may not add to totals.

SOURCE: U.S. Department of Education, National Center for Education Statistics, Fall Enrollment in Colleges and Universities surveys and Integrated Postsecondary Education Data System (IPEDS) surveys. (This table was prepared June 1993.)

Table 5.—Total enrollment in 2-year institutions of higher education, by sex, attendance status, and control of institution, with alternative projections: 50 States and D.C., fall 1979 to fall 2004

(In thousands)

Year	Total	Sex		Attendance status		Control	
		Men	Women	Full-time	Part-time	Public	Private
1979	4,217	1,924	2,294	1,591	2,627	4,057	160
1980	4,526	2,047	2,479	1,754	2,772	4,329	198
1981	4,716	2,124	2,591	1,796	2,919	4,481	236
1982	4,772	2,170	2,602	1,840	2,932	4,520	252
1983	4,723	2,131	2,592	1,827	2,897	4,459	264
1984	4,531	2,017	2,514	1,704	2,827	4,279	252
1985	4,531	2,002	2,529	1,691	2,840	4,270	261
1986	4,680	2,061	2,619	1,696	2,983	4,414	266
1987	4,776	2,073	2,703	1,709	3,068	4,541	235
1988	4,875	2,090	2,785	1,744	3,132	4,615	260
1989	5,151	2,217	2,934	1,856	3,295	4,884	267
1990	5,240	2,233	3,007	1,884	3,356	4,996	244
1991	5,652	2,402	3,250	2,075	3,577	5,405	247
1992 *	5,498	2,326	3,172	1,962	3,536	5,238	260
Middle alternative projections							
1993	5,671	2,390	3,281	2,012	3,659	5,404	267
1994	5,695	2,392	3,303	2,010	3,685	5,428	267
1995	5,691	2,382	3,309	2,003	3,688	5,425	266
1996	5,704	2,378	3,326	2,008	3,696	5,437	267
1997	5,740	2,390	3,350	2,029	3,711	5,470	270
1998	5,782	2,407	3,375	2,055	3,727	5,510	272
1999	5,849	2,436	3,413	2,101	3,748	5,573	276
2000	5,899	2,462	3,437	2,138	3,761	5,619	280
2001	5,939	2,484	3,455	2,167	3,772	5,657	282
2002	5,977	2,508	3,469	2,197	3,780	5,690	287
2003	5,986	2,519	3,467	2,206	3,780	5,699	287
2004	6,008	2,536	3,472	2,226	3,782	5,719	289
Low alternative projections							
1993	5,526	2,315	3,211	1,957	3,569	5,266	260
1994	5,526	2,319	3,207	1,945	3,581	5,267	259
1995	5,502	2,300	3,202	1,931	3,571	5,244	258
1996	5,498	2,290	3,208	1,931	3,567	5,240	258
1997	5,515	2,293	3,222	1,946	3,569	5,256	259
1998	5,542	2,303	3,239	1,968	3,574	5,281	261
1999	5,591	2,324	3,267	2,009	3,582	5,326	265
2000	5,627	2,340	3,287	2,040	3,587	5,359	268
2001	5,653	2,353	3,300	2,063	3,590	5,383	270
2002	5,677	2,367	3,310	2,086	3,591	5,405	272
2003	5,675	2,370	3,305	2,090	3,585	5,403	272
2004	5,687	2,380	3,307	2,107	3,580	5,413	274
High alternative projections							
1993	5,839	2,474	3,365	2,079	3,760	5,565	274
1994	5,911	2,497	3,414	2,092	3,819	5,633	278
1995	5,926	2,502	3,424	2,085	3,841	5,649	277
1996	5,952	2,507	3,445	2,095	3,857	5,673	279
1997	5,995	2,522	3,473	2,120	3,875	5,714	281
1998	6,047	2,544	3,503	2,152	3,895	5,762	285
1999	6,114	2,574	3,540	2,199	3,915	5,825	289
2000	6,173	2,603	3,570	2,238	3,935	5,878	295
2001	6,216	2,626	3,590	2,267	3,949	5,919	297
2002	6,258	2,651	3,607	2,295	3,963	5,959	299
2003	6,275	2,666	3,609	2,306	3,969	5,974	301
2004	6,302	2,685	3,617	2,326	3,976	6,000	302

* Projected.

NOTE: Projections are based on data through 1991. Because of rounding, details may not add to totals.

SOURCE: U.S. Department of Education, National Center for Education Statistics, Fall Enrollment in Colleges and Universities surveys and Integrated Postsecondary Education Data System (IPEDS) surveys. (This table was prepared June 1993.)

Table 6.—Enrollment in all institutions of higher education, by age, sex, and attendance status, with middle alternative projections: 50 States and D.C., fall 1984, 1989, 1992, 1999, and 2004

(In thousands)

Age	1984 (Estimated) Total	Full-time	Part-time	1989 (Estimated) Total	Full-time	Part-time	1992 (Projected) Total	Full-time	Part-time	1999 (Projected) Total	Full-time	Part-time	2004 (Projected) Total	Full-time	Part-time
Total	12,242	7,098	5,144	13,539	7,661	5,878	14,558	8,139	6,419	15,304	8,511	6,793	15,892	9,087	6,805
14 to 17 years	231	206	25	172	148	24	150	131	19	179	157	22	187	164	23
18 to 19 years	2,609	2,298	312	2,857	2,561	297	2,663	2,344	318	3,173	2,791	382	3,378	2,977	401
20 to 21 years	2,398	1,973	425	2,442	2,031	411	2,718	2,251	466	2,750	2,251	500	3,104	2,517	587
22 to 24 years	2,081	1,307	774	2,194	1,357	837	2,419	1,585	834	2,306	1,487	819	2,626	1,694	932
25 to 29 years	1,964	772	1,192	2,090	718	1,372	2,123	869	1,254	2,056	807	1,249	1,919	753	1,165
30 to 34 years	1,292	309	983	1,353	351	1,003	1,528	412	1,116	1,429	392	1,038	1,360	373	987
35 years and over	1,667	234	1,433	2,431	495	1,935	2,956	545	2,410	3,410	625	2,784	3,317	608	2,709
Men	5,864	3,648	2,216	6,190	3,740	2,450	6,654	3,992	2,662	6,892	4,145	2,747	7,216	4,446	2,770
14 to 17 years	82	74	8	71	59	12	62	52	10	71	59	12	74	62	12
18 to 19 years	1,232	1,083	148	1,342	1,229	113	1,202	1,073	129	1,420	1,274	146	1,537	1,384	154
20 to 21 years	1,214	1,020	194	1,189	991	198	1,289	1,061	228	1,318	1,069	249	1,503	1,201	301
22 to 24 years	1,169	799	370	1,090	723	367	1,294	897	397	1,211	833	378	1,369	940	429
25 to 29 years	1,011	443	568	1,038	399	639	1,093	507	586	1,042	469	573	971	437	534
30 to 34 years	596	147	449	603	164	439	699	195	504	653	193	459	619	183	435
35 years and over	561	82	479	857	175	682	1,013	206	807	1,176	246	930	1,143	239	904
Women	6,378	3,451	2,927	7,349	3,921	3,428	7,904	4,147	3,757	8,412	4,366	4,046	8,676	4,641	4,035
14 to 17 years	149	131	18	101	89	12	89	80	9	108	98	10	113	102	11
18 to 19 years	1,377	1,214	163	1,515	1,331	184	1,459	1,270	189	1,753	1,517	235	1,841	1,594	247
20 to 21 years	1,183	952	231	1,253	1,040	213	1,428	1,190	238	1,432	1,181	251	1,601	1,316	285
22 to 24 years	913	509	404	1,104	634	470	1,125	688	437	1,095	654	441	1,258	754	504
25 to 29 years	953	330	623	1,052	320	732	1,029	362	667	1,013	338	675	947	316	631
30 to 34 years	697	163	534	750	187	563	829	217	612	777	198	578	741	189	552
35 years and over	1,105	152	953	1,574	321	1,253	1,942	338	1,603	2,233	379	1,854	2,175	369	1,805

NOTE: Because of rounding, details may not add to totals.

SOURCE: U.S. Department of Education, National Center for Education Statistics, Fall Enrollment in Colleges and Universities surveys and Integrated Postsecondary Education Data System (IPEDS) surveys; and U.S. Department of Commerce, Bureau of the Census, Unpublished tabulations. (This table was prepared June 1993.)

Table 7.—Enrollment in all institutions of higher education, by age, sex, and attendance status, with low alternative projections: 50 States and D.C., fall 1984, 1989, 1992, 1999, and 2004

(In thousands)

Age	1984 (Estimated)			1989 (Estimated)			1992 (Projected)			1999 (Projected)			2004 (Projected)		
	Total	Full-time	Part-time	Total	Full-time	Part-time	Total	Full-time	Part-time	Total	Full-time	Part-time	Total	Full-time	Part-time
Total	12,242	7,098	5,144	13,539	7,661	5,878	14,558	8,139	6,419	14,649	8,131	6,518	15,083	8,604	6,479
14 to 17 years	231	206	25	172	148	24	150	131	19	172	152	20	180	159	21
18 to 19 years	2,609	2,298	312	2,857	2,561	297	2,663	2,344	318	3,016	2,666	351	3,168	2,800	368
20 to 21 years	2,398	1,973	425	2,442	2,031	411	2,718	2,251	466	2,549	2,103	446	2,839	2,343	496
22 to 24 years	2,081	1,307	774	2,194	1,357	837	2,419	1,585	834	2,167	1,425	742	2,443	1,607	836
25 to 29 years	1,964	772	1,192	2,090	718	1,372	2,123	869	1,254	1,966	794	1,172	1,835	741	1,094
30 to 34 years	1,292	309	983	1,353	351	1,003	1,528	412	1,116	1,394	387	1,008	1,327	368	959
35 years and over	1,667	234	1,433	2,431	495	1,935	2,956	545	2,410	3,383	603	2,780	3,291	586	2,705
Men	5,864	3,648	2,216	6,190	3,740	2,450	6,654	3,992	2,662	6,564	3,899	2,665	6,784	4,128	2,656
14 to 17 years	82	74	8	71	59	12	62	52	10	64	54	10	67	57	11
18 to 19 years	1,232	1,083	148	1,342	1,229	113	1,202	1,073	129	1,317	1,173	144	1,383	1,232	151
20 to 21 years	1,214	1,020	194	1,189	991	198	1,289	1,061	228	1,202	983	219	1,338	1,095	243
22 to 24 years	1,169	799	370	1,090	723	367	1,294	897	397	1,163	802	361	1,312	905	408
25 to 29 years	1,011	443	568	1,038	399	639	1,093	507	586	1,010	456	554	941	425	516
30 to 34 years	596	147	449	603	164	439	699	195	504	644	193	451	611	183	428
35 years and over	561	82	479	857	175	682	1,013	206	807	1,163	237	926	1,130	230	899
Women	6,378	3,451	2,927	7,349	3,921	3,428	7,904	4,147	3,757	8,085	4,232	3,853	8,299	4,476	3,823
14 to 17 years	149	131	18	101	89	12	89	80	9	108	98	10	113	102	11
18 to 19 years	1,377	1,214	163	1,515	1,331	184	1,459	1,270	189	1,699	1,493	206	1,784	1,567	217
20 to 21 years	1,183	952	231	1,253	1,040	213	1,428	1,190	238	1,347	1,120	227	1,501	1,248	253
22 to 24 years	913	509	404	1,104	634	470	1,125	688	437	1,004	624	380	1,131	702	428
25 to 29 years	953	330	623	1,052	320	732	1,029	362	667	956	338	618	894	316	578
30 to 34 years	697	163	534	750	187	563	829	217	612	750	193	557	716	184	532
35 years and over	1,105	152	953	1,574	321	1,253	1,942	338	1,603	2,220	366	1,854	2,161	356	1,805

NOTE: Because of rounding, details may not add to totals.

SOURCE: U.S. Department of Education, National Center for Education Statistics, Fall Enrollment in Colleges and Universities surveys and Integrated Postsecondary Education Data System (IPEDS) surveys; and U.S. Department of Commerce, Bureau of the Census, Unpublished tabulations. (This table was prepared June 1993.)

Table 8.—Enrollment in all institutions of higher education, by age, sex, and attendance status, with high alternative projections: 50 States and D.C., fall 1984, 1989, 1992, 1999, and 2004

(In thousands)

Age	1984 (Estimated)			1989 (Estimated)			1992 (Projected)			1999 (Projected)			2004 (Projected)		
	Total	Full-time	Part-time	Total	Full-time	Part-time	Total	Full-time	Part-time	Total	Full-time	Part-time	Total	Full-time	Part-time
Total	12,242	7,098	5,144	13,539	7,661	5,878	14,558	8,139	6,419	16,054	8,963	7,091	16,699	9,551	7,148
14 to 17 years	231	206	25	172	148	24	150	131	19	185	163	22	194	171	23
18 to 19 years	2,609	2,298	312	2,857	2,561	297	2,663	2,344	318	3,257	2,846	410	3,472	3,036	435
20 to 21 years	2,398	1,973	425	2,442	2,031	411	2,718	2,251	466	2,913	2,395	518	3,291	2,678	612
22 to 24 years	2,081	1,307	774	2,194	1,357	837	2,419	1,585	834	2,449	1,590	859	2,766	1,795	971
25 to 29 years	1,964	772	1,192	2,090	718	1,372	2,123	869	1,254	2,198	896	1,301	2,091	836	1,255
30 to 34 years	1,292	309	983	1,353	351	1,003	1,528	412	1,116	1,542	412	1,130	1,467	392	1,075
35 years and over	1,667	234	1,433	2,431	495	1,935	2,956	545	2,410	3,513	661	2,852	3,418	643	2,775
Men	5,864	3,648	2,216	6,190	3,740	2,450	6,654	3,992	2,662	7,291	4,367	2,924	7,638	4,682	2,956
14 to 17 years	82	74	8	71	59	12	62	52	10	71	59	12	75	62	13
18 to 19 years	1,232	1,083	148	1,342	1,229	113	1,202	1,073	129	1,436	1,278	157	1,559	1,390	170
20 to 21 years	1,214	1,020	194	1,189	991	198	1,289	1,061	228	1,409	1,148	261	1,610	1,289	321
22 to 24 years	1,169	799	370	1,090	723	367	1,294	897	397	1,278	875	402	1,447	991	456
25 to 29 years	1,011	443	568	1,038	399	639	1,093	507	586	1,147	534	613	1,068	497	571
30 to 34 years	596	147	449	603	164	439	699	195	504	724	205	519	686	194	492
35 years and over	561	82	479	857	175	682	1,013	206	807	1,228	268	959	1,193	261	932
Women	6,378	3,451	2,927	7,349	3,921	3,428	7,904	4,147	3,757	8,763	4,596	4,167	9,061	4,869	4,192
14 to 17 years	149	131	18	101	89	12	89	80	9	114	104	10	119	109	11
18 to 19 years	1,377	1,214	163	1,515	1,331	184	1,459	1,270	189	1,821	1,568	253	1,912	1,647	266
20 to 21 years	1,183	952	231	1,253	1,040	213	1,428	1,190	238	1,504	1,247	257	1,680	1,390	291
22 to 24 years	913	509	404	1,104	634	470	1,125	688	437	1,171	714	457	1,319	804	514
25 to 29 years	953	330	623	1,052	320	732	1,029	362	667	1,051	363	688	1,023	339	684
30 to 34 years	697	163	534	750	187	563	829	217	612	819	207	611	781	198	583
35 years and over	1,105	152	953	1,574	321	1,253	1,942	338	1,603	2,285	393	1,892	2,225	383	1,843

NOTE: Because of rounding, details may not add to totals.

SOURCE: U.S. Department of Education, National Center for Education Statistics, Fall Enrollment in Colleges and Universities surveys and Integrated Postsecondary Education Data System (IPEDS) surveys; and U.S. Department of Commerce, Bureau of the Census, Unpublished tabulations. (This table was prepared June 1993.)

Table 9.—Total enrollment in all institutions of higher education, by sex and attendance status, with alternative projections: 50 States and D.C., fall 1979 to fall 2004

(In thousands)

Year	Total	Men		Women	
		Full-time	Part-time	Full-time	Part-time
1979	11,570	3,544	2,142	3,249	2,636
1980	12,097	3,689	2,185	3,409	2,814
1981	12,372	3,714	2,262	3,469	2,927
1982	12,426	3,753	2,278	3,468	2,927
1983	12,465	3,760	2,264	3,501	2,940
1984	12,242	3,648	2,216	3,451	2,927
1985	12,247	3,608	2,211	3,468	2,961
1986	12,504	3,599	2,285	3,521	3,098
1987	12,767	3,611	2,321	3,620	3,214
1988	13,055	3,662	2,340	3,775	3,278
1989	13,539	3,740	2,450	3,921	3,428
1990	13,820	3,808	2,477	4,013	3,522
1991	14,359	3,929	2,572	4,186	3,671
1992 *	14,558	3,992	2,662	4,147	3,757
Middle alternative projections					
1993	14,994	4,104	2,738	4,251	3,901
1994	15,005	4,071	2,760	4,241	3,933
1995	14,946	4,031	2,750	4,211	3,954
1996	14,938	4,010	2,742	4,210	3,976
1997	14,999	4,024	2,741	4,233	4,001
1998	15,111	4,067	2,744	4,279	4,021
1999	15,304	4,145	2,747	4,366	4,046
2000	15,462	4,218	2,752	4,439	4,053
2001	15,607	4,285	2,756	4,510	4,056
2002	15,738	4,354	2,762	4,569	4,053
2003	15,802	4,396	2,765	4,596	4,045
2004	15,892	4,446	2,770	4,641	4,035
Low alternative projections					
1993	14,589	3,938	2,670	4,166	3,815
1994	14,549	3,904	2,698	4,125	3,822
1995	14,448	3,847	2,686	4,091	3,824
1996	14,396	3,806	2,674	4,087	3,829
1997	14,424	3,810	2,669	4,107	3,838
1998	14,500	3,837	2,667	4,150	3,846
1999	14,649	3,899	2,665	4,232	3,853
2000	14,776	3,956	2,664	4,299	3,857
2001	14,887	4,008	2,662	4,362	3,855
2002	14,985	4,059	2,661	4,416	3,849
2003	15,017	4,087	2,658	4,436	3,836
2004	15,083	4,128	2,656	4,476	3,823
High alternative projections					
1993	15,493	4,263	2,844	4,410	3,976
1994	15,619	4,247	2,895	4,436	4,041
1995	15,599	4,207	2,917	4,410	4,065
1996	15,634	4,199	2,917	4,426	4,092
1997	15,718	4,229	2,916	4,451	4,122
1998	15,858	4,288	2,919	4,504	4,147
1999	16,054	4,367	2,924	4,596	4,167
2000	16,225	4,441	2,930	4,671	4,183
2001	16,382	4,513	2,936	4,741	4,192
2002	16,525	4,584	2,944	4,799	4,198
2003	16,597	4,627	2,951	4,825	4,194
2004	16,699	4,682	2,956	4,869	4,192

* Projected.

NOTE: Projections are based on data through 1991. Because of rounding, details may not add to totals.

SOURCE: U.S. Department of Education, National Center for Education Statistics, Fall Enrollment in Colleges and Universities surveys and Integrated Postsecondary Education Data System (IPEDS) surveys. (This table was prepared June 1993.)

Table 10.—Total enrollment in public 4-year institutions of higher education, by sex and attendance status, with alternative projections: 50 States and D.C., fall 1979 to fall 2004

(In thousands)

Year	Total	Men		Women	
		Full-time	Part-time	Full-time	Part-time
1979	4,980	1,833	676	1,661	810
1980	5,129	1,873	685	1,719	851
1981	5,166	1,877	692	1,741	858
1982	5,176	1,889	698	1,734	855
1983	5,223	1,910	698	1,755	860
1984	5,198	1,880	694	1,749	874
1985	5,210	1,864	693	1,760	893
1986	5,300	1,865	706	1,792	937
1987	5,432	1,882	723	1,854	973
1988	5,546	1,910	722	1,932	982
1989	5,694	1,938	743	1,997	1,017
1990	5,848	1,982	764	2,051	1,050
1991	5,905	2,006	765	2,083	1,050
1992 *	6,139	2,072	841	2,100	1,126
Middle alternative projections					
1993	6,318	2,131	865	2,154	1,168
1994	6,308	2,112	874	2,144	1,178
1995	6,270	2,087	872	2,126	1,185
1996	6,259	2,073	870	2,124	1,192
1997	6,276	2,076	868	2,133	1,199
1998	6,326	2,097	868	2,157	1,204
1999	6,413	2,135	867	2,201	1,210
2000	6,489	2,172	866	2,240	1,211
2001	6,563	2,209	865	2,280	1,209
2002	6,628	2,245	865	2,312	1,206
2003	6,666	2,269	865	2,329	1,203
2004	6,712	2,296	864	2,353	1,199
Low alternative projections					
1993	6,142	2,045	844	2,107	1,146
1994	6,112	2,024	856	2,083	1,149
1995	6,059	1,992	853	2,063	1,151
1996	6,028	1,967	850	2,059	1,152
1997	6,036	1,966	848	2,067	1,155
1998	6,071	1,979	847	2,088	1,157
1999	6,142	2,009	845	2,131	1,157
2000	6,206	2,039	844	2,166	1,157
2001	6,265	2,067	842	2,201	1,155
2002	6,317	2,095	839	2,231	1,152
2003	6,341	2,112	838	2,244	1,147
2004	6,378	2,134	836	2,266	1,142
High alternative projections					
1993	6,538	2,216	898	2,235	1,189
1994	6,573	2,204	917	2,243	1,209
1995	6,551	2,180	926	2,228	1,217
1996	6,558	2,173	925	2,235	1,225
1997	6,587	2,185	923	2,245	1,234
1998	6,649	2,214	923	2,272	1,240
1999	6,739	2,253	922	2,320	1,244
2000	6,818	2,291	921	2,359	1,247
2001	6,898	2,330	921	2,399	1,248
2002	6,967	2,368	920	2,431	1,248
2003	7,006	2,392	921	2,447	1,246
2004	7,058	2,422	920	2,471	1,245

* Projected.

NOTE: Projections are based on data through 1991. Because of rounding, details may not add to totals.

SOURCE: U.S. Department of Education, National Center for Education Statistics, Fall Enrollment in Colleges and Universities surveys and Integrated Postsecondary Education Data System (IPEDS) surveys. (This table was prepared June 1993.)

Table 11.—Total enrollment in public 2-year institutions of higher education, by sex and attendance status, with alternative projections: 50 States and D.C., fall 1979 to fall 2004

(In thousands)

Year	Total	Men		Women	
		Full-time	Part-time	Full-time	Part-time
1979	4,057	739	1,123	728	1,468
1980	4,329	812	1,152	784	1,581
1981	4,481	827	1,192	803	1,658
1982	4,520	851	1,195	810	1,664
1983	4,459	827	1,175	807	1,650
1984	4,279	762	1,138	756	1,623
1985	4,270	743	1,138	754	1,635
1986	4,414	742	1,193	764	1,715
1987	4,541	744	1,225	787	1,785
1988	4,615	746	1,231	822	1,817
1989	4,884	793	1,302	881	1,907
1990	4,996	811	1,318	906	1,962
1991	5,405	882	1,414	1,004	2,105
1992 *	5,238	833	1,380	943	2,082
		Middle alternative projections			
1993	5,404	855	1,419	967	2,163
1994	5,428	850	1,427	970	2,181
1995	5,425	847	1,420	967	2,191
1996	5,437	848	1,415	970	2,204
1997	5,470	858	1,416	979	2,217
1998	5,510	871	1,419	990	2,230
1999	5,573	893	1,424	1,010	2,246
2000	5,619	911	1,430	1,025	2,253
2001	5,657	926	1,436	1,037	2,258
2002	5,690	941	1,442	1,048	2,259
2003	5,699	948	1,446	1,050	2,255
2004	5,719	958	1,452	1,058	2,251
		Low alternative projections			
1993	5,266	821	1,383	951	2,111
1994	5,267	815	1,393	946	2,113
1995	5,244	806	1,384	942	2,112
1996	5,240	803	1,377	945	2,115
1997	5,256	809	1,374	953	2,120
1998	5,281	818	1,374	964	2,125
1999	5,326	836	1,375	983	2,132
2000	5,359	850	1,376	997	2,136
2001	5,383	860	1,378	1,008	2,137
2002	5,405	871	1,380	1,018	2,136
2003	5,403	874	1,380	1,019	2,130
2004	5,413	882	1,381	1,026	2,124
		High alternative projections			
1993	5,565	881	1,474	1,002	2,208
1994	5,633	881	1,496	1,013	2,243
1995	5,649	877	1,505	1,011	2,256
1996	5,673	881	1,506	1,016	2,270
1997	5,714	894	1,507	1,026	2,287
1998	5,762	910	1,511	1,038	2,303
1999	5,825	932	1,517	1,059	2,317
2000	5,878	951	1,524	1,075	2,328
2001	5,919	966	1,531	1,087	2,335
2002	5,959	982	1,539	1,097	2,341
2003	5,974	989	1,546	1,099	2,340
2004	6,000	1,000	1,553	1,107	2,340

* Projected.

NOTE: Projections are based on data through 1991. Because of rounding, details may not add to totals.

SOURCE: U.S. Department of Education, National Center for Education Statistics, Fall Enrollment in Colleges and Universities surveys and Integrated Postsecondary Education Data System (IPEDS) surveys. (This table was prepared June 1993.)

Table 12.—Total enrollment in private 4-year institutions of higher education, by sex and attendance status, with alternative projections: 50 States and D.C., fall 1979 to fall 2004

(In thousands)

Year	Total	Men		Women	
		Full-time	Part-time	Full-time	Part-time
1979	2,373	924	329	784	336
1980	2,442	936	333	816	357
1981	2,489	939	344	830	376
1982	2,478	933	341	824	380
1983	2,518	935	350	834	399
1984	2,512	926	346	839	401
1985	2,506	917	342	844	403
1986	2,524	910	343	856	415
1987	2,558	908	346	878	426
1988	2,634	933	347	918	436
1989	2,693	933	360	938	463
1990	2,731	944	361	959	467
1991	2,802	962	367	990	483
1992 *	2,921	1,009	406	996	510
Middle alternative projections					
1993	3,005	1,038	418	1,020	529
1994	3,002	1,030	423	1,016	533
1995	2,985	1,018	422	1,008	537
1996	2,975	1,010	421	1,005	539
1997	2,983	1,010	421	1,009	543
1998	3,003	1,018	421	1,019	545
1999	3,042	1,034	420	1,040	548
2000	3,074	1,050	420	1,057	547
2001	3,105	1,064	419	1,075	547
2002	3,133	1,080	418	1,089	546
2003	3,150	1,091	417	1,097	545
2004	3,172	1,103	417	1,109	543
Low alternative projections					
1993	2,921	996	408	999	518
1994	2,911	989	414	988	520
1995	2,887	974	414	978	521
1996	2,870	961	412	975	522
1997	2,873	960	412	978	523
1998	2,887	964	411	988	524
1999	2,916	976	410	1,006	524
2000	2,943	988	409	1,022	524
2001	2,969	1,001	407	1,038	523
2002	2,991	1,012	407	1,051	521
2003	3,001	1,020	405	1,057	519
2004	3,018	1,030	404	1,067	517
High alternative projections					
1993	3,116	1,084	435	1,059	538
1994	3,135	1,080	444	1,064	547
1995	3,122	1,068	448	1,056	550
1996	3,124	1,063	448	1,059	554
1997	3,136	1,067	448	1,063	558
1998	3,162	1,079	447	1,075	561
1999	3,201	1,095	447	1,096	563
2000	3,234	1,110	446	1,114	564
2001	3,268	1,127	445	1,131	565
2002	3,300	1,143	446	1,146	565
2003	3,316	1,154	445	1,153	564
2004	3,339	1,167	444	1,165	563

* Projected.

NOTE: Projections are based on data through 1991. Because of rounding, details may not add to totals.

SOURCE: U.S. Department of Education, National Center for Education Statistics, Fall Enrollment in Colleges and Universities surveys and Integrated Postsecondary Education Data System (IPEDS) surveys. (This table was prepared June 1993.)

Table 13.—Total enrollment in private 2-year institutions of higher education, by sex and attendance status, with alternative projections: 50 States and D.C., fall 1979 to fall 2004

(In thousands)

Year	Total	Men		Women	
		Full-time	Part-time	Full-time	Part-time
1979	160	48	14	76	22
1980	198	68	15	90	24
1981	236	71	34	95	35
1982	252	80	45	99	28
1983	264	88	41	105	30
1984	252	79	37	106	29
1985	261	84	38	110	30
1986	266	83	43	108	32
1987	235	76	30	102	29
1988	260	73	40	103	44
1989	267	76	45	105	41
1990	244	71	34	96	43
1991	247	80	27	109	32
1992 *	260	78	35	108	39
		Middle alternative projections			
1993	267	80	36	110	41
1994	267	79	36	111	41
1995	266	79	36	110	41
1996	267	79	36	111	41
1997	270	80	36	112	42
1998	272	81	36	113	42
1999	276	83	36	115	42
2000	280	85	36	117	42
2001	282	86	36	118	42
2002	287	88	37	120	42
2003	287	88	37	120	42
2004	289	89	37	121	42
		Low alternative projections			
1993	260	76	35	109	40
1994	259	76	35	108	40
1995	258	75	35	108	40
1996	258	75	35	108	40
1997	259	75	35	109	40
1998	261	76	35	110	40
1999	265	78	35	112	40
2000	268	79	35	114	40
2001	270	80	35	115	40
2002	272	81	35	116	40
2003	272	81	35	116	40
2004	274	82	35	117	40
		High alternative projections			
1993	274	82	37	114	41
1994	278	82	38	116	42
1995	277	82	38	115	42
1996	279	82	38	116	43
1997	281	83	38	117	43
1998	285	85	38	119	43
1999	289	87	38	121	43
2000	295	89	39	123	44
2001	297	90	39	124	44
2002	299	91	39	125	44
2003	301	92	39	126	44
2004	302	93	39	126	44

* Projected.

NOTE: Projections are based on data through 1991. Because of rounding, details may not add to totals.

SOURCE: U.S. Department of Education, National Center for Education Statistics, Fall Enrollment in Colleges and Universities surveys and Integrated Postsecondary Education Data System (IPEDS) surveys. (This table was prepared June 1993.)

Table 14.—Undergraduate enrollment in all institutions, by sex and attendance status, with alternative projections: 50 States and D.C., fall 1979 to fall 2004

(In thousands)

Year	Total	Men		Women	
		Full-time	Part-time	Full-time	Part-time
1979	9,998	3,087	1,734	2,993	2,185
1980	10,475	3,227	1,773	3,135	2,340
1981	10,755	3,261	1,848	3,188	2,458
1982	10,825	3,299	1,871	3,184	2,470
1983	10,846	3,304	1,854	3,210	2,478
1984	10,618	3,195	1,812	3,153	2,459
1985	10,597	3,156	1,806	3,163	2,471
1986	10,798	3,146	1,871	3,206	2,575
1987	11,046	3,164	1,905	3,299	2,679
1988	11,317	3,206	1,931	3,436	2,743
1989	11,742	3,279	2,032	3,562	2,869
1990	11,959	3,337	2,043	3,640	2,940
1991	12,439	3,436	2,135	3,786	3,082
1992 *	12,450	3,427	2,165	3,740	3,118
		Middle alternative projections			
1993	12,823	3,520	2,227	3,838	3,238
1994	12,815	3,483	2,243	3,825	3,264
1995	12,761	3,452	2,232	3,798	3,279
1996	12,765	3,440	2,224	3,804	3,297
1997	12,833	3,461	2,223	3,832	3,317
1998	12,949	3,508	2,226	3,881	3,334
1999	13,147	3,591	2,231	3,969	3,356
2000	13,309	3,667	2,237	4,041	3,364
2001	13,462	3,738	2,243	4,112	3,369
2002	13,596	3,807	2,251	4,169	3,369
2003	13,659	3,847	2,256	4,192	3,364
2004	13,747	3,895	2,262	4,233	3,357
		Low alternative projections			
1993	12,469	3,377	2,171	3,758	3,163
1994	12,406	3,332	2,190	3,717	3,167
1995	12,313	3,281	2,178	3,688	3,166
1996	12,278	3,252	2,166	3,691	3,169
1997	12,313	3,261	2,161	3,716	3,175
1998	12,396	3,293	2,159	3,762	3,182
1999	12,555	3,361	2,159	3,846	3,189
2000	12,687	3,420	2,160	3,913	3,194
2001	12,806	3,475	2,160	3,977	3,194
2002	12,910	3,528	2,161	4,030	3,191
2003	12,944	3,554	2,161	4,047	3,182
2004	13,011	3,592	2,162	4,085	3,172
		High alternative projections			
1993	13,227	3,634	2,312	3,980	3,301
1994	13,309	3,608	2,351	3,996	3,354
1995	13,287	3,575	2,367	3,972	3,373
1996	13,334	3,578	2,367	3,994	3,395
1997	13,423	3,615	2,365	4,024	3,419
1998	13,568	3,679	2,369	4,079	3,441
1999	13,770	3,763	2,375	4,173	3,459
2000	13,944	3,841	2,383	4,246	3,474
2001	14,108	3,916	2,391	4,318	3,483
2002	14,253	3,989	2,400	4,374	3,490
2003	14,325	4,030	2,409	4,397	3,489
2004	14,424	4,082	2,416	4,437	3,489

* Projected.

NOTE: Projections are based on data through 1991. Because of rounding, details may not add to totals.

SOURCE: U.S. Department of Education, National Center for Education Statistics, Fall Enrollment in Colleges and Universities surveys and Integrated Postsecondary Education Data System (IPEDS) surveys. (This table was prepared June 1993.)

Table 15.—Undergraduate enrollment in public institutions, by sex and attendance status, with alternative projections: 50 States and D.C., fall 1979 to fall 2004

(In thousands)

Year	Total	Men		Women	
		Full-time	Part-time	Full-time	Part-time
1979	8,046	2,316	1,551	2,229	1,952
1980	8,441	2,426	1,588	2,334	2,093
1981	8,648	2,452	1,639	2,373	2,185
1982	8,713	2,487	1,653	2,373	2,201
1983	8,697	2,482	1,635	2,385	2,195
1984	8,494	2,390	1,600	2,325	2,179
1985	8,478	2,357	1,596	2,331	2,193
1986	8,661	2,351	1,652	2,367	2,291
1987	8,919	2,375	1,701	2,449	2,393
1988	9,103	2,399	1,714	2,550	2,439
1989	9,488	2,470	1,801	2,663	2,553
1990	9,710	2,527	1,826	2,734	2,623
1991	10,148	2,610	1,921	2,851	2,766
1992 *	10,097	2,587	1,928	2,801	2,781
		Middle alternative projections			
1993	10,403	2,657	1,983	2,875	2,888
1994	10,406	2,631	1,997	2,866	2,912
1995	10,367	2,608	1,987	2,847	2,925
1996	10,374	2,600	1,980	2,852	2,942
1997	10,428	2,617	1,979	2,873	2,959
1998	10,520	2,653	1,982	2,910	2,975
1999	10,673	2,716	1,987	2,975	2,995
2000	10,797	2,773	1,993	3,028	3,003
2001	10,914	2,827	1,999	3,080	3,008
2002	11,014	2,878	2,006	3,122	3,008
2003	11,060	2,908	2,011	3,138	3,003
2004	11,126	2,944	2,017	3,168	2,997
		Low alternative projections			
1993	10,119	2,550	1,933	2,815	2,821
1994	10,077	2,517	1,950	2,786	2,824
1995	10,005	2,479	1,938	2,765	2,823
1996	9,980	2,458	1,928	2,768	2,826
1997	10,008	2,466	1,923	2,787	2,832
1998	10,072	2,491	1,922	2,821	2,838
1999	10,193	2,542	1,922	2,884	2,845
2000	10,293	2,587	1,923	2,933	2,850
2001	10,381	2,627	1,924	2,980	2,850
2002	10,459	2,667	1,925	3,019	2,848
2003	10,482	2,686	1,925	3,031	2,840
2004	10,530	2,714	1,926	3,059	2,831
		High alternative projections			
1993	10,729	2,743	2,059	2,981	2,946
1994	10,805	2,725	2,093	2,994	2,993
1995	10,796	2,701	2,107	2,978	3,010
1996	10,834	2,704	2,107	2,994	3,029
1997	10,907	2,733	2,106	3,017	3,051
1998	11,019	2,781	2,110	3,057	3,071
1999	11,176	2,845	2,116	3,127	3,088
2000	11,309	2,904	2,123	3,181	3,101
2001	11,434	2,960	2,131	3,234	3,109
2002	11,545	3,015	2,139	3,275	3,116
2003	11,599	3,045	2,148	3,291	3,115
2004	11,675	3,084	2,155	3,321	3,115

* Projected.

NOTE: Projections are based on data through 1991. Because of rounding, details may not add to totals.

SOURCE: U.S. Department of Education, National Center for Education Statistics, Fall Enrollment in Colleges and Universities surveys and Integrated Postsecondary Education Data System (IPEDS) surveys. (This table was prepared June 1993.)

Table 16.—Undergraduate enrollment in private institutions, by sex and attendance status, with alternative projections: 50 States and D.C., fall 1979 to fall 2004

(In thousands)

Year	Total	Men		Women	
		Full-time	Part-time	Full-time	Part-time
1979	1,951	772	184	762	233
1980	2,033	800	185	801	246
1981	2,106	809	209	816	272
1982	2,112	812	219	811	270
1983	2,149	823	219	824	283
1984	2,124	805	212	827	280
1985	2,120	800	210	832	278
1986	2,137	796	219	839	284
1987	2,128	788	204	850	286
1988	2,213	807	217	886	304
1989	2,255	808	231	899	316
1990	2,250	810	217	905	317
1991	2,291	825	215	935	316
1992 *	2,353	840	237	939	337
Middle alternative projections					
1993	2,420	863	244	963	350
1994	2,409	852	246	959	352
1995	2,394	844	245	951	354
1996	2,391	840	244	952	355
1997	2,405	844	244	959	358
1998	2,429	855	244	971	359
1999	2,474	875	244	994	361
2000	2,512	894	244	1,013	361
2001	2,548	911	244	1,032	361
2002	2,582	929	245	1,047	361
2003	2,599	939	245	1,054	361
2004	2,621	951	245	1,065	360
Low alternative projections					
1993	2,350	827	238	943	342
1994	2,329	815	240	931	343
1995	2,308	802	240	923	343
1996	2,298	794	238	923	343
1997	2,305	795	238	929	343
1998	2,324	802	237	941	344
1999	2,362	819	237	962	344
2000	2,394	833	237	980	344
2001	2,425	848	236	997	344
2002	2,451	861	236	1,011	343
2003	2,462	868	236	1,016	342
2004	2,481	878	236	1,026	341
High alternative projections					
1993	2,498	891	253	999	355
1994	2,504	883	258	1,002	361
1995	2,491	874	260	994	363
1996	2,500	874	260	1,000	366
1997	2,516	882	259	1,007	368
1998	2,549	898	259	1,022	370
1999	2,594	918	259	1,046	371
2000	2,635	937	260	1,065	373
2001	2,674	956	260	1,084	374
2002	2,708	974	261	1,099	374
2003	2,726	985	261	1,106	374
2004	2,749	998	261	1,116	374

* Projected.

NOTE: Projections are based on data through 1991. Because of rounding, details may not add to totals.

SOURCE: U.S. Department of Education, National Center for Education Statistics, Fall Enrollment in Colleges and Universities surveys and Integrated Postsecondary Education Data System (IPEDS) surveys. (This table was prepared June 1993.)

Table 17.—Graduate enrollment in all institutions, by sex and attendance status, with alternative projections: 50 States and D.C., fall 1979 to fall 2004

(In thousands)

Year	Total	Men		Women	
		Full-time	Part-time	Full-time	Part-time
1979	1,309	280	389	196	444
1980	1,343	281	394	204	466
1981	1,343	277	397	207	462
1982	1,322	280	390	205	447
1983	1,340	286	391	211	452
1984	1,345	286	386	215	459
1985	1,376	289	388	220	479
1986	1,435	294	399	228	514
1987	1,452	294	400	233	525
1988	1,472	304	393	249	526
1989	1,522	309	401	263	548
1990	1,586	321	416	278	571
1991	1,639	341	419	300	578
1992 *	1,790	383	477	302	628
Middle alternative projections					
1993	1,844	396	490	307	651
1994	1,861	399	496	309	657
1995	1,859	392	497	307	663
1996	1,852	386	497	302	667
1997	1,848	381	497	298	672
1998	1,847	379	497	296	675
1999	1,843	375	495	295	678
2000	1,841	374	494	296	677
2001	1,833	370	492	296	675
2002	1,829	370	490	297	672
2003	1,830	372	489	300	669
2004	1,831	374	488	303	666
Low alternative projections					
1993	1,802	380	479	303	640
1994	1,822	388	488	303	643
1995	1,817	384	488	299	646
1996	1,805	375	488	294	648
1997	1,802	372	488	291	651
1998	1,797	369	488	288	652
1999	1,789	364	486	287	652
2000	1,786	364	484	287	651
2001	1,779	361	482	287	649
2002	1,772	359	480	287	646
2003	1,769	361	477	289	642
2004	1,768	364	474	291	639
High alternative projections					
1993	1,919	426	511	319	663
1994	1,956	433	521	327	675
1995	1,960	429	527	325	679
1996	1,953	421	527	321	684
1997	1,952	416	528	318	690
1998	1,949	413	527	316	693
1999	1,945	410	526	314	695
2000	1,943	407	524	316	696
2001	1,937	405	522	314	696
2002	1,935	403	521	316	695
2003	1,934	405	519	318	692
2004	1,935	407	517	321	690

* Projected.

NOTE: Projections are based on data through 1991. Because of rounding, details may not add to totals.

SOURCE: U.S. Department of Education, National Center for Education Statistics, Fall Enrollment in Colleges and Universities surveys and Integrated Postsecondary Education Data System (IPEDS) surveys. (This table was prepared June 1993.)

Table 18.—Graduate enrollment in public institutions, by sex and attendance status, with alternative projections: 50 States and D.C., fall 1979 to fall 2004

(In thousands)

Year	Total	Men Full-time	Men Part-time	Women Full-time	Women Part-time
1979	884	182	246	133	325
1980	900	180	245	137	337
1981	887	177	242	138	329
1982	870	180	237	136	317
1983	872	184	235	140	313
1984	870	182	229	142	317
1985	891	181	232	144	333
1986	941	188	244	150	358
1987	945	185	244	152	364
1988	949	193	236	163	357
1989	978	195	242	171	369
1990	1,023	203	253	180	388
1991	1,050	215	255	192	388
1992*	1,152	242	290	195	425
Middle alternative projections					
1993	1,187	250	298	198	441
1994	1,198	252	301	200	445
1995	1,197	248	302	198	449
1996	1,193	244	302	195	452
1997	1,191	241	302	193	455
1998	1,190	240	302	191	457
1999	1,187	237	301	190	459
2000	1,186	236	300	191	459
2001	1,181	234	299	191	457
2002	1,179	234	298	192	455
2003	1,179	235	297	194	453
2004	1,179	236	296	196	451
Low alternative projections					
1993	1,161	240	291	196	434
1994	1,173	245	296	196	436
1995	1,170	243	296	193	438
1996	1,162	237	296	190	439
1997	1,160	235	296	188	441
1998	1,157	233	296	186	442
1999	1,152	230	295	185	442
2000	1,150	230	294	185	441
2001	1,146	228	293	185	440
2002	1,141	227	291	185	438
2003	1,140	228	290	187	435
2004	1,139	230	288	188	433
High alternative projections					
1993	1,234	269	310	206	449
1994	1,258	274	316	211	457
1995	1,261	271	320	210	460
1996	1,256	266	320	207	463
1997	1,255	263	320	205	467
1998	1,254	261	320	204	469
1999	1,251	259	319	203	470
2000	1,250	257	318	204	471
2001	1,247	256	317	203	471
2002	1,245	255	316	204	470
2003	1,244	256	315	205	468
2004	1,245	257	314	207	467

*Projected.

NOTE: Projections are based on data through 1991. Because of rounding, details may not add to totals.

SOURCE: U.S. Department of Education, National Center for Education Statistics, Fall Enrollment in Colleges and Universities surveys and Integrated Postsecondary Education Data System (IPEDS) surveys. (This table was prepared June 1993.)

Table 19.—Graduate enrollment in private institutions, by sex and attendance status, with alternative projections: 50 States and D.C., fall 1979 to fall 2004

(In thousands)

Year	Total	Men		Women	
		Full-time	Part-time	Full-time	Part-time
1979	424	98	144	63	119
1980	442	100	147	67	128
1981	456	100	155	69	132
1982	453	100	153	69	131
1983	468	103	156	71	138
1984	476	104	156	75	142
1985	486	108	156	76	147
1986	494	106	155	78	156
1987	507	108	156	82	161
1988	522	111	157	86	168
1989	544	114	159	92	179
1990	563	118	163	98	184
1991	589	126	164	109	190
1992 *	638	141	187	107	203
Middle alternative projections					
1993	657	146	192	109	210
1994	663	147	195	109	212
1995	662	144	195	109	214
1996	659	142	195	107	215
1997	657	140	195	105	217
1998	657	139	195	105	218
1999	656	138	194	105	219
2000	655	138	194	105	218
2001	652	136	193	105	218
2002	650	136	192	105	217
2003	651	137	192	106	216
2004	652	138	192	107	215
Low alternative projections					
1993	641	140	188	107	206
1994	649	143	192	107	207
1995	647	141	192	106	208
1996	643	138	192	104	209
1997	642	137	192	103	210
1998	640	136	192	102	210
1999	637	134	191	102	210
2000	636	134	190	102	210
2001	633	133	189	102	209
2002	631	132	189	102	208
2003	629	133	187	102	207
2004	629	134	186	103	206
High alternative projections					
1993	685	157	201	113	214
1994	698	159	205	116	218
1995	699	158	207	115	219
1996	697	155	207	114	221
1997	697	153	208	113	223
1998	695	152	207	112	224
1999	694	151	207	111	225
2000	693	150	206	112	225
2001	690	149	205	111	225
2002	690	148	205	112	225
2003	690	149	204	113	224
2004	690	150	203	114	223

* Projected.

NOTE: Projections are based on data through 1991. Because of rounding, details may not add to totals.

SOURCE: U.S. Department of Education, National Center for Education Statistics, Fall Enrollment in Colleges and Universities surveys and Integrated Postsecondary Education Data System (IPEDS) surveys. (This table was prepared June 1993.)

Table 20.—First-professional enrollment in all institutions, by sex and attendance status, with alternative projections: 50 States and D.C., fall 1979 to fall 2004

(In thousands)

Year	Total	Men		Women	
		Full-time	Part-time	Full-time	Part-time
1979	263	176	17	63	7
1980	278	181	18	70	9
1981	275	175	18	73	9
1982	278	174	17	78	9
1983	279	169	19	81	10
1984	279	166	19	83	10
1985	274	162	17	84	10
1986	270	159	15	87	9
1987	268	154	16	88	10
1988	267	151	16	90	10
1989	274	153	16	95	10
1990	274	150	17	96	11
1991	281	152	18	100	11
1992 *	318	182	20	105	11
Middle alternative projections					
1993	327	188	21	106	12
1994	329	189	21	107	12
1995	326	187	21	106	12
1996	321	184	21	104	12
1997	318	182	21	103	12
1998	315	180	21	102	12
1999	314	179	21	102	12
2000	312	177	21	102	12
2001	312	177	21	102	12
2002	313	177	21	103	12
2003	313	177	20	104	12
2004	314	177	20	105	12
Low alternative projections					
1993	318	181	20	105	12
1994	321	184	20	105	12
1995	318	182	20	104	12
1996	313	179	20	102	12
1997	309	177	20	100	12
1998	307	175	20	100	12
1999	305	174	20	99	12
2000	303	172	20	99	12
2001	302	172	20	98	12
2002	303	172	20	99	12
2003	304	172	20	100	12
2004	304	172	20	100	12
High alternative projections					
1993	347	203	21	111	12
1994	354	206	23	113	12
1995	352	203	23	113	13
1996	347	200	23	111	13
1997	343	198	23	109	13
1998	341	196	23	109	13
1999	339	194	23	109	13
2000	338	193	23	109	13
2001	337	192	23	109	13
2002	337	192	23	109	13
2003	338	192	23	110	13
2004	340	193	23	111	13

* Projected.

NOTE: Projections are based on data through 1991. Because of rounding, details may not add to totals.

SOURCE: U.S. Department of Education, National Center for Education Statistics, Fall Enrollment in Colleges and Universities surveys and Integrated Postsecondary Education Data System (IPEDS) surveys. (This table was prepared June 1993.)

Table 21.—First-professional enrollment in public institutions, by sex and attendance status, with alternative projections: 50 States and D.C., fall 1979 to fall 2004

(In thousands)

Year	Total	Men		Women	
		Full-time	Part-time	Full-time	Part-time
1979	106	74	2	27	1
1980	114	79	4	32	2
1981	112	75	3	33	2
1982	113	73	3	35	2
1983	113	71	3	37	2
1984	114	70	3	38	2
1985	111	69	3	38	2
1986	112	67	3	39	2
1987	110	65	3	40	2
1988	109	64	2	41	2
1989	113	65	2	43	2
1990	112	63	3	44	2
1991	111	62	3	45	2
1992 *	128	76	3	47	2
Middle alternative projections					
1993	132	79	3	48	2
1994	132	79	3	48	2
1995	131	78	3	48	2
1996	129	77	3	47	2
1997	127	76	3	46	2
1998	126	75	3	46	2
1999	126	75	3	46	2
2000	125	74	3	46	2
2001	125	74	3	46	2
2002	125	74	3	46	2
2003	126	74	3	47	2
2004	126	74	3	47	2
Low alternative projections					
1993	128	76	3	47	2
1994	129	77	3	47	2
1995	128	76	3	47	2
1996	126	75	3	46	2
1997	124	74	3	45	2
1998	123	73	3	45	2
1999	123	73	3	45	2
2000	122	72	3	45	2
2001	121	72	3	44	2
2002	122	72	3	45	2
2003	122	72	3	45	2
2004	122	72	3	45	2
High alternative projections					
1993	140	85	3	50	2
1994	143	86	4	51	2
1995	143	85	4	51	3
1996	141	84	4	50	3
1997	139	83	4	49	3
1998	138	82	4	49	3
1999	137	81	4	49	3
2000	137	81	4	49	3
2001	136	80	4	49	3
2002	136	80	4	49	3
2003	137	80	4	50	3
2004	138	81	4	50	3

* Projected.

NOTE: Projections are based on data through 1991. Because of rounding, details may not add to totals.

SOURCE: U.S. Department of Education, National Center for Education Statistics, Fall Enrollment in Colleges and Universities surveys and Integrated Postsecondary Education Data System (IPEDS) surveys. (This table was prepared June 1993.)

Table 22.—First-professional enrollment in private institutions, by sex and attendance status, with alternative projections: 50 states and D.C., fall 1979 to fall 2004

(In thousands)

Year	Total	Men		Women	
		Full-time	Part-time	Full-time	Part-time
1979	157	102	15	35	6
1980	163	104	16	38	7
1981	162	101	14	40	7
1982	165	101	14	43	7
1983	165	97	16	44	8
1984	164	96	16	43	8
1985	162	93	14	46	8
1986	158	91	12	48	7
1987	158	88	14	48	8
1988	158	87	14	49	8
1989	162	87	14	52	9
1990	162	86	15	52	9
1991	169	90	15	55	9
1992 *	190	106	17	58	9
Middle alternative projections					
1993	195	109	18	58	10
1994	197	110	18	59	10
1995	195	109	18	58	10
1996	192	107	18	57	10
1997	191	106	18	57	10
1998	189	105	18	56	10
1999	188	104	18	56	10
2000	187	103	18	56	10
2001	187	103	18	56	10
2002	188	103	18	57	10
2003	187	103	17	57	10
2004	188	103	17	58	10
Low alternative projections					
1993	190	105	17	58	10
1994	192	107	17	58	10
1995	190	106	17	57	10
1996	187	104	17	56	10
1997	185	103	17	55	10
1998	184	102	17	55	10
1999	182	101	17	54	10
2000	181	100	17	54	10
2001	181	100	17	54	10
2002	181	100	17	54	10
2003	182	100	17	55	10
2004	182	100	17	55	10
High alternative projections					
1993	207	118	18	61	10
1994	211	120	19	62	10
1995	209	118	19	62	10
1996	206	116	19	61	10
1997	204	115	19	60	10
1998	203	114	19	60	10
1999	202	113	19	60	10
2000	201	112	19	60	10
2001	201	112	19	60	10
2002	201	112	19	60	10
2003	201	112	19	60	10
2004	202	112	19	61	10

* Projected.

NOTE: Projections are based on data through 1991. Because of rounding, details may not add to totals.

SOURCE: U.S. Department of Education, National Center for Education Statistics, Fall Enrollment in Colleges and Universities surveys and Integrated Postsecondary Education Data System (IPEDS) surveys. (This table was prepared June 1993.)

Table 23.—Full-time-equivalent enrollment in all institutions of higher education, by level of student and type of institution, with alternative projections: 50 States and D.C., fall 1979 to fall 2004

(In thousands)

Year	Total	Undergraduate		Graduate	First-professional
		4-year	2-year	4-year	4-year
1979	8,487	4,989	2,471	778	249
1980	8,819	5,109	2,658	790	263
1981	9,015	5,188	2,765	801	262
1982	9,092	5,194	2,843	790	266
1983	9,166	5,254	2,841	805	266
1984	8,952	5,215	2,659	814	263
1985	8,943	5,204	2,649	829	261
1986	9,064	5,241	2,704	859	259
1987	9,230	5,363	2,743	868	256
1988	9,467	5,517	2,800	892	256
1989	9,781	5,628	2,967	922	265
1990	9,984	5,744	3,016	963	261
1991	10,361	5,804	3,280	1,010	267
1992 *	10,454	5,903	3,154	1,093	304
		Middle alternative projections			
1993	10,751	6,068	3,246	1,124	313
1994	10,727	6,026	3,253	1,133	315
1995	10,662	5,976	3,247	1,127	312
1996	10,644	5,966	3,254	1,117	307
1997	10,689	5,995	3,280	1,110	304
1998	10,787	6,067	3,312	1,107	301
1999	10,962	6,194	3,365	1,103	300
2000	11,112	6,306	3,406	1,102	298
2001	11,252	6,419	3,439	1,096	298
2002	11,382	6,515	3,472	1,096	299
2003	11,448	6,569	3,481	1,099	299
2004	11,540	6,636	3,501	1,103	300
		Low alternative projections			
1993	10,444	5,884	3,160	1,096	304
1994	10,382	5,814	3,153	1,108	307
1995	10,287	5,747	3,135	1,101	304
1996	10,240	5,719	3,134	1,088	299
1997	10,265	5,737	3,149	1,083	295
1998	10,337	5,793	3,173	1,077	293
1999	10,483	5,904	3,217	1,071	291
2000	10,608	5,999	3,250	1,070	289
2001	10,721	6,094	3,274	1,065	288
2002	10,823	6,176	3,297	1,061	289
2003	10,865	6,214	3,299	1,063	290
2004	10,941	6,271	3,314	1,066	290
		High alternative projections			
1993	11,133	6,276	3,347	1,178	333
1994	11,186	6,266	3,380	1,201	339
1995	11,136	6,221	3,380	1,199	336
1996	11,154	6,239	3,396	1,189	331
1997	11,219	6,282	3,427	1,183	327
1998	11,341	6,372	3,465	1,179	325
1999	11,521	6,504	3,519	1,174	323
2000	11,678	6,617	3,565	1,173	322
2001	11,825	6,737	3,599	1,168	321
2002	11,959	6,838	3,631	1,168	321
2003	12,028	6,892	3,644	1,170	322
2004	12,128	6,964	3,667	1,173	324

* Projected.

NOTE: Projections are based on data through 1991. Because of rounding, details may not add to totals.

SOURCE: U.S. Department of Education, National Center for Education Statistics, Fall Enrollment in Colleges and Universities surveys and Integrated Postsecondary Education Data System (IPEDS) surveys. (This table was prepared June 1993.)

Table 24.—Full-time-equivalent enrollment in public institutions of higher education, by level of student and type of institution, with alternative projections: 50 States and D.C., fall 1979 to fall 2004

(In thousands)

Year	Total	Undergraduate		Graduate	First-professional
		4-year	2-year	4-year	4-year
1979	6,393	3,438	2,333	519	103
1980	6,642	3,524	2,484	522	113
1981	6,781	3,575	2,573	524	110
1982	6,851	3,597	2,630	514	110
1983	6,881	3,635	2,616	520	111
1984	6,685	3,605	2,447	521	111
1985	6,668	3,601	2,428	529	110
1986	6,778	3,629	2,483	556	110
1987	6,938	3,731	2,542	557	108
1988	7,097	3,827	2,592	571	107
1989	7,372	3,921	2,752	587	112
1990	7,558	4,015	2,819	615	109
1991	7,863	4,046	3,068	640	109
1992*	7,872	4,111	2,939	696	126
Middle alternative projections					
1993	8,098	4,226	3,026	716	130
1994	8,082	4,198	3,032	722	130
1995	8,036	4,162	3,027	718	129
1996	8,029	4,156	3,034	712	127
1997	8,067	4,176	3,058	708	125
1998	8,143	4,226	3,087	706	124
1999	8,275	4,313	3,136	702	124
2000	8,389	4,391	3,173	702	123
2001	8,496	4,470	3,204	699	123
2002	8,592	4,537	3,233	699	123
2003	8,641	4,574	3,242	701	124
2004	8,707	4,621	3,260	702	124
Low alternative projections					
1993	7,868	4,098	2,946	699	126
1994	7,822	4,050	2,939	706	127
1995	7,753	4,003	2,923	702	126
1996	7,722	3,983	2,921	693	124
1997	7,744	3,996	2,936	690	122
1998	7,800	4,035	2,958	686	121
1999	7,912	4,112	2,997	682	121
2000	8,006	4,178	3,027	681	120
2001	8,090	4,243	3,049	678	119
2002	8,167	4,300	3,070	676	120
2003	8,196	4,327	3,072	678	120
2004	8,251	4,366	3,086	679	120
High alternative projections					
1993	8,379	4,371	3,120	750	138
1994	8,420	4,364	3,150	765	140
1995	8,389	4,334	3,152	763	140
1996	8,406	4,346	3,166	757	138
1997	8,460	4,376	3,195	753	136
1998	8,553	4,437	3,230	751	135
1999	8,691	4,530	3,279	748	134
2000	8,809	4,608	3,320	747	134
2001	8,921	4,691	3,352	744	133
2002	9,021	4,762	3,383	744	133
2003	9,072	4,799	3,394	745	134
2004	9,146	4,849	3,415	747	135

*Projected.

NOTE: Projections are based on data through 1991. Because of rounding, details may not add to totals.

SOURCE: U.S. Department of Education, National Center for Education Statistics, Fall Enrollment in Colleges and Universities surveys and Integrated Postsecondary Education Data System (IPEDS) surveys. (This table was prepared June 1993.)

Table 25.—Full-time-equivalent enrollment in private institutions of higher education, by level of student and type of institution, with alternative projections: 50 States and D.C., fall 1979 to fall 2004

(In thousands)

Year	Total	Undergraduate		Graduate	First-professional
		4-year	2-year	4-year	4-year
1979	2,095	1,552	138	259	146
1980	2,177	1,585	174	268	150
1981	2,233	1,612	192	277	152
1982	2,241	1,596	213	276	156
1983	2,285	1,619	226	285	155
1984	2,267	1,610	212	293	152
1985	2,276	1,603	221	300	151
1986	2,286	1,613	221	303	149
1987	2,292	1,632	201	311	148
1988	2,370	1,690	209	321	149
1989	2,409	1,707	216	335	153
1990	2,426	1,729	197	348	152
1991	2,498	1,758	212	370	158
1992 *	2,583	1,792	215	397	179
Middle alternative projections					
1993	2,653	1,842	220	408	183
1994	2,644	1,828	220	411	185
1995	2,625	1,814	219	409	183
1996	2,615	1,810	220	405	180
1997	2,624	1,820	223	402	179
1998	2,644	1,841	225	401	177
1999	2,686	1,881	229	400	176
2000	2,723	1,915	233	400	175
2001	2,757	1,949	235	398	175
2002	2,790	1,978	239	397	176
2003	2,808	1,995	239	399	175
2004	2,832	2,015	241	400	176
Low alternative projections					
1993	2,576	1,786	215	397	178
1994	2,560	1,764	214	402	180
1995	2,534	1,744	213	399	178
1996	2,518	1,735	213	395	175
1997	2,521	1,741	214	393	173
1998	2,537	1,758	216	391	172
1999	2,571	1,792	220	389	170
2000	2,602	1,821	223	388	169
2001	2,631	1,851	225	387	169
2002	2,657	1,876	227	385	169
2003	2,669	1,887	227	385	170
2004	2,690	1,905	229	386	170
High alternative projections					
1993	2,755	1,905	227	428	195
1994	2,766	1,902	229	436	198
1995	2,747	1,887	228	435	196
1996	2,748	1,893	230	432	193
1997	2,760	1,906	232	430	191
1998	2,789	1,934	236	428	190
1999	2,830	1,975	240	427	189
2000	2,868	2,009	245	426	188
2001	2,904	2,045	247	424	188
2002	2,938	2,077	249	424	188
2003	2,957	2,093	251	425	188
2004	2,982	2,115	252	426	189

* Projected.

NOTE: Projections are based on data through 1991. Because of rounding, details may not add to totals.

SOURCE: U.S. Department of Education, National Center for Education Statistics, Fall Enrollment in Colleges and Universities surveys and Integrated Postsecondary Education Data System (IPEDS) surveys. (This table was prepared June 1993.)

Chapter 3

High School Graduates

The number of high school graduates is projected to increase each year through 2003–2004. This increase in the number of high school graduates reflects the overall change in the 18-year-old population during the same period (figure 29). Increases in the number of graduates are expected for both public and private schools.

The tabulations below provide the following information about trends in the number of high school graduates: (1) the average annual rate of change (in percent) for 1978–79 to 1991–92 and the projected growth rate for 1991–92 to 2003–2004 and (2) the rates of change for 1978–79 to 1985–86 and 1985–86 to 1991–92 and the projected growth rates for 1991–92 to 1997–98 and 1997–98 to 2003–2004.

Average annual rate of change (in percent)

	1978–79 to 1991–92	Projected
		1991–92 to 2003–2004
Total	-1.6	1.8
Public	-1.7	1.8
Private	-1.2	1.9

Average annual rate of change (in percent)

	1978–79 to 1985–86	1985–86 to 1991–92	Projected	
			1991–92 to 1997–98	1997–98 to 2003–2004
Total	-2.3	-0.9	2.4	1.3
Public	-2.4	-1.0	2.4	1.3
Private	-2.0	-0.3	2.4	1.3

Total High School Graduates

The number of high school graduates from public and private schools decreased from 3.1 million in 1978–79 to 2.6 million in 1985–86 (table 26 and figure 30). After 1985–86, this number increased to 2.8 million in 1987–

88. Then, it decreased to about 2.5 million in 1991–92, a decrease of 19 percent from 1978–79, or an average annual rate of decline of 1.6 percent. Over the projection period, the total number of high school graduates is expected to remain around 2.5 million in 1992–93 and 1993–94. Thereafter, it is projected to rise to 3.1 million by 2003–2004, an increase of 25 percent from 1991–92, or an average annual growth rate of 1.8 percent. During the projection period, the growth rate will be higher in the first half of the projection period (1991–92 to 1997–98) than the growth rate in the second half (1997–98 to 2003–2004), 2.4 percent per year versus 1.3 percent per year.

High School Graduates, by Control of Institution

The number of graduates of public high schools decreased from 2.8 million in 1978–79 to 2.4 million in 1985–86 (figure 31). Then, it increased to 2.5 million in 1987–88 before declining to about 2.2 million in 1991–92, a decrease of 20 percent from 1978–79, or an average annual rate of decline of 1.7 percent. Over the projection period, public high school graduates are projected to increase to 2.8 million by 2003–2004, an increase of 25 percent from 1991–92, or an average annual growth rate of 1.8 percent. During the projection period, the growth rate will be higher in the first half of the projection period (1991–92 to 1997–98) that the growth rate in the second half (1997–98 to 2003–2004), 2.4 percent per year versus 1.3 percent per year (figure 32).

The number of graduates of private high schools is projected to increase from 256,000 in 1991–92 to 319,000 by 2003–2004, an increase of 25 percent, or an average annual growth rate of 1.9 percent. During the projection period, the growth rate will be higher in the first half of the projection period (1991–92 to 1997–98) than the growth rate in the second half (1997–98 to 2003–2004), 2.4 percent per year versus 1.3 percent per year.

Figure 29
18-year-old population, with projections:1979 to 2004

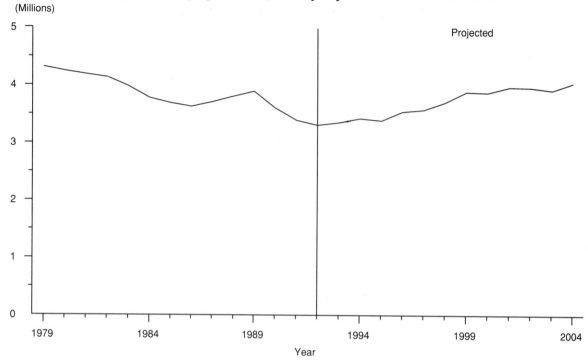

Figure 30
High school graduates, with projections: 1978-79 to 2003-2004

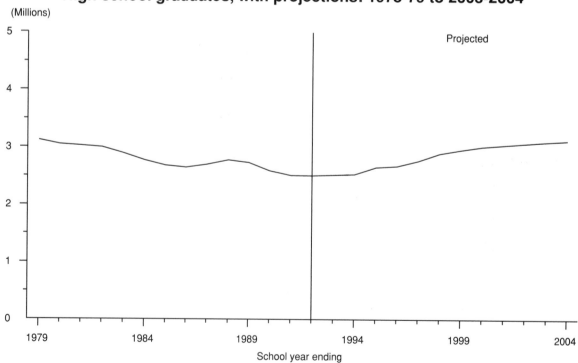

Figure 31
High school graduates, by control of institution, with projections: 1978-79 to 2002-2003

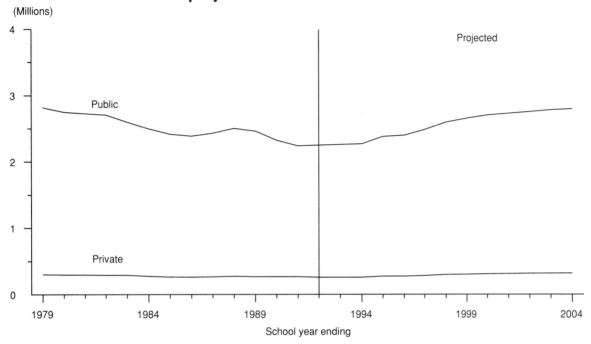

Figure 32
Average annual rates of change for high school graduates

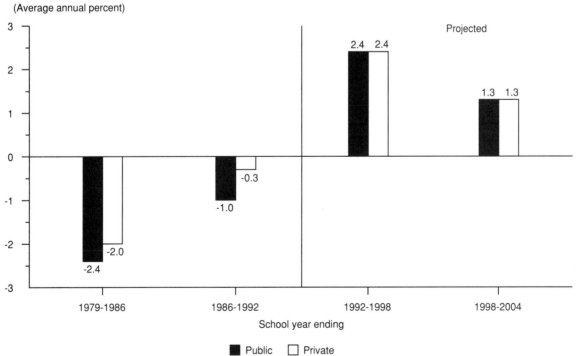

Table 26.—High school graduates, by control of institution, with projections:
50 States and D.C., 1978–79 to 2003–2004

(In thousands)

Year ending	Total	Public	Private
1979	3,101	2,801	300
1980	3,043	2,748	295
1981	3,020	2,725	295
1982	2,995	2,705	290
1983	2,888	2,598	290
1984	2,767	2,495	272
1985	2,677	2,414	263
1986	2,643	2,383	260
1987	2,694	2,429	265
1988	2,773	2,500	273
1989	2,727	2,459	268
1990	2,586	2,320	266
1991	2,506	2,238	268
1992 *	2,502	2,246	256
Projected			
1993	2,514	2,257	257
1994	2,526	2,267	258
1995	2,648	2,377	271
1996	2,669	2,396	273
1997	2,763	2,480	283
1998	2,890	2,595	296
1999	2,955	2,653	302
2000	3,009	2,701	308
2001	3,039	2,728	311
2002	3,066	2,753	314
2003	3,096	2,779	317
2004	3,116	2,797	319

*Estimate

NOTE: Prior to 1989–90, numbers for private high school graduates were estimated by NCES. Because of rounding, details may not add to totals.

SOURCE: U.S. Department of Education, National Center for Education Statistics, *Statistics of Public Elementary and Secondary Schools*; Common Core of Data surveys; "Selected Public and Private Elementary and Secondary Education Statistics," *NCES Bulletin*, October 23, 1979; "Private Elementary and Secondary Education, 1983: Enrollment, Teachers, and Schools," *NCES Bulletin*, December 1984; 1985 Private School Survey; "Key Statistics for Public Elementary and Secondary Education: School Year 1989–90," *Early Estimates*; "Key Statistics for Private Elementary and Secondary Education: School Year 1988–89," *Early Estimates*; "Key Statistics for Private Elementary and Secondary Education: School Year 1989–90," *Early Estimates*; "Key Statistics for Public and Private Elementary and Secondary Education: School Year 1990–91," *Early Estimates*; "Public and Private Elementary and Secondary Education Statistics: School Year 1991–92," *Early Estimates*; and "Public and Private Elementary and Secondary Education Statistics: School Year 1992–93," *Early Estimates*. (This table was prepared June 1993.)

Chapter 4

Earned Degrees Conferred

The historical growth in enrollment of women in institutions of higher education led to an increase in the number of earned degrees conferred. Between 1978–79 and 1991–92, the number of degrees awarded to women rose at all levels. Degrees conferred on men at the associate, bachelor's, master's, and doctor's levels also showed increases over 1978–79. In 1991–92, women earned the majority of associate, bachelor's, and master's degrees, and nearly two-fifths of doctor's and first-professional degrees. Over the projection period, the number of degrees awarded to women will continue to rise at most levels. With the exception of doctor's degrees, the number of degrees awarded to men will increase over the projection period.

Three alternative projections of earned degrees by level and sex were developed. In general, the number of degrees was related to college-age populations and higher education enrollment by level enrolled and attendance status.

Associate Degrees

Between 1978–79 and 1979–80, the number of associate degrees decreased from 403,000 to 401,000 and then increased to 456,000 in 1982–83, before declining to 435,000 in 1987–88. Since then, it increased to an estimated 485,000 in 1991–92 (table 27 and figure 33). Under the middle alternative, this number is expected to increase to 560,000 by 2003–2004, an increase of 15 percent from 1991–92. Under the low and high alternatives, the number of associate degrees is projected to range between 536,000 and 586,000 by 2003–2004. The number of associate degrees awarded to men decreased from 192,000 in 1978–79 to 184,000 in 1979–80. Thereafter, it rose to 207,000 in 1982–83 and then decreased to 186,000 in 1988–89, before rising to an estimated 204,000 in 1991–92 (figure 34). Under the middle alternative, this number is projected to increase to 233,000 by 2003–2004, an increase of 14 percent from 1991–92. Under the low and high alternatives, the number of associate degrees awarded to men is expected to range between 218,000 and 243,000 by 2003–2004. The number of associate degrees awarded to women increased from 211,000 in 1978–79 to 283,000 in 1990–91. In 1991–92, this number is estimated to be 281,000. Under the middle alternative, this number is projected to increase to 327,000 by 2003–2004, an increase of 16 percent from 1991–92. Under the low and high alternatives, the number of associate degrees awarded to women is projected to range between 318,000 and 343,000 by 2003–2004.

Bachelor's Degrees

The number of bachelor's degrees increased from 921,000 in 1978–79 to an estimated 1,120,000 in 1991–92, an increase of 22 percent (table 28 and figure 35). Under the middle alternative, this number is expected to rise to 1,214,000 in 1995–96, decrease slightly to 1,190,000 in 1999–2000, and then increase to 1,278,000 by 2003–2004, an increase of 14 percent from 1991–92. Under the low and high alternatives in 2003–2004, the number of bachelor's degrees is projected to range between 1,208,000 and 1,354,000. The number of bachelor's degrees awarded to men declined from 477,000 in 1978–79 to 470,000 in 1980–81. Then, this number increased to 486,000 in 1985–86 and declined for two more years, before rising to an estimated 518,000 in 1991–92 (figure 36). Under the middle alternative, this number is expected to increase to 598,000 by 2003–2004, an increase of 15 percent from 1991–92. Under the low and high alternatives, the number of bachelor's degrees awarded to men is projected to range between 552,000 and 635,000 by 2003–2004. The number of bachelor's degrees awarded to women increased from 444,000 in 1978–79 to an estimated 602,000 in 1991–92, an increase of 36 percent. Under the middle alternative, this number is expected to increase to 680,000 by 2003–2004, an increase of 13 percent from 1991–92. Under the low and high alternatives, the number of bachelor's degrees awarded to women is projected to range between 656,000 and 719,000 by 2003–2004.

Master's Degrees

The number of master's degrees decreased from 301,000 in 1978–79 to 284,000 in 1983–84, before rising to an estimated 349,000 in 1991–92, an increase of 23 percent from 1983–84 (table 29 and figure 37). Under the middle alternative, this number is expected to increase to 389,000 in 1996–97, before decreasing to 363,000 by 2003–2004. Under the low and high alternatives, the number of master's degrees is projected to range between 347,000 and 379,000 by 2003–2004. The number of master's degrees awarded to men decreased from 153,000 in 1978–79 to 141,000 in 1986–87. Then, it increased to an estimated 163,000 in 1991–92 (figure 38). Under the middle alternative, this number is projected to increase to 194,000 in 1996–97, before decreasing to 170,000 by 2003–2004. Under the low and high alternatives, the number of master's degrees awarded to men is projected to range between 163,000 and 177,000 by 2003–2004. The number of master's degrees awarded to women decreased from 148,000 in 1978–79 to 147,000 in 1979–80. Then, it rose to 150,000 in 1981–82 and declined to 141,000 in 1983–84. Since then, it increased to an estimated 186,000 in 1991–92. Under the middle alternative, this number is expected to increase to 193,000 by 2003–2004, an increase of 4 percent from 1991–92. Under the low and high alternatives, the number of master's degrees awarded to women is projected to range between 184,000 and 202,000 by 2003–2004.

Doctor's Degrees

The number of doctor's degrees increased from 32,700 in 1978–79 to about 40,100 in 1991–92, an increase of 23 percent (table 30 and figure 39). Under the middle alternative, this number is expected to increase slightly to 41,400 in 2003–2004, an increase of 3 percent from 1991–92. Under the low and high alternatives, the number of doctor's degrees is projected to range between 39,900 and 47,300 by 2003–2004. The number of doctor's degrees awarded to men decreased from 23,500 in 1978–79 to 21,900 in 1982–83. Then, it increased to 22,100 in 1983–84 before decreasing to 21,700 in 1984–85. Thereafter, it increased to an estimated 25,200 in 1991–92. Under the middle alternative, this number is expected to fall to 21,200 by 2003–2004, a decrease of 16 percent from 1991–92 (figure 40). Under the low and high alternatives, the number of doctor's degrees awarded to men is projected to range between 19,800 and 27,000 by 2003–2004. The number of degrees awarded to women rose from 9,200 in 1978–79 to an estimated 14,900 in 1991–92, an increase of 62 percent. Over the projection period, this pattern is expected to continue. Under the middle alternative, the number of doctor's degrees awarded to women is projected to climb to 20,200 by 2003–2004, an increase of 36 percent from 1991–92. Under the low and high alternatives, the number of doctor's degrees awarded to women is projected

to range between 20,100 and 20,300 by 2003–2004. The share of doctor's degrees awarded to women, which was 28 percent in 1978–79 and 37 percent in 1991–92, is projected to climb to 49 percent by 2003–2004.

First-Professional Degrees

The number of first-professional degrees awarded rose from 68,800 in 1978–79 to 75,100 in 1984–85. Then, it decreased to 70,700 in 1987–88. Thereafter, it increased to 71,900 in 1990–91 before declining slightly to an estimated 71,600 in 1991–92 (table 31 and figure 41). Under the middle alternative, this number is expected to increase to 75,300 in 1995–96 and then decrease to 74,000 by 2003–2004, a decrease of 2 percent from 1995–96. Under the low and high alternatives, the number of first-professional degrees is projected to range between 72,000 and 77,000 by 2003–2004. The number of first-professional degrees awarded to men decreased from 52,700 in 1978–79 to about 43,200 in 1991–92, a decrease of 18 percent (figure 42). Under the middle alternative, this number is projected to increase to 44,200 in 1995–96, before decreasing to 43,400 by 2003–2004. Under the low and high alternatives, the number of first-professional degrees awarded to men is projected to range between 42,500 and 44,300 by 2003–2004. The number of first-professional degrees awarded to women increased from 16,200 in 1978–79 to an estimated 28,400 in 1991–92, an increase of 75 percent. Under the middle alternative, this number is expected to increase to 30,600 by 2003–2004, an increase of 8 percent from 1991–92. Under the low and high alternatives, the number of first-professional degrees awarded to women is projected to range between 29,500 and 32,700 by 2003–2004. The women's proportion of first-professional degrees rose from 24 percent in 1978–79 to 40 percent in 1991–92. By 2003–2004, this proportion is expected to be 41 percent.

Figure 33
Associate degrees, with alternative projections: 1978-1979 to 2003-2004

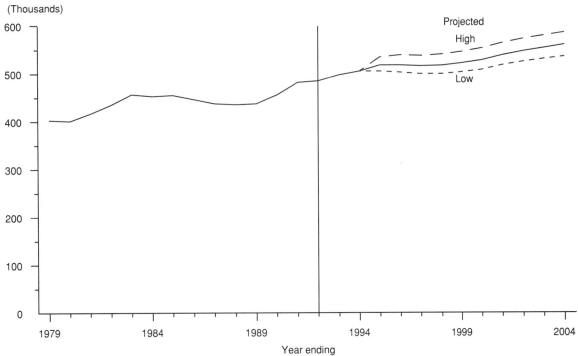

Figure 34
Associate degrees, by sex of recipient,
with middle alternative projections: 1978-79 to 2003-2004

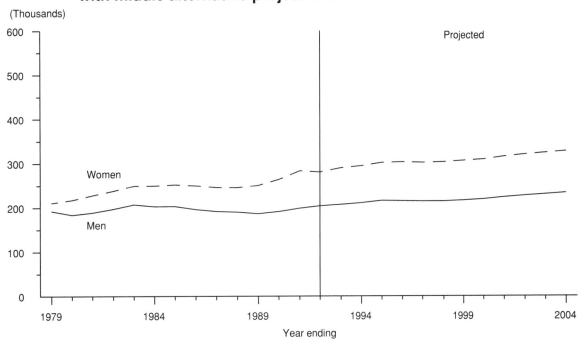

Figure 35
Bachelor's degrees, with alternative projections: 1978-79 to 2003-2004

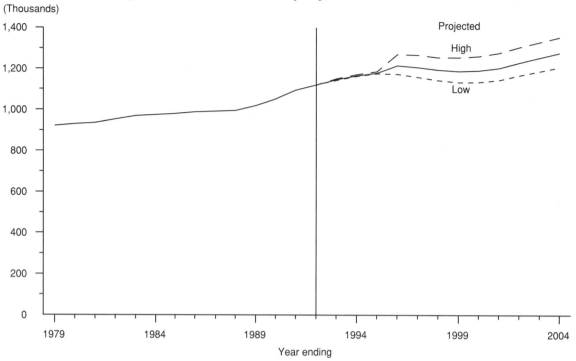

Figure 36

Bachelor's degrees, by sex of recipient,
with middle alternative projections: 1978-79 to 2003-2004

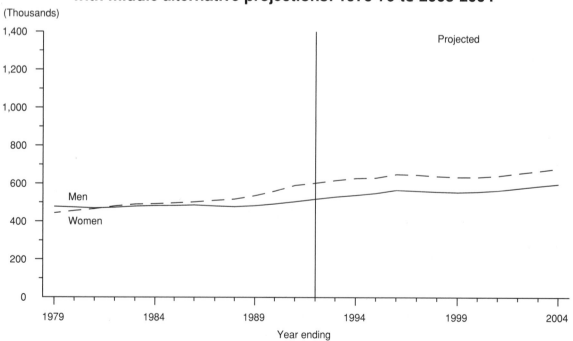

Figure 37
Master's degrees, with alternative projections: 1978-79 to 2003-2004

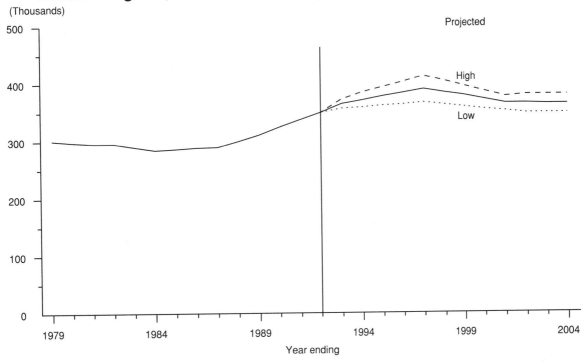

Figure 38
Master's degrees, by sex of recipient,
with middle alternative projections: 1978-79 to 2003-2004

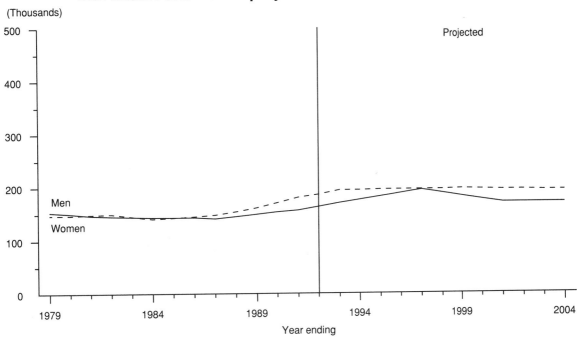

Figure 39
Doctor's degrees, with alternative projections: 1978-79 to 2003-2004

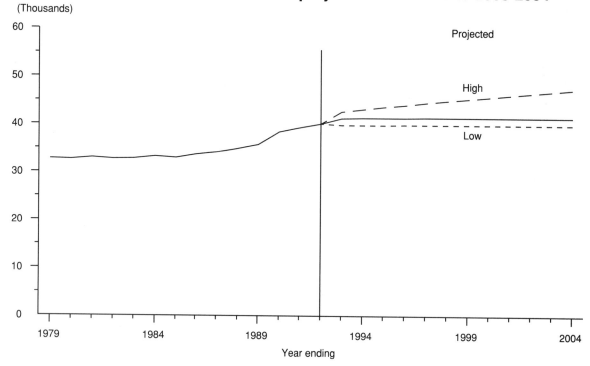

Figure 40
Doctor's degrees, by sex of recipient,
with middle alternative projections: 1978-79 to 2003-2004

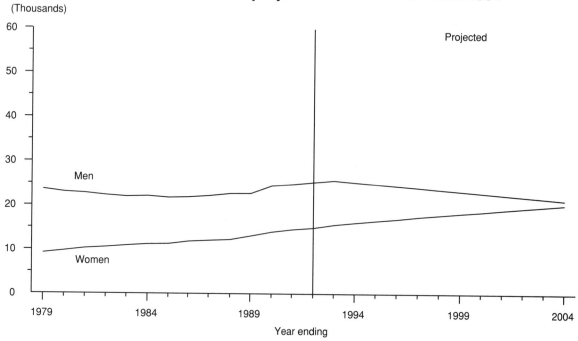

Figure 41
First-professional degrees, with alternative projections: 1978-79 to 2003-2004

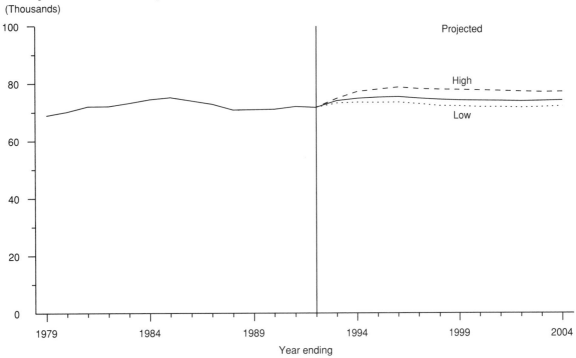

Figure 42
First-professional degrees, by sex of recipient,
with middle alternative projections: 1978-79 to 2003-2004

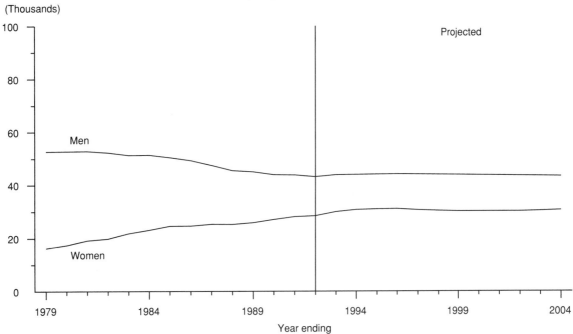

Table 27.—Associate degrees, by sex of recipient, with alternative projections: 50 States and D.C., 1978–79 to 2003–2004

Year ending	Total	Men	Women
1979	402,702	192,091	210,611
1980	400,910	183,737	217,173
1981	416,377	188,638	227,739
1982	434,515	196,939	237,576
1983	456,441	207,141	249,300
1984	452,416	202,762	249,654
1985	454,712	202,932	251,780
1986	446,047	196,166	249,881
1987	437,137	191,525	245,612
1988	435,085	190,047	245,038
1989	436,764	186,316	250,448
1990	455,102	191,195	263,907
1991	481,720	198,634	283,086
1992 *	485,000	204,000	281,000
Middle alternative projections			
1993	497,000	207,000	290,000
1994	504,000	210,000	294,000
1995	518,000	216,000	302,000
1996	518,000	215,000	303,000
1997	516,000	214,000	302,000
1998	517,000	214,000	303,000
1999	522,000	216,000	306,000
2000	528,000	219,000	309,000
2001	538,000	223,000	315,000
2002	547,000	227,000	320,000
2003	554,000	230,000	324,000
2004	560,000	233,000	327,000
Low alternative projections			
1993	497,000	207,000	290,000
1994	504,000	210,000	294,000
1995	505,000	208,000	297,000
1996	502,000	207,000	295,000
1997	499,000	205,000	294,000
1998	499,000	204,000	295,000
1999	503,000	205,000	298,000
2000	508,000	207,000	301,000
2001	518,000	211,000	307,000
2002	525,000	214,000	311,000
2003	531,000	216,000	315,000
2004	536,000	218,000	318,000
High alternative projections			
1993	497,000	207,000	290,000
1994	504,000	210,000	294,000
1995	535,000	222,000	313,000
1996	538,000	222,000	316,000
1997	538,000	222,000	316,000
1998	540,000	223,000	317,000
1999	545,000	225,000	320,000
2000	552,000	228,000	324,000
2001	564,000	233,000	331,000
2002	573,000	237,000	336,000
2003	580,000	240,000	340,000
2004	586,000	243,000	343,000

* Projected.

NOTE: Projections are based on data through 1990–91. Because of rounding, details may not add to totals.

SOURCE: U.S. Department of Education, National Center for Education Statistics, ''Degrees and Other Formal Awards Conferred'' survey and Integrated Postsecondary Education Data System (IPEDS), ''Completions'' survey. (This table was prepared June 1993.)

Table 28.—Bachelor's degrees, by sex of recipient, with alternative projections: 50 States and D.C., 1978–79 to 2003–2004

Year ending	Total	Men	Women
1979	921,390	477,344	444,046
1980	929,417	473,611	455,806
1981	935,140	469,883	465,257
1982	952,998	473,364	479,634
1983	969,510	479,140	490,370
1984	974,309	482,319	491,990
1985	979,477	482,528	496,949
1986	987,823	485,923	501,900
1987	991,339	480,854	510,485
1988	994,829	477,203	517,626
1989	1,018,755	483,346	535,409
1990	1,051,344	491,696	559,648
1991	1,094,538	504,045	590,493
1992 *	1,120,000	518,000	602,000
Middle alternative projections			
1993	1,145,000	529,000	616,000
1994	1,165,000	537,000	628,000
1995	1,178,000	548,000	630,000
1996	1,214,000	565,000	649,000
1997	1,206,000	560,000	646,000
1998	1,194,000	556,000	638,000
1999	1,187,000	553,000	634,000
2000	1,190,000	556,000	634,000
2001	1,203,000	563,000	640,000
2002	1,229,000	575,000	654,000
2003	1,254,000	587,000	667,000
2004	1,278,000	598,000	680,000
Low alternative projections			
1993	1,143,000	527,000	616,000
1994	1,163,000	535,000	628,000
1995	1,176,000	546,000	630,000
1996	1,173,000	539,000	634,000
1997	1,159,000	533,000	626,000
1998	1,143,000	525,000	618,000
1999	1,134,000	520,000	614,000
2000	1,135,000	521,000	614,000
2001	1,144,000	525,000	619,000
2002	1,167,000	534,000	633,000
2003	1,187,000	543,000	644,000
2004	1,208,000	552,000	656,000
High alternative projections			
1993	1,150,000	534,000	616,000
1994	1,171,000	543,000	628,000
1995	1,186,000	556,000	630,000
1996	1,269,000	592,000	677,000
1997	1,267,000	588,000	679,000
1998	1,254,000	583,000	671,000
1999	1,254,000	583,000	671,000
2000	1,261,000	589,000	672,000
2001	1,277,000	599,000	678,000
2002	1,305,000	611,000	694,000
2003	1,329,000	623,000	706,000
2004	1,354,000	635,000	719,000

* projected.

NOTE: Projections are based on data through 1990–91. Because of rounding, details may not add to totals.

SOURCE: U.S. Department of Education, National Center for Education Statistics, ''Degrees and Other Formal Awards Conferred'' survey and Integrated Postsecondary Education Data System (IPEDS), ''Completions'' survey. (This table was prepared June 1993.)

Table 29.—Master's degrees, by sex of recipient, with alternative projections: 50 States and D.C., 1978–79 to 2003–2004

Year ending	Total	Men	Women
1979	301,079	153,370	147,709
1980	298,081	150,749	147,332
1981	295,739	147,043	148,696
1982	295,546	145,532	150,014
1983	289,921	144,697	145,224
1984	284,263	143,595	140,668
1985	286,251	143,390	142,861
1986	288,567	143,508	145,059
1987	289,557	141,363	148,194
1988	299,317	145,163	154,154
1989	310,621	149,354	161,267
1990	324,301	153,653	170,648
1991	337,168	156,482	180,686
1992 *	349,000	163,000	186,000
Middle alternative projections			
1993	364,000	170,000	194,000
1994	370,000	176,000	194,000
1995	377,000	182,000	195,000
1996	383,000	188,000	195,000
1997	389,000	194,000	195,000
1998	383,000	188,000	195,000
1999	378,000	182,000	196,000
2000	371,000	176,000	195,000
2001	364,000	170,000	194,000
2002	364,000	170,000	194,000
2003	363,000	170,000	193,000
2004	363,000	170,000	193,000
Low alternative projections			
1993	356,000	166,000	190,000
1994	358,000	169,000	189,000
1995	361,000	172,000	189,000
1996	363,000	175,000	188,000
1997	366,000	178,000	188,000
1998	362,000	175,000	187,000
1999	358,000	172,000	186,000
2000	354,000	169,000	185,000
2001	351,000	166,000	185,000
2002	347,000	163,000	184,000
2003	347,000	163,000	184,000
2004	347,000	163,000	184,000
High alternative projections			
1993	372,000	174,000	198,000
1994	384,000	183,000	201,000
1995	393,000	192,000	201,000
1996	402,000	201,000	201,000
1997	412,000	210,000	202,000
1998	403,000	201,000	202,000
1999	394,000	192,000	202,000
2000	385,000	183,000	202,000
2001	376,000	174,000	202,000
2002	379,000	177,000	202,000
2003	379,000	177,000	202,000
2004	379,000	177,000	202,000

* Projected.

NOTE: Projections are based on data through 1990–91. Because of rounding, details may not add to totals.

SOURCE: U.S. Department of Education, National Center for Education Statistics, ''Degrees and Other Formal Awards Conferred'' survey and Integrated Postsecondary Education Data System (IPEDS), ''Completions'' survey. (This table was prepared June 1993.)

Table 30.—Doctor's degrees, by sex of recipient, with alternative projections: 50 States and D.C., 1978–79 to 2003–2004

Year ending	Total	Men	Women
1979	32,730	23,541	9,189
1980	32,615	22,943	9,672
1981	32,958	22,711	10,247
1982	32,707	22,224	10,483
1983	32,775	21,902	10,873
1984	33,209	22,064	11,145
1985	32,943	21,700	11,243
1986	33,653	21,819	11,834
1987	34,120	22,099	12,021
1988	34,870	22,615	12,255
1989	35,720	22,648	13,072
1990	38,371	24,401	13,970
1991	39,294	24,756	14,538
1992 *	40,100	25,200	14,900
Middle alternative projections			
1993	41,200	25,600	15,600
1994	41,300	25,200	16,100
1995	41,300	24,800	16,500
1996	41,300	24,400	16,900
1997	41,400	24,000	17,400
1998	41,400	23,600	17,800
1999	41,400	23,200	18,200
2000	41,400	22,800	18,600
2001	41,400	22,400	19,000
2002	41,400	22,000	19,400
2003	41,400	21,600	19,800
2004	41,400	21,200	20,200
Low alternative projections			
1993	39,800	24,200	15,600
1994	39,800	23,800	16,000
1995	39,800	23,400	16,400
1996	39,900	23,000	16,900
1997	39,900	22,600	17,300
1998	39,900	22,200	17,700
1999	39,900	21,800	18,100
2000	39,900	21,400	18,500
2001	39,900	21,000	18,900
2002	39,900	20,600	19,300
2003	39,900	20,200	19,700
2004	39,900	19,800	20,100
High alternative projections			
1993	42,600	27,000	15,600
1994	43,100	27,000	16,100
1995	43,600	27,000	16,600
1996	44,000	27,000	17,000
1997	44,500	27,000	17,500
1998	44,900	27,000	17,900
1999	45,300	27,000	18,300
2000	45,700	27,000	18,700
2001	46,100	27,000	19,100
2002	46,500	27,000	19,500
2003	46,900	27,000	19,900
2004	47,300	27,000	20,300

* Projected.

NOTE: Projections are based on data through 1990–91. Because of rounding, details may not add to totals.

SOURCE: U.S. Department of Education, National Center for Education Statistics, ''Degrees and Other Formal Awards Conferred'' survey and Integrated Postsecondary Education Data System (IPEDS), ''Completions'' survey. (This table was prepared June 1993.)

Table 31.—First-professional degrees, by sex of recipient, with alternative projections: 50 States and D.C., 1978–79 to 2003–2004

Year ending	Total	Men	Women
1979	68,848	52,652	16,196
1980	70,131	52,716	17,415
1981	71,956	52,792	19,164
1982	72,032	52,223	19,809
1983	73,136	51,310	21,826
1984	74,407	51,334	23,073
1985	75,063	50,455	24,608
1986	73,910	49,261	24,649
1987	72,750	47,460	25,290
1988	70,735	45,484	25,251
1989	70,856	45,046	25,810
1990	70,988	43,961	27,027
1991	71,948	43,846	28,102
1992 *	71,600	43,200	28,400
Middle alternative projections			
1993	73,900	43,900	30,000
1994	74,700	44,000	30,700
1995	75,100	44,100	31,000
1996	75,300	44,200	31,100
1997	74,700	44,100	30,600
1998	74,300	44,000	30,300
1999	74,000	43,900	30,100
2000	73,900	43,800	30,100
2001	73,800	43,700	30,100
2002	73,700	43,600	30,100
2003	73,800	43,500	30,300
2004	74,000	43,400	30,600
Low alternative projections			
1993	73,100	43,100	30,000
1994	73,400	43,000	30,400
1995	73,300	42,900	30,400
1996	73,400	42,800	30,600
1997	72,800	42,700	30,100
1998	72,100	42,600	29,500
1999	72,000	42,500	29,500
2000	71,700	42,500	29,200
2001	71,700	42,500	29,200
2002	71,500	42,500	29,000
2003	71,700	42,500	29,200
2004	72,000	42,500	29,500
High alternative projections			
1993	74,700	44,700	30,000
1994	77,100	45,000	32,100
1995	77,900	45,300	32,600
1996	78,600	45,600	33,000
1997	78,000	45,500	32,500
1998	77,800	45,400	32,400
1999	77,700	45,300	32,400
2000	77,500	45,100	32,400
2001	77,300	44,900	32,400
2002	77,100	44,700	32,400
2003	76,900	44,500	32,400
2004	77,000	44,300	32,700

* 'rojected.

NOTE: Projections are based on data through 1990–91. Because of rounding, details may not add to totals.

SOURCE: U.S. Department of Education, National Center for Education Statistics, ''Degrees and Other Formal Awards Conferred'' survey and Integrated Postsecondary Education Data System (IPEDS), ''Completions'' survey. (This table was prepared June 1993.)

Chapter 5

Classroom Teachers

Between 1992 and 2004, the number of classroom teachers in elementary and secondary schools is projected to rise, primarily due to the increase in school enrollment during this period. Increases are expected in the numbers of both elementary and secondary teachers. The number of secondary teachers will increase at a faster rate than the number of elementary teachers. Public and private teachers are projected to grow at similar rates.

Three alternative projections of the numbers of classroom teachers were developed to indicate a range of possible outcomes. These alternatives are based on different assumptions about the growth paths for two of the key variables in the teacher model—disposable income per capita and education revenue receipts from state sources per capita. Under the middle alternative, disposable income per capita is projected to increase by 12 percent between 1992 and 2004, while education revenue receipts from state sources per capita will rise by 19 percent during this period. The low alternative assumes that disposable income per capita and education revenue receipts from state sources per capita will increase by 8 percent and 12 percent, respectively. The high alternative assumes that disposable income per capita and education revenue receipts from state sources per capita will increase by 16 percent and 25 percent, respectively. The third variable in the teacher model, enrollment by organizational level, is the same for all three alternatives.

For classroom teachers, the following tabulations show: (1) the average annual rate of change (in percent) for 1979–92 and the three alternative projected rates of change for 1992–2004 and (2) the rates of change for 1979–86 and 1986–92 and the middle alternative projected rates of change for 1992–98 and 1998–2004.

Average annual rate of change (in percent)

| | 1979–92 | 1992–2004 | | |
		Low	Middle	High
Total	1.0	1.1	1.3	1.6
Elementary	1.8	0.7	1.0	1.3
Secondary	-0.0	1.7	1.9	2.1
Public	0.9	1.1	1.3	1.7
Private	2.1	1.0	1.2	1.6

Average annual rate of change (in percent)
(Middle alternative projections)

| | 1979–86 | 1986–92 | Projected | |
			1992–98	1998–2004
Total	0.7	1.4	1.7	1.0
Elementary	1.4	2.2	1.2	0.7
Secondary	-0.1	0.1	2.4	1.3
Public	0.4	1.5	1.7	1.0
Private	3.4	0.7	1.5	0.9

Elementary and Secondary School Teachers

The number of classroom teachers in elementary and secondary schools decreased from 2.46 million in 1979 to 2.44 million in 1981, a decrease of 1 percent (table 32 and figure 43). Thereafter, this number increased steadily to about 2.81 million in 1992, an increase of 15 percent from 1981. Under the middle alternative, the number of classroom teachers is projected to increase to 3.30 million by the year 2004, increasing at an average annual growth rate of 1.3 percent, for a 17-percent increase over the projection period. The growth rate will be higher in the first half of the projection period (1992–98) than in the second half (1998–2004), 1.7 percent per year versus 1.0 percent (figure 44). Under the low and high alternatives, the number of classroom teachers is projected to range between 3.22 million and 3.42 million by the year 2004. For the low alternative, this will be an average annual growth rate of 1.1 percent. For the high alternative, this will be a growth rate of 1.6 percent.

Classroom Teachers, by Organizational Level

While elementary enrollment decreased from 1979 to 1983, the number of elementary teachers rose slightly, from 1.38 million in 1979 to 1.43 million in 1983 (figure 45). Then, the number continued to increase to about 1.74 million in 1992, an increase of 26 percent from 1979. Under the middle alternative, the number of elementary teachers is projected to increase to 1.95 million by 2004, an increase of 12 percent from 1992; this increase represents an average annual growth rate of 1.0 percent per year. During the projection period, the growth rate in the 1992–

98 period will be 1.2 percent, while the growth rate in the 1998–2004 period will be 0.7 percent (figure 46). Under the low and high alternatives, elementary teachers are projected to range between 1.90 million and 2.04 million by the year 2004. For the low alternative, this will be an average annual growth rate of 0.7 percent. For the high alternative, this will be a growth rate of 1.3 percent.

The number of secondary classroom teachers decreased from 1.08 million in 1979 to 1.04 million in 1981. Then, the number of secondary classroom teachers increased to about 1.08 million in 1992, an increase of 4 percent from 1981. This moderate increase in the number of secondary teachers occurred even though secondary enrollment decreased for most years between 1981 and 1992. Under the middle alternative, the number of secondary teachers is projected to increase from 1.08 million in 1992 to 1.35 million by the year 2004, resulting in an increase of 25 percent. This increase will represent an average annual growth rate of 1.9 percent over the projection period. During the projection period, the growth rate in the 1992–98 period will be 2.4 percent, while the growth rate in the 1998–2004 period will be 1.3 percent. Under the low and high alternatives, secondary teachers are projected to range between 1.32 million and 1.39 million by the year 2004. For the low alternative, this will be an average annual growth rate of 1.7 percent. For the high alternative, this will be a growth rate of 2.1 percent.

Classroom Teachers, by Control of School

The number of classroom teachers in public elementary and secondary schools decreased from 2.18 million in 1979 to 2.13 million in 1981. Then, the number of public school teachers increased to about 2.45 million in 1992, an increase of 15 percent from 1981 (figure 47). Under the middle alternative, the number of public school teachers is projected to increase to 2.88 million by the year 2004, resulting in an increase of 17 percent from 1992. This increase will represent an average annual growth rate of 1.3 percent. During the projection period, the growth rate in the 1992–98 period will be 1.7 percent, while the growth rate in the 1998–2004 period will be 1.0 percent (figure 48). Under the low and high alternatives, public school teachers are projected to range between 2.81 million and 2.99 million by the year 2004. For the low alternative, this will be an average annual growth rate of 1.1 percent. For the high alternative, this will be a growth rate of 1.7 percent.

The number of classroom teachers in private elementary and secondary schools was about 363,000 in 1992. This number is projected to increase to 420,000 by the year 2004, an increase of 16 percent from 1992. This increase will represent an average annual growth rate of 1.2 percent. During the projection period, the growth rate in the 1992–98 period will be 1.5 percent, while the growth rate in the 1998–2004 period will be 0.9 percent. Under the low and high alternatives, private school teachers are projected

to range between 411,000 and 437,000 by the year 2004. For the low alternative, this will be an average annual growth rate of 1.0 percent. For the high alternative, this will be a growth rate of 1.6 percent.

Pupil-Teacher Ratios

A broad relationship between the number of pupils and teachers can be described by the pupil-teacher ratio. The pupil-teacher ratios were computed based on elementary and secondary enrollment by organizational level and the number of classroom teachers by organizational level.

The pupil-teacher ratio in elementary schools decreased from 20.5 in 1979 to 18.4 in 1989 (table 33 and figure 49). Then, the pupil-teacher ratio increased to 18.5 in 1990 and held steady through 1992. Under the middle alternative, this ratio is projected to increase to 19.0 in 1994, before declining to 18.4 by the year 2004. Under the low and high alternatives, the pupil-teacher ratio in elementary schools is expected to range between 17.6 and 18.9 by the year 2004.

For public elementary schools, under the middle alternative, the pupil-teacher ratio is projected to increase from 18.9 in 1992 to 19.4 in 1994 and then decline to 18.8 by the year 2004 (figure 50). Under the low and high alternatives, the pupil-teacher ratio in public elementary schools is projected to range between 18.0 and 19.3 by the year 2004. For private elementary schools, under the middle alternative, the pupil-teacher ratio is projected to increase from 16.2 in 1992 to 16.7 in 1994 and then decline to 16.3 by the year 2004. Under the low and high alternatives, the pupil-teacher ratio in private elementary schools is expected to range between 15.6 and 16.7 by the year 2004.

For secondary schools, the pupil-teacher ratio decreased from 17.0 in 1979 to 14.3 in 1990. Then, it increased to about 14.8 in 1992. Under the middle alternative, this ratio is projected to increase to 15.0 in 1993, fluctuate in a narrow range, and then fall slightly to 14.7 by the year 2004. Under the low and high alternatives, the pupil-teacher ratio in secondary schools is projected to range between 14.3 and 15.0 by the year 2004.

For public secondary schools, under the middle alternative, the pupil-teacher ratio is projected to increase from 15.2 in 1992 to 15.4 in 1993. Then, the ratio will fall to 15.0 in 1993, fluctuate in a narrow range, and then rise slightly to 15.1 by 2004. Under the low and high alternatives, the pupil-teacher ratio in public secondary schools is expected to range between 14.7 and 15.4 by the year 2004. For private secondary schools, under the middle alternative, the pupil-teacher ratio is projected to increase from 11.3 in 1992 to 11.5 in 1993, fluctuate in a narrow range, and then fall to 11.2 by the year 2004. Under the low and high alternatives, the pupil-teacher ratio in private secondary schools is projected to range between 10.9 and 11.5 by the year 2004.

Although private school classroom teachers represented 13 percent of total classroom teachers in 1992, private school enrollment was 11 percent of total enrollment. This indicates that private schools have more teachers for a given number of students than do public schools; that is, private school pupil-teacher ratios are smaller than public school pupil-teacher ratios.

Figure 43
Elementary and secondary classroom teachers, with alternative projections: Fall 1979 to fall 2004

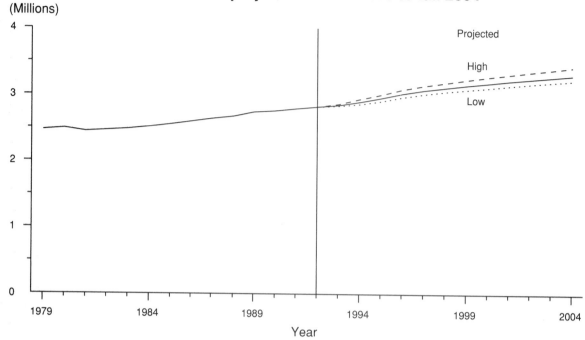

Figure 44
Average annual growth rates for classroom teachers

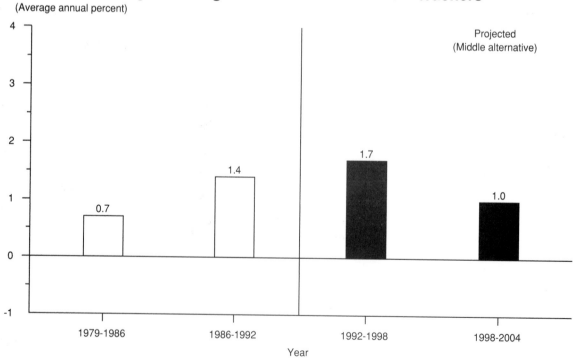

Figure 45
Elementary and secondary classroom teachers, by organizational level, with middle alternative projections: Fall 1979 to fall 2004

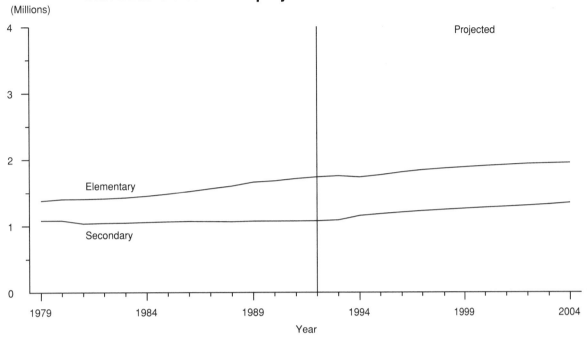

Figure 46
Average annual rates of change for classroom teachers, by organizational level

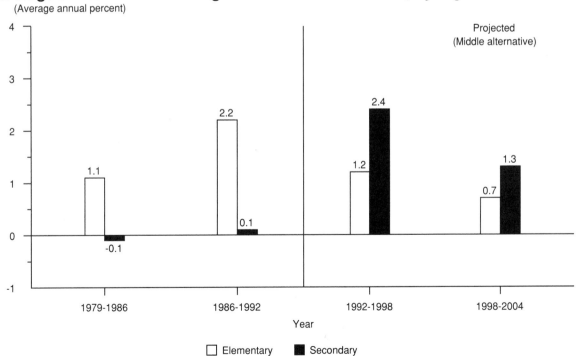

Figure 47
Elementary and secondary classroom teachers, by control of institution, with middle alternative projections: Fall 1979 to fall 2004

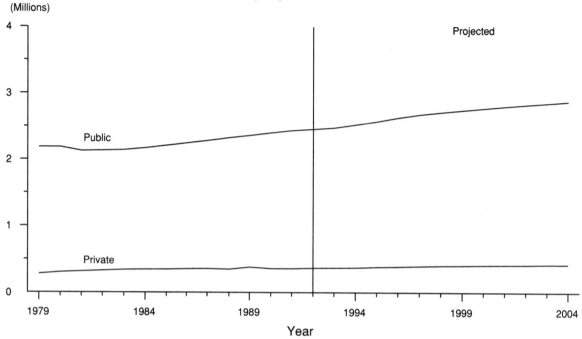

Figure 48
Average annual growth rates for classroom teachers, by control of institution

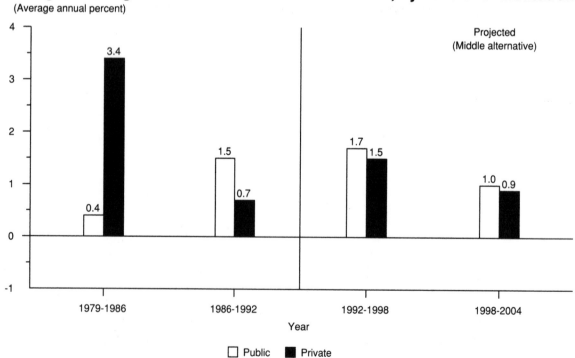

Figure 49
Pupil-teacher ratios, by organizational level,
with middle alternative projections: Fall 1979 to fall 2004

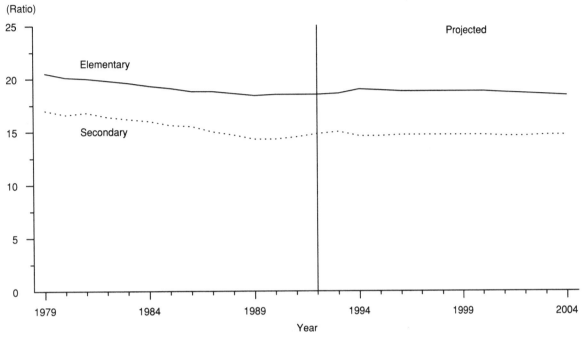

Figure 50
Pupil-teacher ratios, by organizational level and control,
with middle alternative projections: Fall 1979 to fall 2004

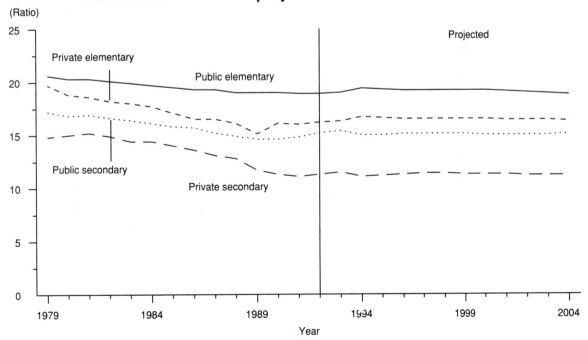

Table 32.—Classroom teachers in elementary and secondary schools, by control of institution and organizational level, with alternative projections: 50 States and D.C., fall 1979 to fall 2004

(In thousands)

Year	Total			Public			Private		
	K–12	Elementary	Secondary	K–12	Elementary	Secondary	K–12	Elementary	Secondary
1979	2,461	1,379	1,082	2,185	1,191	994	[1]276	188	88
1980	2,486	1,402	1,084	2,185	1,190	995	301	212	89
1981	2,440	1,404	1,037	2,127	1,183	945	[1]313	221	92
1982	2,458	1,413	1,045	2,133	1,182	951	[1]325	231	94
1983	2,476	1,426	1,050	2,139	1,186	953	337	240	97
1984	2,508	1,451	1,057	2,168	1,208	960	[1]340	243	97
1985	2,549	1,483	1,066	2,206	1,237	969	343	246	97
1986	2,592	1,521	1,071	2,244	1,271	973	[1]348	250	98
1987	2,632	1,564	1,068	2,279	1,307	973	[2]353	257	95
1988	2,668	1,604	1,064	2,323	1,353	970	[2]345	251	94
1989	2,734	1,662	1,072	2,357	1,387	970	[2]377	275	102
1990	2,753	1,680	1,073	2,398	1,426	972	[2]355	254	101
1991	2,787	1,713	1,074	2,432	1,459	973	[2]355	254	101
1992[2]	2,814	1,738	1,076	2,451	1,478	973	363	260	103
Middle alternative projections									
1993	2,841	1,753	1,088	2,475	1,491	984	366	262	104
1994	2,890	1,736	1,155	2,520	1,476	1,044	370	260	111
1995	2,950	1,768	1,181	2,572	1,504	1,068	378	265	113
1996	3,017	1,810	1,207	2,630	1,539	1,091	386	271	116
1997	3,070	1,843	1,227	2,677	1,568	1,109	393	276	117
1998	3,109	1,866	1,243	2,711	1,587	1,124	398	279	119
1999	3,145	1,885	1,260	2,742	1,603	1,140	403	282	121
2000	3,179	1,903	1,276	2,772	1,618	1,154	407	285	122
2001	3,211	1,920	1,291	2,800	1,633	1,167	411	287	124
2002	3,241	1,935	1,306	2,827	1,645	1,181	414	289	125
2003	3,268	1,943	1,325	2,851	1,653	1,198	418	291	127
2004	3,296	1,949	1,347	2,875	1,658	1,218	420	292	129
Low alternative projections									
1993	2,828	1,746	1,082	2,463	1,485	978	365	261	104
1994	2,856	1,717	1,139	2,490	1,460	1,030	366	257	109
1995	2,904	1,741	1,163	2,532	1,481	1,052	372	260	111
1996	2,963	1,775	1,188	2,584	1,510	1,074	379	266	114
1997	3,012	1,804	1,208	2,626	1,534	1,093	385	270	116
1998	3,048	1,826	1,223	2,658	1,553	1,106	390	273	117
1999	3,078	1,842	1,236	2,684	1,566	1,118	394	275	118
2000	3,109	1,859	1,250	2,711	1,581	1,131	398	278	120
2001	3,140	1,874	1,266	2,738	1,594	1,145	402	280	121
2002	3,170	1,889	1,281	2,765	1,606	1,159	405	283	123
2003	3,196	1,896	1,299	2,788	1,613	1,175	408	284	124
2004	3,220	1,900	1,319	2,809	1,616	1,193	411	284	126
High alternative projections									
1993	2,856	1,763	1,094	2,488	1,499	989	368	264	105
1994	2,933	1,761	1,171	2,557	1,498	1,059	376	263	112
1995	3,002	1,801	1,201	2,618	1,532	1,086	384	269	115
1996	3,078	1,850	1,228	2,684	1,573	1,111	394	277	118
1997	3,137	1,888	1,250	2,735	1,605	1,130	402	282	120
1998	3,183	1,915	1,268	2,775	1,629	1,146	408	287	121
1999	3,228	1,941	1,288	2,815	1,650	1,165	414	290	123
2000	3,270	1,964	1,306	2,851	1,671	1,181	419	294	125
2001	3,309	1,987	1,322	2,885	1,690	1,195	424	297	127
2002	3,346	2,007	1,340	2,918	1,706	1,211	428	300	128
2003	3,383	2,022	1,361	2,950	1,719	1,231	433	302	130
2004	3,422	2,036	1,386	2,985	1,731	1,253	437	305	133

[1] Estimated by NCES.
[2] Estimate.

NOTE: The numbers of elementary and secondary teachers reported separately by the National Education Association were prorated to the NCES totals for each year. Projections are based on data through 1992. Because of rounding, details may not add to totals.

SOURCE: U.S. Department of Education, National Center for Education Statistics, *Statistics of Public Elementary and Secondary Schools*; Common Core of Data surveys; "Selected Public and Private Elementary and Secondary Education Statistics,"*NCES Bulletin*, October 23, 1979; "Private Elementary and Secondary Education, 1983: Enrollment, Teachers, and Schools," *NCES Bulletin*, December 1984; 1985 Private School Survey; "Key Statistics for Private Elementary and Secondary Education: School Year 1988-89," *Early Estimates*; "Key Statistics for Private Elementary and Secondary Education: School Year 1989-90," *Early Estimates*; "Key Statistics for Public and Private Elementary and Secondary Education: School Year 1990-91," *Early Estimates*; "Public and Private Elementary and Secondary Education: School Year 1991-92," *Early Estimates*; and "Public and Private Elementary and Secondary Education: School Year 1992-93," *Early Estimates*. (This table was prepared June 1993.)

Table 33.—Pupil-teacher ratios in elementary and secondary schools, by control of institution and organizational level, with alternative projections: 50 States and D.C., fall 1979 to fall 2004

Year	Total		Public		Private	
	Elementary	Secondary	Elementary	Secondary	Elementary	Secondary
1979	20.5	17.0	20.6	17.2	[1]19.7	[1]14.8
1980	20.1	16.6	20.3	16.8	18.8	15.0
1981	20.0	16.8	20.3	16.9	[1]18.6	[1]15.2
1982	19.8	16.4	20.2	16.6	[1]18.2	[1]14.9
1983	19.6	16.2	19.9	16.4	18.0	14.4
1984	19.3	16.0	19.7	16.1	[1]17.7	[1]14.4
1985	19.1	15.6	19.5	15.8	17.1	14.0
1986	18.8	15.5	19.3	15.7	[1]16.5	[1]13.6
1987	18.8	15.0	19.3	15.2	[2]16.4	[2]13.1
1988	18.6	14.7	19.0	14.9	[2]16.1	[2]12.8
1989	18.4	14.3	19.0	14.6	[2]15.1	[2]11.7
1990	18.5	14.3	19.0	14.6	[2]16.1	[2]11.3
1991	18.5	14.5	18.9	14.8	[2]16.0	[2]11.1
1992	18.5	14.8	18.9	15.2	[2]16.2	[2]11.3
			Middle alternative projections			
1993	18.6	15.0	19.0	15.4	16.3	11.5
1994	19.0	14.6	19.4	15.0	16.7	11.1
1995	18.9	14.6	19.3	15.0	16.6	11.2
1996	18.8	14.7	19.2	15.1	16.5	11.3
1997	18.8	14.7	19.2	15.1	16.5	11.4
1998	18.8	14.7	19.2	15.1	16.5	11.4
1999	18.8	14.7	19.2	15.1	16.5	11.3
2000	18.8	14.7	19.2	15.0	16.5	11.3
2001	18.7	14.6	19.1	15.0	16.4	11.3
2002	18.6	14.6	19.0	15.0	16.4	11.2
2003	18.5	14.7	18.9	15.0	16.4	11.2
2004	18.4	14.7	18.8	15.1	16.3	11.2
			Low alternative projections (Based on high alternative projections of teachers)			
1993	18.5	14.9	18.9	15.3	16.2	11.3
1994	18.7	14.4	19.1	14.8	16.4	11.0
1995	18.6	14.4	18.9	14.8	16.3	11.0
1996	18.4	14.4	18.8	14.8	16.2	11.1
1997	18.3	14.5	18.7	14.8	16.1	11.1
1998	18.3	14.5	18.7	14.8	16.1	11.1
1999	18.3	14.4	18.6	14.7	16.0	11.1
2000	18.2	14.3	18.6	14.7	16.0	11.0
2001	18.1	14.3	18.5	14.6	15.9	11.0
2002	18.0	14.3	18.3	14.6	15.8	11.0
2003	17.8	14.3	18.2	14.6	15.7	10.9
2004	17.6	14.3	18.0	14.7	15.6	10.9
			High alternative projections (Based on low alternative projections of teachers)			
1993	18.7	15.1	19.1	15.5	16.4	11.5
1994	19.2	14.8	19.6	15.2	16.9	11.3
1995	19.2	14.9	19.6	15.2	16.9	11.4
1996	19.2	14.9	19.6	15.3	16.8	11.5
1997	19.2	15.0	19.6	15.3	16.8	11.5
1998	19.2	15.0	19.6	15.4	16.8	11.6
1999	19.2	15.0	19.6	15.3	16.9	11.5
2000	19.2	15.0	19.6	15.3	16.9	11.5
2001	19.2	14.9	19.6	15.3	16.8	11.5
2002	19.1	14.9	19.5	15.3	16.8	11.5
2003	19.0	15.0	19.4	15.3	16.8	11.4
2004	18.9	15.0	19.3	15.4	16.7	11.5

[1] Estimated by NCES.
[2] Estimate.

NOTE: The pupil-teachers ratios were derived from tables 2 and 32. Some data have been revised from previously published figures. Projections are based on data through 1992. Because of rounding, details may not add to totals.

SOURCE: U.S. Department of Education, National Center for Education Statistics, *Statistics of Public Elementary and Secondary Schools*; Common Core of Data surveys; "Selected Public and Private Elementary and Secondary Education Statistics,"*NCES Bulletin*, October 23, 1979; "Private Elementary and Secondary Education, 1983: Enrollment, Teachers, and Schools," *NCES bulletin*, December1984; 1985 Private School Survey; "Key Statistics for Private Elementary and Secondary Education: School Year 1988-89," *Early Estimates*; "Key Statistics for Private Elementary and Secondary Education: School Year 1989-90," *Early Estimates*; "Key Statistics for Public and Private Elementary and Secondary Education: School Year 1990-91," *Early Estimates*; "Public and Private Elementary and Secondary Education Statistics: School Year 1991-92," *Early Estimates*; and "Public and Private Elementary and Secondary Education Statistics: School Year 1992-93," *Early Estimates*. (This table was prepared June 1993.)

Chapter 6

Expenditures of Public Elementary and Secondary Schools

Current expenditures are projected to increase by 36.7 percent and average annual teacher salaries in public elementary and secondary schools are projected to increase by 12.9 percent between school years 1990–91 and 2003–2004 in the middle set of projections presented in this chapter. These projections are based on assumptions concerning economic growth and assistance by state governments to local governments; these assumptions are discussed in this chapter. Other sets of projections, based on alternative economic scenarios, are also discussed. No projections for private schools are presented as there are no regular data collections for private school expenditures.

Current Expenditures

Past Trends

Current expenditures, which had already been in a period of growth, have continued to increase since 1978–79. Current expenditures, in constant 1991–92 dollars, amounted to $159.4 billion in 1978–79. These expenditures reached $208.0 percent in 1990–91, an increase of 30.5 percent, and are estimated to reach $211.9 billion in 1992–93, an estimated increase of 33.0 percent from 1978–79 (table 34 and figure 51). From 1978–79 to 1990–91, current expenditures per pupil in average daily attendance rose 32.7 percent to $5,413 (table 34 and figures 52 and 53). Current expenditures per pupil in average daily attendance increased an estimated 31.3 percent from 1978–79 to 1992–93. Current expenditures per pupil in fall enrollment (table 35) increased 34.7 percent from 1978–79 to 1990–91.

Historically, education expenditures have followed a path similar to general economic trends. For most of the period since 1978–79, the economy has been rising. Current expenditures have also been rising during that period. (See figure 54 for a comparison of the growth rates of current expenditures per pupil and one major indicator of the state of the economy, disposable income per capita.)

The amount that local governments spend on education is also historically associated with the amount of state education aid to local governments. There was also a rapid rise in state education aid to local governments during the period from 1978–79 to 1990–91. (See figure 55 for a comparison of the growth rates of current expenditures per pupil and revenue receipts from state sources per capita).

The only time in the past 15 years in which current expenditures decreased was from 1978–79 to 1981–82. The following three events may account for part of that decline. First, disposable income per capita and state education aid per capita were in periods of either slow growth or decline at that time. Second, this was the period of the "tax revolt," when many voters expressed their displeasure at the spending habits of state or local governments by voting for measures that would limit taxes or spending. It was also a period of high inflation, when state and local governments may have had difficulty anticipating the rapid rise in school costs.

Current expenditures have increased each year since 1981–82. The percent increase has not been constant over that time however. Most of the largest of the percent increases occurred from 1984–85 to 1988–89. That was the period when disposable income per capita and state education aid per capita were also increasing most rapidly. Since 1988–89, current expenditures have not been increasing as rapidly. Disposable income per capita and state education aid per capita have been increasing at lower rates than in the mid-1980s as well.

The percentage of total disposable income spent on public elementary and secondary school current expenditures is virtually the same in 1990–91 as it was in 1978–79 (4.9 percent in both years). This percentage was not stable during this period however. It fell from 4.9 percent in 1978–79 to 4.3 percent in 1983–84 before beginning to rise again. The year 1983–84 is also important because average daily attendance that year reached its lowest level since 1962–63 and has been increasing annually since then.

Continuing an earlier trend, current expenditures per pupil as a percentage of disposable income per capita rose from 27.9 percent in 1978–79 to an estimated 31.8 percent in 1990–91.

Alternative Projections

The level of spending on elementary and secondary education has followed a path similar to the economic climate of the nation and the amount of revenue receipts provided by state governments to local governments for education. Regression equations were used to develop the forecasts for current expenditures, with a measure of the state of the economy (disposable income per capita) and the amount of revenue receipts from state sources for education used as two factors associated with current expenditures. Several plausible growth paths for disposable income per capita and revenue receipts from state sources were used to produce alternative sets of projections for current expenditures. Hence, the forecasts for current expenditures depend on the forecasts for these inputs. Another important factor is that the relationships that have existed among the variables in the past continue throughout the projection period.

Three sets of projections are presented for current expenditures in this chapter. These sets of forecasts are based on alternative projections for disposable income per capita and local government revenue receipts from state sources per capita. The U.S. Quarterly Model of the economic consulting firm DRI/McGraw-Hill (DRI) was used in developing forecasts of both disposable income per capita and revenue receipts from state sources. The assumptions underlying each set of alternative projections for current expenditures are described briefly. For more information about these assumptions and about the methodology used to compute these forecasts, see appendix A5. The values of disposable income per capita and local government revenue receipts from state sources per capita are shown in Appendix B.

The middle alternative projections are based on the assumptions that disposable income per capita will increase at rates between 0.7 and 1.4 percent during the period from 1993–94 to 2003–2004 and that revenue receipts from state sources per capita will increase at rates between 0.7 percent and 4.4 percent.

The low alternative projections are based on the assumptions that disposable income per capita will change at rates between -1.3 and 1.2 percent and that revenue receipts from state sources per capita will increase at rates between 0.0 percent and 2.4 percent.

The high alternative projections are based on the assumptions that disposable income will increase at rates between 0.7 and 3.9 percent and that revenue receipts from state sources will increase at rates between 0.8 percent and 5.4 percent.

A third factor influencing the growth in current expenditures in these projections is the ratio of enrollment (as measured by average daily attendance) to the population. The same projections for enrollment and the population are used in the production of all sets of projections for current expenditures presented in this chapter.

Enrollments are projected to increase steadily during the forecast period. With enrollments rising, communities should have less money to spend per pupil than if enrollments had remained unchanged. However, this expected increase in enrollment should also have a strong positive effect on total expenditures. With enrollments expected to rise, total expenditures should grow at a higher rate than expenditures per pupil.

The projections in this chapter are presented in both constant 1991–92 dollars and in current dollars. The projections were developed in constant dollars and then placed in current dollars using projections for the Consumer Price Index (CPI). Three alternative sets of projections for the

CPI were developed, one for each of the alternative sets of projections for current expenditures. These three alternative sets of projections for the CPI were developed simultaneously with the alternative sets of projections for disposable income per capita using the U.S. Quarterly Model. Since the set of projections for the CPI developed for use with the low alternative projections is rising at the fastest rate and that developed for use with the high alternative projections is rising at the slowest rate, it will frequently be the case that the current dollar projections from the low alternative set of projections are higher than those from the other two alternative sets of projections.

In the middle alternative projections, current expenditures in constant 1991–92 dollars are projected to grow slowly at first, as the economy comes out of the downturn of the early 1990s, and then continue to rise thereafter, reaching $284.4 billion in 2003–2004. This is an increase of 36.7 percent over the 1990–91 level, and a 34.2 percent over the estimated level for 1992–93.

Current expenditures per pupil in average daily attendance are projected to increase by 14.9 percent to $6,218 from 1990–91 to 2003–2004 (table 34 and figures 51 and 51). The projected rate of increase is not steady from 1990–91 to 2003–2004. With the slow economic growth of the early 1990s, current expenditures per pupil is estimated to have dropped slightly from 1990–91 to 1992–93. Current expenditures per pupil is projected to increase each year after that. As mentioned above, due to the increases projected for enrollments, total current expenditures are projected to increase more rapidly than expenditures per pupil.

In the middle alternative projection, total current expenditures as a percentage of total disposable income are projected to increase from 4.9 percent in 1990–91 to 5.3 percent in 2003–2004. One cause of this projected increase is the 19.0-percent increase in enrollment projected for this period.

Current expenditures per pupil as a percentage of disposable income per capita are also projected to increase, from 31.8 percent to 32.7 percent. This increase is smaller than that which occurred from 1978–79 to 1990–91. The rapid increase projected for enrollment compared with the increase projected for the population (19.0 percent for enrollment, 13.4 percent for the population) is one cause of this relatively small increase.

In the low alternative projections, both disposable income per capita and revenue receipts from state sources are projected to increase more slowly than in the middle set of projections. As a result, both current expenditures and current expenditures per pupil are projected to increase more slowly than in the middle set of projections. Current expenditures are projected to increase by 29.1 percent from 1990–91 to 2003–2004 reaching $268.6 billion at the end of the forecast period. Current expenditures per pupil in average daily attendance are projected to increase by 8.5 percent to $5,874.

In current dollars, current expenditures are projected to reach $317.9 billion dollars in 1997–98 using the low alternative projections. This is greater than the amount projected for 1997–98 using the middle set of alternative projections. This happens because the set of projections for the Consumer Price Index (CPI) used to place the low set of projections for current expenditures into current dollars is rising at a faster rate than the set of CPI projections used to place the middle set of projections for current expenditures into current dollars.

In the high alternative projections, both disposable income per capita and revenue receipts from state sources are projected to increase more rapidly than in the middle set of projections. Current expenditures are projected to increase by approximately 43.8 percent to $299.2 billion in 2003–2004. Current expenditures per pupil in average daily attendance are projected to increase by 20.9 percent to $6,543.

When examined in current dollars, the current expenditures projections for 1997–98 from the high alternative projections are less than those from the low alternative projections because the 1997–98 projection for the CPI is so much lower for the high alternative set of projections for current expenditures.

Teacher Salaries

Past Trends

The period from 1978–79 to 1992–93 has been dominated by three different patterns for teacher salaries in constant dollars (table 36 and figures 56 and 57).

Teacher salaries, already in a period of decline, fell 7.1 percent from 1978–79 to 1980–81, from $30,340 to $28,171 (average annual salary) in constant 1991–92 dollars. The period of greatest decline coincided with the period when the decline in enrollments was greatest. (See figure 58 for a comparison of the growth rates for teacher salaries and average daily attendance.) It also coincided with the period when the economy and current expenditures were falling. (See figure 59 for a comparison of the growth rates for teacher salaries and current expenditures per pupil.)

After this period of decline, teacher salaries entered a period of steady and relatively rapid growth. From 1980–81 to 1986–87, teacher salaries increased 17.2 percent, from $28,171 to $33,011. During this period, the revenues of state governments were increasing rapidly. It was during that period when enrollment, which had also been in a period of steady decline, began increasing again.

Since 1986–87, teacher salaries increased only 4.0 percent, with a 0.2 percent decline occurring from 1989–90 to 1991–92. Since 1986–87, the economy and revenues of state and local governments have not been increasing as rapidly as in the middle of the 1980s.

In the 1970s, the number of people preparing to become teachers was much greater than the number of openings for newly qualified teachers. The drop in teacher salaries during this time may be attributed, in part, to excess supply. Then the number of people preparing to become teachers

dropped, and eventually, the decline in teacher salaries stopped. Some of the increase in teacher salaries that occurred during the 1980s may be a result of the reforms enacted to encourage more people to enter the teaching profession.

Alternative Projections

As with current expenditures, a multiple linear regression model was developed for teacher salaries. Teacher salaries are seen as being related to current expenditures and enrollments. (See appendix A5.) Also like current expenditures, these projections depend on the projections of these inputs, and assume that the relationships that have existed among the variables in the past will continue throughout the projection period.

Three sets of alternative projections of teacher salaries—middle, low, and high—have been developed. Each alternative is based on one of the alternative sets of projections for current expenditures presented earlier in this chapter.

The projections for average daily attendance were produced by using the growth rates of the projections for fall enrollment presented in chapter 1. The same projections for average daily attendance were used for each of the three sets of projections for teacher salaries. Enrollments are projected to increase throughout the projection period, with the greatest percent increase occurring in the early and mid-1990s.

As with current expenditures, the three alternative sets of projections for the Consumer Price Index (CPI) developed using the U.S. Quarterly Model were used to place the constant dollar projections into current dollars. As the set of projections for the CPI developed for use with the low alternative projections is rising at the most rapid rate and that developed for use with the high alternative projections is rising at the slowest rate, in some years, the current dollar teacher salary projections from the low alternative set of projections are higher than those from the other two alternative sets of projections.

In the middle alternative projections, the average teacher salary in constant 1991–92 dollars is projected to reach $38,572 in 2003–2004 (table 36 and figure 56). This is a 12.4-percent increase from the level estimated for 1992–93. The greatest percent increases in salaries are projected to occur from 1993–94 to 1996–97. One reason for this is that this period is when the most rapid increases in enrollments are projected (figure 56).

In the low alternative projections, teacher salaries are projected to rise slowly throughout the projection period. The average salary is projected to reach $37,121 in 2003–2004, an increase of about 8.2 percent from 1992–93. (See figure 57 for a comparison of the growth rates for the alternative sets of projections.)

In the high alternative projections, the average teacher salary is projected to reach $39,939 in 2003–2004, an increase of about 16.4 percent.

Figure 51
Current expenditures of public schools (in constant 1991-92 dollars), with alternative projections: 1978-79 to 2003-2004

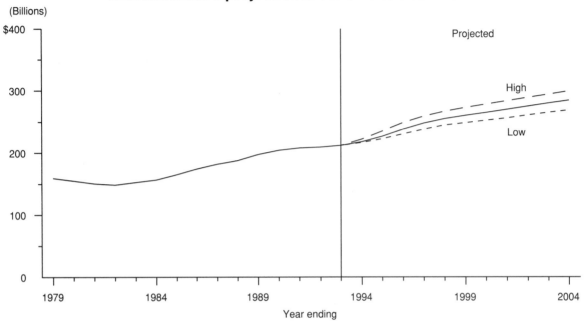

NOTE: Data for 1991-92 and 1992-93 are estimated using past data.

Figure 52
Current expenditures per pupil in average daily attendance (in constant 1991-92 dollars) of public schools, with alternative projections: 1978-79 to 2003-2004

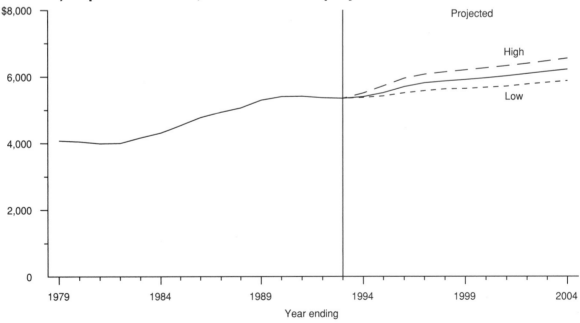

NOTE: Data for 1991-92 and 1992-93 are estimated using past data.

Figure 53
Percent change in current expenditures per pupil in average daily attendance (in constant dollars) of public schools, with alternative projections: 1978-79 to 2003-2004

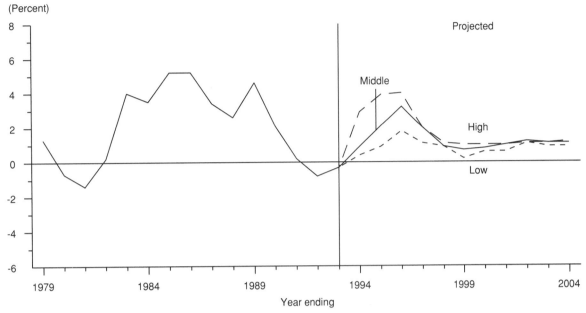

NOTE: Data for 1991-92 and 1992-93 are estimated using past data.

Figure 54
Percent change in current expenditures per pupil in average daily attendance of public schools and disposable income per capita (both in constant dollars), with middle alternative projections: 1978-79 to 2003-2004

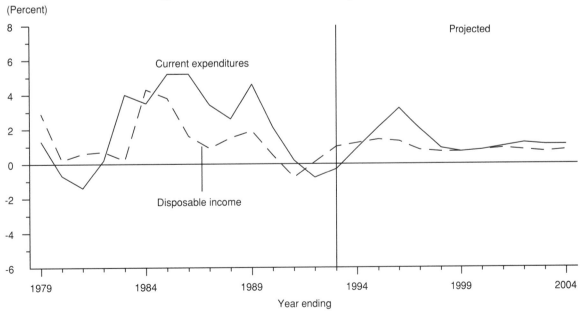

NOTE: Data for current expenditures for 1991-92 and 1992-93 are estimated using past data.

Figure 55
Percent change in current expenditures per pupil in average daily attendance of public schools and education revenue receipts from state sources per capita (both in constant dollars), with middle alternative projections: 1978-79 to 2003-2004

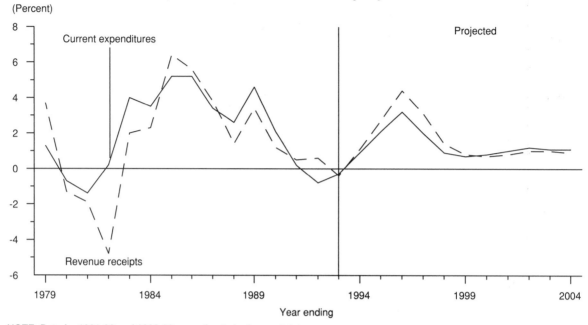

NOTE: Data for 1991-92 and 1992-93 are estimated using past data.

Figure 56
Average annual salaries of teachers (in constant 1991-92 dollars) in public schools, with alternative projections: 1978-79 to 2003-2004

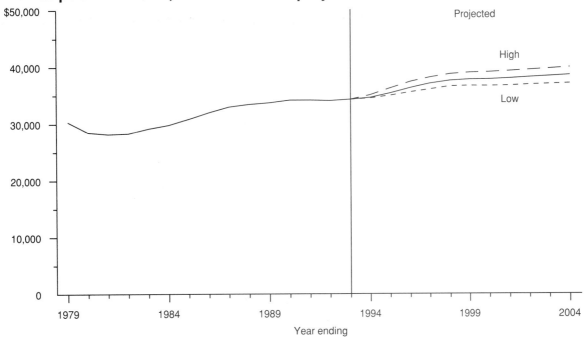

Figure 57
Percent change in average annual salaries of teachers (in constant dollars) in public schools, with alternative projections: 1978-79 to 2003-2004

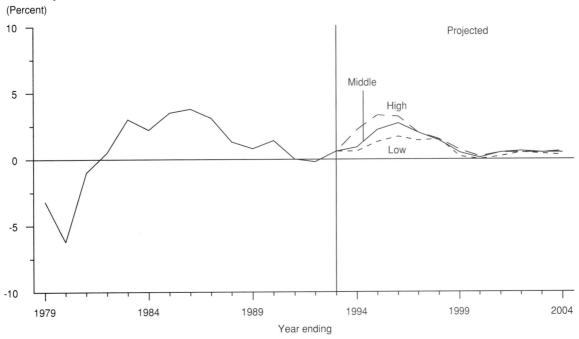

Figure 58
Percent change in average annual salaries of teachers (in constant dollars) in public schools and average daily attendance, with middle alternative projections: 1978-79 to 2003-2004

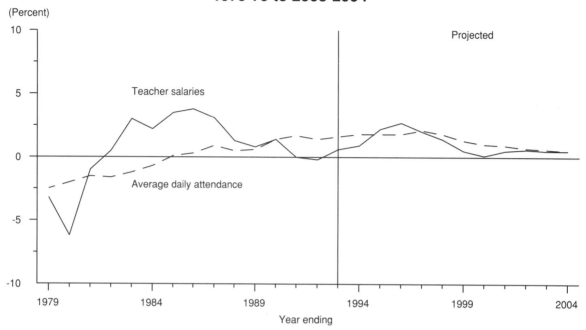

Figure 59
Percent change in average annual salaries of teachers in public schools, and current expenditures per pupil in average daily attendance of public schools (both in constant dollars), with middle alternative projections: 1978-79 to 2003-2004

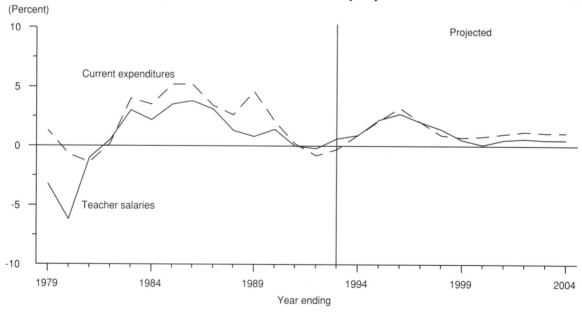

NOTE: Data for current expenditures for 1991-92 and 1992-93 are estimated using past data.

Table 34.—Current expenditures and current expenditures per pupil in average daily attendance (ADA) in public elementary and secondary schools, with alternative projections: 50 States and D.C., 1978–79 to 2003–2004

Year ending	ADA (in thousands)	Current expenditures			
		Constant 1991–92 dollars [1]		Current dollars [2]	
		Total (in billions)	Per pupil in ADA	Total (in billions)	Per pupil in ADA
1979	39,076	$159.4	$4,078	$79.0	$2,020
1980	38,289	155.0	4,049	87.0	2,272
1981	37,704	150.6	3,994	94.3	2,502
1982	37,095	148.5	4,003	101.1	2,726
1983	36,636	152.6	4,164	108.3	2,955
1984	36,363	156.8	4,311	115.4	3,173
1985	36,404	165.2	4,537	126.3	3,470
1986	36,523	174.2	4,771	137.2	3,756
1987	36,864	181.9	4,933	146.4	3,970
1988	37,051	187.5	5,060	157.1	4,240
1989	37,268	197.3	5,293	173.0	4,641
1990	37,799	204.2	5,403	187.6	4,962
1991	38,427	208.0	5,413	201.5	5,245
1992 [3]	38,972	209.2	5,368	209.2	5,368
1993 [3]	39,594	211.9	5,352	218.2	5,511
		Middle alternative projections			
1994	40,321	217.7	5,400	230.8	5,724
1995	41,063	226.5	5,515	247.9	6,036
1996	41,801	238.0	5,694	269.1	6,439
1997	42,672	247.9	5,810	289.6	6,788
1998	43,458	254.9	5,865	308.2	7,093
1999	44,010	260.0	5,907	—	—
2000	44,472	264.8	5,955	—	—
2001	44,859	269.8	6,015	—	—
2002	45,193	275.0	6,085	—	—
2003	45,480	279.8	6,152	—	—
2004	45,727	284.4	6,218	—	—
		Low alternative projections			
1994	40,321	216.7	5,373	232.2	5,759
1995	41,063	222.5	5,420	250.0	6,088
1996	41,801	230.5	5,514	272.1	6,510
1997	42,672	237.9	5,576	294.7	6,905
1998	43,458	244.6	5,628	317.9	7,315
1999	44,010	248.3	5,642	—	—
2000	44,472	252.5	5,678	—	—
2001	44,859	256.1	5,709	—	—
2002	45,193	260.8	5,771	—	—
2003	45,480	264.9	5,825	—	—
2004	45,727	268.6	5,874	—	—
		High alternative projections			
1994	40,321	222.0	5,507	234.3	5,810
1995	41,063	234.9	5,720	254.2	6,191
1996	41,801	248.6	5,947	275.9	6,601
1997	42,672	259.0	6,069	295.2	6,919
1998	43,458	266.7	6,137	313.4	7,211
1999	44,010	272.7	6,197	—	—
2000	44,472	278.2	6,257	—	—
2001	44,859	283.5	6,320	—	—
2002	45,193	288.8	6,391	—	—
2003	45,480	294.0	6,463	—	—
2004	45,727	299.2	6,543	—	—

[1] Based on the Consumer Price Index for all urban consumers, Bureau of Labor Statistics, U.S. Department of Labor.

[2] Projections in current dollars are not shown after 1998 due to the uncertain behavior of inflation over the long term.

[3] Current expenditures and average daily attendance are estimated on the basis of past data.

SOURCE: U.S. Department of Education, National Center for Education Statistics, *Statistics of State School Systems*; Common Core of Data survey; and the Early Estimates survey; and National Education Association, annual *Estimates of State School Statistics*. (Latest edition 1992–93. Copyright 1993 by the National Education Association. All rights reserved.) (This table prepared June 1993.)

Table 35.—Current expenditures and current expenditures per pupil in fall enrollment in public elementary and secondary schools, with alternative projections: 50 States and D.C., 1978–79 to 2003–2004

| Year ending | Fall enrollment [1] (in thousands) | Current expenditures | | | |
| | | Constant 1991–92 dollars [2] | | Current dollars [3] | |
		Total (in billions)	Per pupil in fall enrollment	Total (in billions)	Per pupil in fall enrollment
1979	42,551	$159.4	$3,745	$79.0	$1,855
1980	41,651	155.0	3,722	87.0	2,088
1981	40,877	150.6	3,684	94.3	2,307
1982	40,044	148.5	3,708	101.1	2,525
1983	39,566	152.6	3,856	108.3	2,736
1984	39,252	156.8	3,994	115.4	2,940
1985	39,208	165.2	4,212	126.3	3,222
1986	39,422	174.2	4,420	137.2	3,479
1987	39,753	181.9	4,575	146.4	3,682
1988	40,007	187.5	4,686	157.1	3,927
1989	40,189	197.3	4,908	173.0	4,304
1990	40,543	204.2	5,037	187.6	4,626
1991	41,217	208.0	5,046	201.5	4,890
1992 [4]	42,000	209.2	4,981	209.2	4,981
1993 [4]	42,670	211.9	4,967	218.2	5,114
Middle alternative projections					
1994	43,454	217.7	5,010	230.8	5,311
1995	44,254	226.5	5,118	247.9	5,601
1996	45,049	238.0	5,284	269.1	5,975
1997	45,988	247.9	5,391	289.6	6,298
1998	46,835	254.9	5,442	308.2	6,581
1999	47,430	260.0	5,481	—	—
2000	47,927	264.8	5,526	—	—
2001	48,345	269.8	5,581	—	—
2002	48,705	275.0	5,647	—	—
2003	49,014	279.8	5,709	—	—
2004	49,280	284.4	5,770	—	—
Low alternative projections					
1994	43,454	216.7	4,986	232.2	5,344
1995	44,254	222.5	5,029	250.0	5,649
1996	45,049	230.5	5,117	272.1	6,040
1997	45,988	237.9	5,174	294.7	6,407
1998	46,835	244.6	5,223	317.9	6,788
1999	47,430	248.3	5,235	—	—
2000	47,927	252.5	5,268	—	—
2001	48,345	256.1	5,298	—	—
2002	48,705	260.8	5,355	—	—
2003	49,014	264.9	5,405	—	—
2004	49,280	268.6	5,451	—	—
High alternative projections					
1994	43,454	222.0	5,110	234.3	5,391
1995	44,254	234.9	5,308	254.2	5,744
1996	45,049	248.6	5,519	275.9	6,125
1997	45,988	259.0	5,631	295.2	6,420
1998	46,835	266.7	5,695	313.4	6,691
1999	47,430	272.7	5,750	—	—
2000	47,927	278.2	5,806	—	—
2001	48,345	283.5	5,864	—	—
2002	48,705	288.8	5,930	—	—
2003	49,014	294.0	5,997	—	—
2004	49,280	299.2	6,071	—	—

[1] Each enrollment number is for the fall of the school year ending in the school year shown in column 1. Hence, the enrollment number listed for 1979 is for fall 1978.

[2] Based on the Consumer Price Index for all urban consumers, Bureau of Labor Statistics, U.S. Department of Labor.

[3] Projections in current dollars are not shown after 1998 due to the uncertain behavior of inflation over the long term.

[4] Current expenditures are early estimates.

SOURCE: U.S. Department of Education, National Center for Education Statistics, *Statistics of State School Systems*; *Statistics of Public Elementary and Secondary Schools*; ''Selected Public and Private Elementary and Secondary Education Statistics,'' NCES Bulletin, October 23, 1979; Common Core of Data survey; and the Early Estimates survey; and National Education Association, annual *Estimates of State School Statistics*. (Latest edition 1992–93. Copyright 1993 by the National Education Association. All rights reserved.) (This table prepared June 1993.)

Table 36.—Average annual salaries of classroom teachers in public elementary and secondary schools, with alternative projections: 50 States and D.C., 1978–79 to 2003–2004

Year ending	Constant 1991–92 dollars [1]	Current dollars [2]
1979	$30,340	$15,032
1980	28,464	15,970
1981	28,171	17,644
1982	28,306	19,274
1983	29,162	20,695
1984	29,802	21,935
1985	30,851	23,600
1986	32,011	25,199
1987	33,011	26,569
1988	33,452	28,034
1989	33,721	29,568
1990	34,179	31,391
1991	34,172	33,114
1992	34,098	34,098
1993	34,316	35,334
Middle alternative projections		
1994	34,632	36,711
1995	35,388	38,729
1996	36,330	41,081
1997	37,055	43,289
1998	37,589	45,459
1999	37,774	—
2000	37,819	—
2001	37,995	—
2002	38,205	—
2003	38,397	—
2004	38,572	—
Low alternative projections		
1994	34,520	36,997
1995	34,985	39,301
1996	35,572	41,993
1997	36,066	44,665
1998	36,592	47,560
1999	36,657	—
2000	36,647	—
2001	36,705	—
2002	36,879	—
2003	37,015	—
2004	37,121	—
High alternative projections		
1994	35,084	37,016
1995	36,251	39,236
1996	37,398	41,509
1997	38,146	43,487
1998	38,737	45,515
1999	38,995	—
2000	39,090	—
2001	39,280	—
2002	39,494	—
2003	39,708	—
2004	39,939	—

[1] Based on the Consumer Price Index for all urban consumers, Bureau of Labor Statistics, U.S. Department of Labor.

[2] Projections in current dollars are not shown after 1998 due to the uncertain behavior of inflation over the long term.

SOURCE: National Education Association, annual *Estimates of State School Statistics*. (Latest edition 1992–93. Copyright 1993 by the National Education Association. All rights reserved.) (This table prepared June 1993.)

Chapter 7

Expenditures of Institutions of Higher Education

The steady growth in higher education expenditures that has marked the 1980s is expected to continue throughout the 1990s. Key assumptions behind these projections are that the economy continues to grow at a steady rate, that inflation rates remain near current levels, and that enrollments increase as in the middle alternative projections presented in chapter 2. Projections based on alternative economic scenarios are discussed below.

The higher education system is examined by both control of institution (public versus private) and by type of institution (4-year versus 2-year). For each of these sectors of higher education, two different types of expenditures—current-fund expenditures and educational and general expenditures—are examined. All expenditure data have been adjusted for inflation. Since the historical trends and the projections of current-fund expenditures and educational and general expenditures are very similar, emphasis is given to current-fund expenditures.

Past Trends

Following a well-established trend, current-fund expenditures have increased significantly since 1978–79 (table 37 and figure 60). In real terms, current-fund expenditures increased 47.3 percent from 1978–79 to 1990–91. (1990–91 is the last year for which there are actual data.) From 1978–79 to 1992–93, current-fund expenditures are estimated to have increased 56.1 percent. The rate of increase in current-fund expenditures during this period has not been consistent. There have been years of rapid growth and slow growth, and even decline. Factors that can be associated with current-fund expenditures during these periods include: (1) the economy as a whole, and, for public institutions, the economic situation of state and local governments; (2) the inflation rate; and (3) enrollments.

Current-fund expenditures grew slowly from 1978–79 to 1981–82. During that period, current–fund expenditures increased 0.9 percent, from $102.4 billion to $103.3 billion in constant 1991–92 dollars. The economy was in a period of slow growth at that time. One measure of the state of the economy, disposable income per capita, rose only 1.5 percent. Inflation was also increasing rapidly. The average annual inflation rate for that period was over 10 percent as measured by the Consumer Price Index.

Current-fund expenditures have risen steadily since 1981–82. From 1981–82 to 1990–91, current-fund expenditures increased 45.9 percent.

The greatest increases occurred from 1981–82 to 1986–87, when current–fund expenditures rose 27.2 percent. The economy was increasing steadily during that period with disposable income per capita rising 11.1 percent.

Much of the 14.7 percent increase that occurred from 1986–87 to 1990–91 was due to the rapid increase in enrollments that occurred during that time. The number of students as measured by full-time-equivalent enrollment rose 10.1 percent. From 1981–82 to 1986–87, full-time-equivalent enrollment rose by 0.6 percent.

While current-fund expenditures in both public and private institutions rose, they did not rise at the same rate. From 1978–79 to 1990–91, current-fund expenditures increased 40.9 percent in public institutions and 59.9 percent in private institutions.

For the period under examination, educational and general expenditures have been an almost constant percentage of current-fund expenditures (about 78 percent). Hence, the trend for educational and general expenditures is virtually identical to that for current-fund expenditures (table 38 and figure 61). Total educational and general expenditures in constant dollars increased 46.5 percent from 1978–79 to 1990–91. There was a 38.4 percent increase in educational and general expenditures in public colleges from 1978–79 to 1990–91 and a 64.6 percent increase in private colleges.

Since the trends of current-fund expenditures for the different sectors show some differences, the data are examined separately for each sector, except private 2-year institutions. Expenditures are examined both as a total and per student in full-time-equivalent (FTE) enrollment.

The trend for private 2-year projections is not shown separately because there have been significant additions to the universe of private 2-year institutions since 1978–79. Private 2-year institutions comprise the smallest of the higher education sectors. In 1990–91, they accounted for only 0.9 percent of total current-fund expenditures and 2.0 percent of FTE enrollment.

Public 4-Year Institutions

The trend for current-fund expenditures in public 4-year institutions is very similar to that for all institutions (table 39). The period from 1978–79 to 1981–82 saw current-fund expenditures falling 0.1 percent. Since then, current expenditures have increased steadily. From 1981–82 to 1990–91 current-fund expenditures increased 42.3 percent. As with the trend for all institutions, the most rapid growth occurred from 1981–82 to 1986–87 when current-fund expenditures rose 25.0 percent. During that time, full-time-equivalent enrollment increased by only 2.1 percent.

When current-fund expenditures are examined on a per student basis, a somewhat different pattern emerges. With the slowing down of the economy, the rise in inflation, and the increase in enrollment, current-fund expenditures per student fell 5.2 percent from 1978–79 to 1981–82. As with total current-fund expenditures, current-fund expenditures per student rose each year from 1981–82 to 1990–91. Almost all of the increase occurred from 1981–82 to 1986–87 when current-fund expenditures per student rose 22.5 percent. From 1986–87 to 1990–91, when FTE enrollment rose 10.3 percent, current-fund expenditures per student only rose 3.1 percent.

The trend for educational and general expenditures (table 40) is similar to that for current-fund expenditures.

Public 2-Year Institutions

Public 2-year institutions show a similar trend to public 4-year institutions (table 41). There was a 1.2 percent decrease in current-fund expenditures in public 2-year institutions from 1978–79 to 1981–82. This was followed by an 18.3 percent increase from 1981–82 to 1986–87. A further 15.8 increase occurred from 1986–87 to 1990–91, when enrollments rose 13.5 percent.

As with public 4-year current-fund expenditures, a somewhat different pattern emerges when public 2-year current-fund expenditures are placed in per student terms. With total current-fund expenditures falling 1.2 percent and enrollments rising 12.7 percent, current-fund expenditures per student fell 12.3 percent from 1978–79 to 1981–82. Between 1981–82 and 1986–87, current-fund expenditures per student rose 22.6 percent. From 1986–87 to 1990–91, current-fund expenditures per student rose only 2.0 percent.

The trend for educational and general expenditures (table 42) is similar to that for current-fund expenditures.

Private 4-Year Institutions

From 1977–78 until 1981–82, current-fund expenditures in private 4-year institutions rose 3.0 percent. Like public institutions, current-fund expenditures rose rapidly throughout the rest of the 1980's. From 1981–82 to 1990–91, current-fund expenditures rose 55.5 percent (table 43).

With the increase in the number of students and the slowdown in the economy, expenditures per student fell 2.3 percent from 1977–78 to 1981–82. Since then, current-fund expenditures per student have been rising. From 1981–82 to 1986–87, current-fund expenditures per student rose 31.9 percent. After that, as enrollments increased, current expenditures per student have continued to increase, but

not at as rapid a rate. From 1986–87 to 1990–91, current expenditures per student rose 7.9 percent.

The trend for educational and general expenditures (table 44) is similar to that for current-fund expenditures.

Alternative Projections

Projections have been prepared for each of the sectors of higher education. With the exception of the private 2-year sector, these projections have been developed using regression models. In most cases, expenditures per student are seen as being related to the state of the economy (as measured by either disposable income per capita or the revenues of state and local governments per capita), the inflation rate, and enrollments. (For more details, see appendix A6.) Hence, the forecasts for higher education expenditures depend on the forecasts for these three types of inputs. Another important factor is that the relationships that have existed among the variables in the past continue throughout the projection period.

Three sets of projections are presented in this chapter. Each is based on an alternative set of assumptions for the state of the economy, specifically, a different growth path for either disposable income per capita or the revenues of state and local governments per capita. These alternative scenarios for the state of the economy were developed using the U.S. Quarterly Model developed by DRI/McGraw–Hill.

The middle alternative projections are based on the assumption that the economy continues to grow at a steady rate (disposable income per capita increases each year at a rate between 0.7 and 1.4 percent and the revenues of state and local governments per capita increase at rates between 0.6 percent and 3.9 percent.) Two alternative sets of projections were developed to show the impact of various economic scenarios. In the low alternative, the economy grows at a lower rate than in the middle alternative set of projections. The growth rate of disposable income per capita varies between -1.3 and 1.2 percent and that for the revenues of state and local governments per capita varies between 0.2 and 3.1 percent. In the high alternative, the economy enters a period of rapid growth and disposable income grows at rates between 0.7 and 3.9 percent and the revenues of state and local governments per capita grow at rates between 0.7 and 5.7 percent.

The three alternative sets of projections are also based on alternative projections for the inflation rate. The projections for the inflation rate were also developed using the U.S. Quarterly Model. For the forecast period, they range from 2.9 percent to 4.0 percent for the middle alternative, 4.0 percent to 5.2 percent for the low alternative, and 2.5 percent to 3.7 percent for the high alternative. The projections of the enrollment are those for the middle alternative projections for full-time-equivalent enrollment presented in chapter 2.

The projections in this chapter are presented in both constant 1991–92 dollars and in current dollars. The projections were developed in constant dollars and then placed in current dollars using projections for the Consumer Price Index (CPI). Three alternative sets of projections for the CPI were developed, one for use with the middle alternative projections, one for use with the low alternative projections, and one for use with the high alternative projections. These three alternative sets of projections for the CPI were developed using the U.S. Quarterly Model. As the set of projections for the CPI developed for use with the low alternative projections is rising at the most rapid rate and that developed for use with the high alternative projections is rising at the slowest rate, it is frequently the case that the current dollar projections from the low alternative set of projections are higher than those from the other two alternative sets of projections.

Due to the short time series of consistent data, only one set of projections was produced for private 2-year institutions. This was included in each of the alternative projections. The set of projections for private 2-year institutions is not examined separately.

All of the alternative projections indicate an increase in current-fund expenditures throughout the remainder of the century. In the middle alternative projection, current-fund expenditures are projected to reach $214.0 billion in 2003–2004. This is a 41.9 percent increase from 1990–91, the last year for which there are actual data. In the low alternative projection, current-fund expenditures are projected to increase to $211.9 billion. In the high alternative projection, the figure for 2003–2004 is $216.6 billion.

A similar pattern is seen for educational and general expenditures. In the middle alternative projection, educational and general expenditures are projected to be $162.9 billion in 2003–2004, a 38.3 percent increase from 1990–91. In the low alternative projection, educational and general expenditures are projected to increase to $160.9 billion. In the high alternative projection, the figure for 2003–2004 is $165.5 billion.

Public 4-Year Institutions

There are only small differences in the trends among the various sectors of higher education. In public 4-year institutions, current-fund expenditures are projected to reach $112.3 billion in the middle alternative projection in 2003–2004 (table 40). This is a 41.9 percent increase from 1990–91 to 2003–2004. In the low alternative projection, the value for 2003–2004 is $111.7 billion and in the high alternative projection, it is $113.3 billion.

Since full-time-equivalent (FTE) enrollment is projected to increase by 13.9 from 1990–91 to 2003–2004, the rate of increase for expenditures is lower on a per student basis. In the middle alternative projection, a 24.6 percent increase is projected for the period from 1990–91 to 2003–2004 compared with 23.9 percent for the low alternative projection and 25.7 percent for the high alternative projection. The most rapid increases are projected to occur from 1994–95 to 1997–98, when the declines in FTE enrollments are projected.

Public 2-Year Institutions

Expenditures are also seen as increasing in public 2-year institutions. For instance, in the middle alternative projection, current-fund expenditures are projected to reach $21.8 billion in 2003–2004 and expenditures per student are projected to increase to $6,711. When the low alternative projection is used, with its lower growth path for revenues of state and local governments per capita, lower values for current expenditure are found. When the high alternative projection is used, with its higher growth path for revenues of state and local governments per capita, higher values are found. The most rapid increases for expenditures per student are projected to occur from 1994–95 to 1996–97, when the slowest growth in FTE enrollments is projected.

Private 4-Year Institutions

The trends for private 4-year institutions exhibit the same patterns as other types of institutions. Total current-fund expenditures are seen as increasing each year. In the middle alternative projection, from 1990–91 to 2003–2004, they are projected to increase 46.3 percent. Current-fund expenditures per student are projected to increase 26.9 percent during the same time. The most rapid growth for expenditures per student is projected to occur from 1994–95 to 1996–97, when FTE enrollments are projected to decline.

Figure 60
Current-fund expenditures (in constant 1991-92 dollars) of public and private institutions of higher education, with middle alternative projections: 1978-79 to 2003-2004

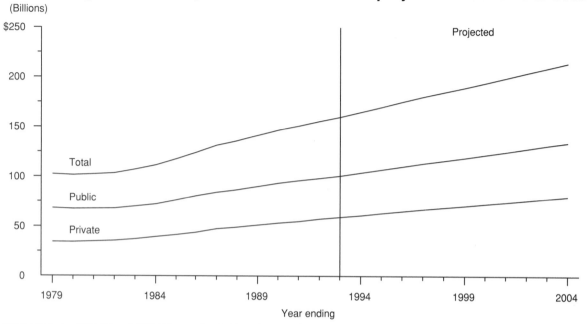

NOTE: Data for 1991-92 and 1992-93 are estimated by using past data.

Figure 61
Educational and general expenditures (in constant 1991-92 dollars) of public and private institutions of higher education, with middle alternative projections: 1978-79 to 2003-2004

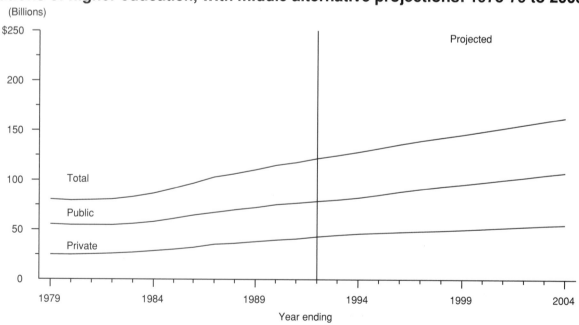

NOTE: Data for 1991-92 and 1992-93 are estimated by using past data.

Table 37.—Current-fund expenditures of public and private institutions of higher education, with alternative projections: 50 States and D.C., 1978–79 to 2003–2004

Year ending	Constant 1991–92 dollars [1] (in billions)			Current dollars (in billions)		
	Total	Public	Private	Total	Public	Private
1979	$102.4	$68.1	$34.3	$50.7	$33.7	$17.0
1980	101.4	67.3	34.1	56.9	37.8	19.1
1981	102.3	67.5	34.8	64.1	42.3	21.8
1982	103.3	67.9	35.4	70.3	46.2	24.1
1983	107.0	69.9	37.1	75.9	49.6	26.4
1984	111.4	72.1	39.3	82.0	53.1	28.9
1985	117.6	76.2	41.4	90.0	58.3	31.6
1986	123.9	80.3	43.6	97.5	63.2	34.3
1987	131.4	84.1	47.4	105.8	67.7	38.1
1988	135.8	86.7	49.1	113.8	72.6	41.1
1989	141.3	90.0	51.2	123.9	78.9	44.9
1990	146.6	93.4	53.2	134.7	85.8	48.9
1991	150.8	95.9	54.8	146.1	93.0	53.1
1992 [2]	155.6	98.3	57.3	155.6	98.3	57.3
1993 [2]	159.8	100.7	59.1	164.6	103.7	60.9
Middle alternative projections						
1994	164.8	103.8	60.9	174.7	110.0	64.6
1995	169.8	106.9	63.0	185.8	116.9	68.9
1996	175.2	110.1	65.0	198.1	124.5	73.5
1997	180.2	113.2	67.0	210.5	132.2	78.3
1998	184.8	116.0	68.8	223.5	140.3	83.2
1999	189.3	118.7	70.5	—	—	—
2000	194.1	121.8	72.4	—	—	—
2001	199.1	124.8	74.2	—	—	—
2002	204.1	128.0	76.1	—	—	—
2003	209.1	131.2	78.0	—	—	—
2004	214.0	134.1	79.9	—	—	—
Low alternative projections						
1994	163.9	103.7	60.2	175.6	111.1	64.5
1995	168.0	106.0	62.0	188.7	119.1	69.6
1996	172.9	109.0	64.0	204.2	128.6	75.5
1997	178.0	112.0	66.0	220.4	138.7	81.7
1998	182.6	114.7	67.8	237.3	149.1	88.2
1999	187.0	117.4	69.6	—	—	—
2000	191.8	120.4	71.4	—	—	—
2001	196.8	123.4	73.3	—	—	—
2002	201.9	126.7	75.2	—	—	—
2003	207.0	129.9	77.1	—	—	—
2004	211.9	132.9	79.0	—	—	—
High alternative projections						
1994	165.4	104.0	61.5	174.5	109.7	64.8
1995	171.5	107.8	63.7	185.6	116.7	68.9
1996	177.4	111.5	65.8	196.9	123.8	73.1
1997	182.4	114.7	67.7	207.9	130.7	77.2
1998	187.0	117.6	69.4	219.7	138.2	81.6
1999	191.6	120.4	71.2	—	—	—
2000	196.6	123.5	73.0	—	—	—
2001	201.5	126.7	74.9	—	—	—
2002	206.6	129.8	76.8	—	—	—
2003	211.7	133.0	78.7	—	—	—
2004	216.6	136.0	80.6	—	—	—

[1] Based on the Consumer Price Index for all urban consumers, Bureau of Labor Statistics, U.S. Department of Labor.

[2] Estimated on the basis of past data.

—Projections in current dollars are not shown after 1998 due to the uncertain behavior of inflation over the long term.

SOURCE: U.S. Department of Education, National Center for Education Statistics, "Financial Statistics of Institutions of Higher Education," and "Fall Enrollment in Colleges and Universities" surveys. (This table was prepared June 1993.)

Table 38.—Educational and general expenditures of public and private institutions of higher education, with alternative projections: 50 States and D.C., 1978–79 to 2003–2004

Year ending	Constant 1991–92 dollars [1] (in billions)			Current dollars (in billions)		
	Total	Public	Private	Total	Public	Private
1979	$80.4	$55.5	$24.9	$39.8	$27.5	$12.3
1980	79.4	54.6	24.8	44.5	30.6	13.9
1981	79.9	54.6	25.4	50.1	34.2	15.9
1982	80.6	54.6	26.0	54.8	37.2	17.7
1983	83.0	56.0	27.1	58.9	39.7	19.2
1984	86.6	57.9	28.7	63.7	42.6	21.1
1985	91.6	61.3	30.3	70.1	46.9	23.2
1986	96.7	64.6	32.1	76.1	50.9	25.3
1987	103.1	67.5	35.5	83.0	54.4	28.6
1988	106.4	70.0	36.4	89.2	58.6	30.5
1989	110.4	72.4	38.0	96.8	63.4	33.4
1990	115.0	75.3	39.7	105.6	69.2	36.4
1991	117.8	76.8	41.0	114.1	74.4	39.7
1992 [2]	121.8	78.7	43.1	121.8	78.7	43.1
1993 [2]	124.9	80.2	44.7	128.6	82.5	46.1
	Middle alternative projections					
1994	128.4	82.3	46.1	136.1	87.3	48.9
1995	132.1	85.1	47.0	144.6	93.2	51.4
1996	136.1	88.3	47.8	153.8	99.8	54.0
1997	139.6	91.1	48.6	163.1	106.4	56.7
1998	142.8	93.5	49.3	172.7	113.1	59.6
1999	145.9	95.7	50.2	—	—	—
2000	149.2	98.0	51.2	—	—	—
2001	152.6	100.4	52.2	—	—	—
2002	156.1	102.8	53.3	—	—	—
2003	159.6	105.3	54.3	—	—	—
2004	162.9	107.7	55.2	—	—	—
	Low alternative projections					
1994	127.6	82.2	45.4	136.7	88.1	48.6
1995	130.3	84.4	46.0	146.4	94.8	51.7
1996	134.0	87.2	46.7	158.1	102.9	55.2
1997	137.5	90.0	47.6	170.3	111.4	58.9
1998	140.7	92.4	48.4	182.9	120.1	62.9
1999	143.7	94.5	49.2	—	—	—
2000	147.0	96.8	50.2	—	—	—
2001	150.4	99.1	51.3	—	—	—
2002	154.0	101.6	52.4	—	—	—
2003	157.6	104.2	53.4	—	—	—
2004	160.9	106.6	54.3	—	—	—
	High alternative projections					
1994	129.1	82.5	46.6	136.2	87.0	49.2
1995	133.7	86.0	47.7	144.7	93.1	51.6
1996	138.1	89.5	48.6	153.3	99.3	54.0
1997	141.7	92.4	49.4	161.6	105.3	56.3
1998	144.9	94.9	50.0	170.3	111.5	58.8
1999	148.1	97.2	50.9	—	—	—
2000	151.6	99.6	52.0	—	—	—
2001	155.0	102.0	53.0	—	—	—
2002	158.5	104.5	54.0	—	—	—
2003	162.0	107.0	55.1	—	—	—
2004	165.5	109.4	56.1	—	—	—

[1] Based on the Consumer Price Index for all urban consumers, Bureau of Labor Statistics, U.S. Department of Labor.

[2] Estimated on the basis of past data.

—Projections in current dollars are not shown after 1998 due to the uncertain behavior of inflation over the long term.

SOURCE: U.S. Department of Education, National Center for Education Statistics, "Financial Statistics of Institutions of Higher Education," and "Fall Enrollment in Colleges and Universities" surveys. (This table was prepared June 1993.)

Table 39.—Current-fund expenditures and current-fund expenditures per full-time equivalent (FTE) student of public 4-year institutions, with alternative projections: 50 States and D.C., 1978–79 to 2003–2004

| Year ending | FTE (in thousands) | Current-fund expenditures | | | |
| | | Constant 1991–92 dollars [1] | | Current dollars | |
		Total (in billions)	Per student in FTE	Total (in billions)	Per student in FTE
1979	3,996	$55.7	$13,940	$27.6	$6,907
1980	4,059	55.2	13,602	31.0	7,632
1981	4,158	55.4	13,315	34.7	8,339
1982	4,209	55.6	13,222	37.9	9,003
1983	4,221	57.2	13,560	40.6	9,623
1984	4,266	59.2	13,882	43.6	10,218
1985	4,238	62.8	14,812	48.0	11,330
1986	4,240	66.3	15,636	52.2	12,309
1987	4,295	69.6	16,199	56.0	13,038
1988	4,396	71.8	16,325	60.1	13,681
1989	4,506	74.5	16,540	65.3	14,503
1990	4,620	77.2	16,702	70.9	15,339
1991	4,740	79.2	16,703	76.7	16,186
1992 [2]	4,796	81.0	16,899	81.0	16,899
1993 [2]	4,933	83.6	16,951	86.1	17,454
Middle alternative projections					
1994	5,072	86.3	17,013	91.5	18,035
1995	5,050	88.8	17,582	97.2	19,242
1996	5,009	91.4	18,242	103.3	20,628
1997	4,995	93.9	18,793	109.7	21,955
1998	5,009	96.3	19,218	116.4	23,242
1999	5,056	98.7	19,526	—	—
2000	5,139	101.4	19,731	—	—
2001	5,216	104.1	19,962	—	—
2002	5,292	106.9	20,203	—	—
2003	5,359	109.7	20,470	—	—
2004	5,399	112.3	20,808	—	—
Low alternative projections					
1994	5,072	86.2	16,999	92.4	18,218
1995	5,050	88.3	17,493	99.2	19,651
1996	5,009	90.8	18,121	107.2	21,392
1997	4,995	93.3	18,669	115.5	23,120
1998	5,009	95.6	19,090	124.3	24,812
1999	5,056	98.0	19,389	—	—
2000	5,139	100.7	19,591	—	—
2001	5,216	103.4	19,825	—	—
2002	5,292	106.2	20,074	—	—
2003	5,359	109.1	20,349	—	—
2004	5,399	111.7	20,691	—	—
High alternative projections					
1994	5,072	86.4	17,030	91.1	17,967
1995	5,050	89.3	17,679	96.6	19,134
1996	5,009	92.1	18,383	102.2	20,404
1997	4,995	94.6	18,945	107.9	21,597
1998	5,009	97.1	19,382	114.1	22,773
1999	5,056	99.6	19,696	—	—
2000	5,139	102.3	19,907	—	—
2001	5,216	105.1	20,140	—	—
2002	5,292	107.9	20,381	—	—
2003	5,359	110.7	20,649	—	—
2004	5,399	113.3	20,992	—	—

[1] Based on the Consumer Price Index for all urban consumers, Bureau of Labor Statistics, U.S. Department of Labor.

[2] Estimated on the basis of past data.

—Projections in current dollars are not shown after 1998 due to the uncertain behavior of inflation over the long term.

SOURCE: U.S. Department of Education, National Center for Education Statistics, ''Financial Statistics of Institutions of Higher Education,'' and ''Fall Enrollment in Colleges and Universities'' surveys. (This table was prepared June 1993.)

Table 40.—Educational and general expenditures and educational and general expenditures per full-time equivalent (FTE) student of public 4-year institutions, with alternative projections: 50 States and D.C., 1978–79 to 2003–2004

Year ending	FTE (in thousands)	Current-fund expenditures			
		Constant 1991–92 dollars [1]		Current dollars	
		Total (in billions)	Per student in FTE	Total (in billions)	Per student in FTE
1979	3,996	$43.9	$10,980	$21.7	$5,440
1980	4,059	43.3	10,666	24.3	5,985
1981	4,158	43.3	10,402	27.1	6,515
1982	4,209	43.2	10,259	29.4	6,986
1983	4,221	44.2	10,475	31.4	7,434
1984	4,266	45.9	10,756	33.8	7,917
1985	4,238	48.8	11,504	37.3	8,800
1986	4,240	51.6	12,169	40.6	9,580
1987	4,295	54.1	12,586	43.5	10,130
1988	4,396	56.1	12,751	47.0	10,686
1989	4,506	57.9	12,852	50.8	11,270
1990	4,620	60.2	13,031	55.3	11,968
1991	4,740	61.2	12,904	59.3	12,504
1992 [2]	4,796	62.6	13,063	62.6	13,063
1993 [2]	4,933	64.3	13,036	66.2	13,423
		Middle alternative projections			
1994	5,072	66.0	13,015	70.0	13,797
1995	5,050	68.3	13,528	74.8	14,805
1996	5,009	70.8	14,127	80.0	15,974
1997	4,995	73.0	14,618	85.3	17,077
1998	5,009	75.1	14,988	90.8	18,127
1999	5,056	77.0	15,239	—	—
2000	5,139	79.0	15,378	—	—
2001	5,216	81.1	15,543	—	—
2002	5,292	83.2	15,717	—	—
2003	5,359	85.3	15,918	—	—
2004	5,399	87.5	16,198	—	—
		Low alternative projections			
1994	5,072	66.0	13,004	70.7	13,937
1995	5,050	68.0	13,460	76.4	15,121
1996	5,009	70.3	14,035	83.0	16,569
1997	4,995	72.6	14,525	89.8	17,988
1998	5,009	74.6	14,891	96.9	19,355
1999	5,056	76.5	15,136	—	—
2000	5,139	78.5	15,273	—	—
2001	5,216	80.5	15,440	—	—
2002	5,292	82.7	15,620	—	—
2003	5,359	84.8	15,827	—	—
2004	5,399	87.0	16,110	—	—
		High alternative projections			
1994	5,072	66.1	13,027	69.7	13,745
1995	5,050	68.7	13,601	74.3	14,720
1996	5,009	71.3	14,233	79.1	15,798
1997	4,995	73.6	14,733	83.9	16,795
1998	5,009	75.7	15,112	88.9	17,756
1999	5,056	77.7	15,367	—	—
2000	5,139	79.7	15,512	—	—
2001	5,216	81.8	15,678	—	—
2002	5,292	83.9	15,851	—	—
2003	5,359	86.0	16,053	—	—
2004	5,399	88.2	16,338	—	—

[1] Based on the Consumer Price Index for all urban consumers, Bureau of Labor Statistics, U.S. Department of Labor.

[2] Estimated on the basis of past data.

—Projections in current dollars are not shown after 1998 due to the uncertain behavior of inflation over the long term.

SOURCE: U.S. Department of Education, National Center for Education Statistics, ''Financial Statistics of Institutions of Higher Education,'' and ''Fall Enrollment in Colleges and Universities'' surveys. (This table was prepared June 1993.)

Table 41.—Current-fund expenditures and current-fund expenditures per full-time equivalent (FTE) student of public 2-year institutions, with alternative projections: 50 States and D.C., 1978–79 to 2003–2004

Year ending	FTE (in thousands)	Constant 1991–92 dollars [1]		Current dollars	
		Total (in billions)	Per student in FTE	Total (in billions)	Per student in FTE
1979	2,283	$12.4	$5,421	$6.1	$2,686
1980	2,333	12.1	5,186	6.8	2,910
1981	2,484	12.1	4,887	7.6	3,061
1982	2,573	12.2	4,755	8.3	3,238
1983	2,630	12.6	4,799	9.0	3,406
1984	2,616	12.9	4,934	9.5	3,631
1985	2,447	13.5	5,502	10.3	4,209
1986	2,428	14.0	5,760	11.0	4,534
1987	2,483	14.5	5,831	11.7	4,693
1988	2,542	14.9	5,870	12.5	4,919
1989	2,591	15.5	5,984	13.6	5,247
1990	2,752	16.2	5,898	14.9	5,417
1991	2,818	16.8	5,947	16.2	5,763
1992 [2]	3,067	17.2	5,613	17.2	5,613
1993 [2]	2,939	17.1	5,804	17.6	5,976
		Middle alternative projections			
1994	3,026	17.5	5,791	18.6	6,139
1995	3,032	18.1	5,958	19.8	6,521
1996	3,027	18.8	6,198	21.2	7,008
1997	3,034	19.3	6,370	22.6	7,442
1998	3,058	19.7	6,451	23.9	7,802
1999	3,087	20.0	6,485	—	—
2000	3,136	20.4	6,493	—	—
2001	3,173	20.7	6,529	—	—
2002	3,204	21.1	6,582	—	—
2003	3,233	21.5	6,639	—	—
2004	3,242	21.8	6,711	—	—
		Low alternative projections			
1994	3,026	17.5	5,768	18.7	6,181
1995	3,032	17.6	5,819	19.8	6,537
1996	3,027	18.2	6,009	21.5	7,094
1997	3,034	18.7	6,178	23.2	7,651
1998	3,058	19.1	6,251	24.8	8,124
1999	3,087	19.4	6,272	—	—
2000	3,136	19.7	6,275	—	—
2001	3,173	20.0	6,316	—	—
2002	3,204	20.4	6,381	—	—
2003	3,233	20.9	6,451	—	—
2004	3,242	21.2	6,529	—	—
		High alternative projections			
1994	3,026	17.6	5,816	18.6	6,136
1995	3,032	18.5	6,109	20.0	6,612
1996	3,027	19.4	6,418	21.6	7,124
1997	3,034	20.0	6,608	22.9	7,533
1998	3,058	20.5	6,706	24.1	7,880
1999	3,087	20.8	6,750	—	—
2000	3,136	21.2	6,769	—	—
2001	3,173	21.6	6,808	—	—
2002	3,204	22.0	6,861	—	—
2003	3,233	22.4	6,919	—	—
2004	3,242	22.7	7,000	—	—

[1] Based on the Consumer Price Index for all urban consumers, Bureau of Labor Statistics, U.S. Department of Labor.

[2] Estimated on the basis of past data.

—Projections in current dollars are not shown after 1998 due to the uncertain behavior of inflation over the long term.

SOURCE: U.S. Department of Education, National Center for Education Statistics, "Financial Statistics of Institutions of Higher Education," and "Fall Enrollment in Colleges and Universities" surveys. (This table was prepared June 1993.)

Table 42.—Educational and general expenditures and educational and general expenditures per full-time equivalent (FTE) student of public 2-year institutions, with alternative projections: 50 States and D.C., 1978–79 to 2003–2004

| Year ending | FTE (in thousands) | Current-fund expenditures | | | |
| | | Constant 1991–92 dollars [1] | | Current dollars | |
		Total (in billions)	Per student in FTE	Total (in billions)	Per student in FTE
1979	2,283	$11.6	$5,084	$5.8	$2,519
1980	2,333	11.3	4,838	6.3	2,715
1981	2,484	11.3	4,552	7.1	2,851
1982	2,573	11.4	4,436	7.8	3,021
1983	2,630	11.7	4,464	8.3	3,168
1984	2,616	12.0	4,582	8.8	3,372
1985	2,447	12.5	5,118	9.6	3,915
1986	2,428	13.0	5,367	10.3	4,225
1987	2,483	13.5	5,428	10.8	4,369
1988	2,542	13.9	5,477	11.7	4,590
1989	2,591	14.4	5,575	12.7	4,888
1990	2,752	15.1	5,490	13.9	5,042
1991	2,818	15.6	5,539	15.1	5,367
1992 [2]	3,067	16.1	5,241	16.1	5,241
1993 [2]	2,939	15.8	5,391	16.3	5,551
		Middle alternative projections			
1994	3,026	16.3	5,386	17.3	5,709
1995	3,032	16.8	5,546	18.4	6,070
1996	3,027	17.5	5,779	19.8	6,535
1997	3,034	18.0	5,945	21.1	6,945
1998	3,058	18.4	6,021	22.3	7,281
1999	3,087	18.7	6,048	—	—
2000	3,136	19.0	6,054	—	—
2001	3,173	19.3	6,086	—	—
2002	3,204	19.7	6,134	—	—
2003	3,233	20.0	6,187	—	—
2004	3,242	20.3	6,249	—	—
		Low alternative projections			
1994	3,026	16.2	5,362	17.4	5,747
1995	3,032	16.4	5,402	18.4	6,068
1996	3,027	16.9	5,583	20.0	6,591
1997	3,034	17.4	5,745	21.6	7,115
1998	3,058	17.8	5,812	23.1	7,554
1999	3,087	18.0	5,827	—	—
2000	3,136	18.3	5,828	—	—
2001	3,173	18.6	5,865	—	—
2002	3,204	19.0	5,926	—	—
2003	3,233	19.4	5,991	—	—
2004	3,242	19.6	6,060	—	—
		High alternative projections			
1994	3,026	16.4	5,412	17.3	5,710
1995	3,032	17.3	5,703	18.7	6,173
1996	3,027	18.2	6,007	20.2	6,668
1997	3,034	18.8	6,191	21.4	7,058
1998	3,058	19.2	6,285	22.6	7,384
1999	3,087	19.5	6,323	—	—
2000	3,136	19.9	6,340	—	—
2001	3,173	20.2	6,376	—	—
2002	3,204	20.6	6,424	—	—
2003	3,233	20.9	6,477	—	—
2004	3,242	21.2	6,548	—	—

[1] Based on the Consumer Price Index for all urban consumers, Bureau of Labor Statistics, U.S. Department of Labor.

[2] Estimated on the basis of past data.

—Projections in current dollars are not shown after 1998 due to the uncertain behavior of inflation over the long term.

SOURCE: U.S. Department of Education, National Center for Education Statistics, ''Financial Statistics of Institutions of Higher Education,'' and ''Fall Enrollment in Colleges and Universities'' surveys. (This table was prepared June 1993.)

Table 43.—Current-fund expenditures and current-fund expenditures per full-time equivalent (FTE) student of private 4-year institutions, with alternative projections: 50 States and D.C., 1978–79 to 2003–2004

Year ending	FTE (in thousands)	Current-fund expenditures			
		Constant 1991–92 dollars [1]		Current dollars	
		Total (in billions)	Per student in FTE	Total (in billions)	Per student in FTE
1979	1,936	$33.4	$17,265	$16.6	$8,554
1980	1,957	33.3	17,016	18.7	9,547
1981	2,003	33.8	16,869	21.2	10,565
1982	2,041	34.4	16,867	23.4	11,485
1983	2,028	36.1	17,801	25.6	12,633
1984	2,059	38.2	18,533	28.1	13,641
1985	2,055	40.2	19,547	30.7	14,952
1986	2,055	42.4	20,635	33.4	16,244
1987	2,065	45.9	22,253	37.0	17,910
1988	2,091	47.7	22,832	40.0	19,134
1989	2,158	49.9	23,139	43.8	20,289
1990	2,194	52.0	23,681	47.7	21,749
1991	2,228	53.5	24,021	51.9	23,277
1992 [2]	2,286	55.9	24,458	55.9	24,458
1993 [2]	2,368	57.7	24,384	59.5	25,108
Middle alternative projections					
1994	2,433	59.5	24,459	63.1	25,928
1995	2,424	61.5	25,380	67.3	27,776
1996	2,406	63.6	26,438	71.9	29,895
1997	2,395	65.6	27,373	76.6	31,979
1998	2,401	67.3	28,037	81.4	33,907
1999	2,419	69.1	28,555	—	—
2000	2,457	70.9	28,845	—	—
2001	2,490	72.7	29,195	—	—
2002	2,522	74.6	29,565	—	—
2003	2,551	76.4	29,958	—	—
2004	2,569	78.3	30,489	—	—
Low alternative projections					
1994	2,433	58.8	24,161	63.0	25,894
1995	2,424	60.5	24,974	68.0	28,055
1996	2,406	62.6	26,000	73.8	30,693
1997	2,395	64.5	26,950	79.9	33,376
1998	2,401	66.4	27,643	86.3	35,929
1999	2,419	68.1	28,168	—	—
2000	2,457	69.9	28,465	—	—
2001	2,490	71.8	28,832	—	—
2002	2,522	73.7	29,216	—	—
2003	2,551	75.6	29,617	—	—
2004	2,569	77.5	30,149	—	—
High alternative projections					
1994	2,433	60.0	24,666	63.3	26,025
1995	2,424	62.2	25,676	67.4	27,789
1996	2,406	64.4	26,773	71.5	29,716
1997	2,395	66.3	27,678	75.6	31,553
1998	2,401	68.0	28,305	79.9	33,258
1999	2,419	69.7	28,821	—	—
2000	2,457	71.5	29,115	—	—
2001	2,490	73.4	29,463	—	—
2002	2,522	75.2	29,831	—	—
2003	2,551	77.1	30,229	—	—
2004	2,569	79.1	30,772	—	—

[1] Based on the Consumer Price Index for all urban consumers, Bureau of Labor Statistics, U.S. Department of Labor.

[2] Estimated on the basis of past data.

—Projections in current dollars are not shown after 1998 due to the uncertain behavior of inflation over the long term.

SOURCE: U.S. Department of Education, National Center for Education Statistics, ''Financial Statistics of Institutions of Higher Education,'' and ''Fall Enrollment in Colleges and Universities'' surveys. (This table was prepared June 1993.)

Table 44.—Educational and general expenditures and educational and general expenditures per full-time equivalent (FTE) student of private 4-year institutions, with alternative projections: 50 States and D.C., 1978–79 to 2003–2004

Year ending	FTE (in thousands)	Current-fund expenditures			
		Constant 1991–92 dollars [1]		Current dollars	
		Total (in billions)	Per student in FTE	Total (in billions)	Per student in FTE
1979	1,936	$24.2	$12,496	$12.0	$6,191
1980	1,957	24.1	12,322	13.5	6,913
1981	2,003	24.5	12,255	15.4	7,675
1982	2,041	25.1	12,297	17.1	8,373
1983	2,028	26.2	12,912	18.6	9,163
1984	2,059	27.8	13,484	20.4	9,924
1985	2,055	29.3	14,245	22.4	10,897
1986	2,055	31.0	15,083	24.4	11,873
1987	2,065	34.3	16,588	27.6	13,351
1988	2,091	35.2	16,827	29.5	14,102
1989	2,158	36.9	17,093	32.3	14,988
1990	2,194	38.5	17,551	35.4	16,119
1991	2,228	39.8	17,874	38.6	17,321
1992 [2]	2,286	41.8	18,292	41.8	18,292
1993 [2]	2,368	43.4	18,343	44.7	18,888
		Middle alternative projections			
1994	2,433	44.8	18,408	47.5	19,514
1995	2,424	45.6	18,829	50.0	20,607
1996	2,406	46.5	19,321	52.6	21,848
1997	2,395	47.3	19,729	55.2	23,049
1998	2,401	48.0	19,986	58.0	24,170
1999	2,419	48.8	20,180	—	—
2000	2,457	49.8	20,282	—	—
2001	2,490	50.8	20,417	—	—
2002	2,522	51.9	20,564	—	—
2003	2,551	52.8	20,716	—	—
2004	2,569	53.8	20,935	—	—
		Low alternative projections			
1994	2,433	44.1	18,110	47.2	19,409
1995	2,424	44.7	18,425	50.2	20,699
1996	2,406	45.4	18,884	53.6	22,293
1997	2,395	46.2	19,304	57.3	23,907
1998	2,401	47.0	19,585	61.1	25,456
1999	2,419	47.9	19,783	—	—
2000	2,457	48.9	19,890	—	—
2001	2,490	49.9	20,041	—	—
2002	2,522	51.0	20,204	—	—
2003	2,551	51.9	20,362	—	—
2004	2,569	52.9	20,579	—	—
		High alternative projections			
1994	2,433	45.3	18,630	47.8	19,656
1995	2,424	46.4	19,142	50.2	20,718
1996	2,406	47.3	19,673	52.5	21,835
1997	2,395	48.0	20,058	54.8	22,866
1998	2,401	48.7	20,284	57.2	23,833
1999	2,419	49.5	20,480	—	—
2000	2,457	50.6	20,589	—	—
2001	2,490	51.6	20,721	—	—
2002	2,522	52.6	20,868	—	—
2003	2,551	53.6	21,028	—	—
2004	2,569	54.6	21,262	—	—

[1] Based on the Consumer Price Index for all urban consumers, Bureau of Labor Statistics, U.S. Department of Labor.

[2] Estimated on the basis of past data.

—Projections in current dollars are not shown after 1998 due to the uncertain behavior of inflation over the long term.

SOURCE: U.S. Department of Education, National Center for Education Statistics, ''Financial Statistics of Institutions of Higher Education,'' and ''Fall Enrollment in Colleges and Universities'' surveys. (This table was prepared June 1993.)

Technical Appendixes

Appendix A

Projection Methodology

The general procedure for *Projections* was to express the variable to be projected as a percent of a "base" variable. These percents were then projected and applied to projections of the "base" variable. For example, the number of 18-year-old college students was expressed as a percent of the 18-year-old population for each year from 1972 through 1991. This percent was then projected through the year 2004 and applied to projections of the 18-year-old population from the Bureau of the Census.

Enrollment projections are based primarily on population projections. Projections of classroom teachers, high school graduates, earned degrees conferred, and expenditures are based primarily on enrollment projections.

Single exponential smoothing, double exponential smoothing, and multiple linear regression are the three major projection techniques used in this publication. Single exponential smoothing is used when the historical data have a basically horizontal pattern. On the other hand, double exponential smoothing is used when the time series is expected to change linearly with time. In general, exponential smoothing places more weight on recent observations than on earlier ones. The weights for observations decrease exponentially as one moves further into the past. As a result, the older data have less influence on projections. The rate at which the weights of older observations decrease is determined by the smoothing constant selected.

$$P = \alpha X_t + \alpha(1-\alpha)X_{t-1} + \alpha(1-\alpha)^2 X_{t-2}$$
$$+ \alpha(1-\alpha)^3 X_{t-3} + \ldots.$$

Where:

P = projected constant

α = smoothing constant ($0 < \alpha < 1$)

X_t = observation for time t

This equation illustrates that the projection is a weighted average based on exponentially decreasing weights. For a high smoothing constant, weights for earlier observations decrease rapidly. For a low smoothing constant, decreases are more moderate. Projections of enrollments and public high school graduates are based on a range of smoothing constants ($\alpha = 0.2$ to 0.9).

In general, the projections in this publication are based on fairly high smoothing constants. The farther apart the observations are spaced in time, it is more likely that there are changes in the underlying social, political, and economic structure. Since the observations are on an annual basis, major shifts in the underlying process are more likely in the time span of just a few observations than if the observations were available on a monthly or weekly basis. As a result, the underlying process tends to be unstable from one observation to the next. Another reason for using high smoothing constants for some time series is that most of the observations are fairly accurate, because most observations are population values rather than sample estimates. Therefore, large shifts tend to indicate actual changes in the process rather than noise in the data.

Multiple linear regression was also used in making projections, primarily in the areas of teachers, earned degrees, and expenditures. This technique was used when it was believed that a strong causal relationship existed between the variable being projected (the dependent variable) and independent causal variables. However, this technique was used only when accurate data and reliable projections of the independent variables were available.

The functional form primarily used was the multiplicative model. When used with two independent variables, this model takes the form:

$$Y = aX_1^{b_1}X_2^{b_2}$$

This equation can easily be transformed into the linear form by taking the natural log(ln) of both sides of the equation:

$$\ln Y = \ln(a) + b_1\ln X_1 + b_2\ln X_2$$

The multiplicative model has a number of advantages; it is a reasonable way to represent human behavior. Constant elasticities are assumed; this says that a 1 percent change in ln X will lead to a given percent change in ln Y. This percent change is equal to b_1. And it lends itself easily to "a priori" analysis because the researcher does not have to worry about units of measurement when specifying relationships. In fact, the multiplicative model is considered the standard in economic problems. For additional information, see *Long-Range Forecasting: From Crystal Ball to Computer* by J. Scott Armstrong (John Wiley and Sons, 1978, pp. 180–181).

Caveats

Because projections are subject to errors from many sources, alternative projections are shown for some statistical series. These alternatives are not statistical confidence intervals, but instead represent judgments made by the authors as to reasonable upper and lower bounds for each projected series. Alternative projections were developed for higher education enrollment, classroom teachers, earned degrees conferred, and expenditures in public elementary and secondary schools and institutions of higher education.

Assumptions

All projections are based on underlying assumptions, and these assumptions determine projection results to a large extent. It is important that users of projections understand the assumptions to determine the acceptability of projected time series for their purposes. In each chapter, there are descriptions of the primary assumptions upon which the projections of time series are based.

For most projections, low, middle, and high alternatives are shown. These alternatives reveal the level of uncertainty involved in making projections, and they also point out the sensitivity of projections to the assumptions on which they are based.

Many of the projections in this publication are demographically based. Bureau of the Census middle series projections of the population by age were used. These middle series population projections are based on the 1990 census. The future fertility rate assumption, which determines projections of the number of births, is the key assumption in making population projections. The middle series population projections assume an ultimate complete cohort fertility rate of 2.15 births per woman by the year 2050 and a net immigration of 880,000 per year. This assumption plays a major role in determining population projections for the age groups enrolled in nursery school, kindergarten, and elementary grades. The effects of the fertility rate assumption are more pronounced toward the end of the projection period.

For enrollments in secondary grades and college, the fertility assumption is of no consequence, since all students enrolled at these levels were already born when the population projections were made. For projections of enrollments in elementary schools, only middle series population projections were considered. Projections of high school graduates are based on projections of the number of high school graduates expressed as a percent of grade 12 enrollment. Projections of associate, bachelor's, master's (women), doctor's (women), and first-professional (women) degrees are based on projections of college-age populations and higher education enrollment, by sex, attendance status and level enrolled by student, and by type of institution. Many of the projections of classroom teachers and expenditures of public elementary and secondary schools and institutions of higher education are based on projections of disposable income per capita and various revenue measures of state and local governments. Disposable income per capita projections were obtained from DRI/McGraw-Hill. Therefore, the many assumptions made in projecting disposable income per capita also apply to those projections based on projections of disposable income per capita.

A1. Enrollment

Enrollment projections were based on projected enrollment rates, by age and sex, which were applied to population projections by age and sex developed by the Bureau of the Census. These enrollment rates were projected by taking into account the most recent trends, as well as the effects of economic conditions and demographic changes on a person's decision to enter college. The enrollment rates were then used in an interactive forecasting model (IFMOD), which consists of age-specific rates by sex and by enrollment levels (nursery school through college). The model has 5 stages. See figure 62.

The first stage of IFMOD is an age-specific enrollment model in which enrollment rates are projected and applied to age-specific population projections. This stage, which is used separately for each sex, includes the following categories: (1) nursery and kindergarten, (2) elementary grades 1–8, (3) secondary grades 9–12, (4) full-time college enrollment, and (5) part-time college enrollment. For each of these enrollment categories, enrollment rates were projected by individual ages 3 through 24 and for the age groups 25 to 29, 30 to 34, and 35 years and over.

Enrollments by age and age groups from the Bureau of the Census were adjusted to NCES totals to compute enrollment rates for 1972 through 1991. Different assumptions were made to produce low, middle, and high alternative projections of enrollment rates to the year 2004.

Elementary Grades 1–8

Projections of elementary enrollment rates were considered for ages 5 through 21. Elementary enrollments are negligible for the remaining ages. Because most elementary enrollment rates have been fluctuating at levels close to 100 percent from 1972 to 1991, alternative enrollment rate projections were not computed. The only set of enrollment rate projections computed was based on the assumption that rates will remain constant through the year 2004 (table A1.1). Several of the rates in table A1.1 exceed 100 percent, as a result of several factors. The enrollment data by age were prorated to agree with NCES totals. The Bureau of the Census does not revise enrollment estimates by age, but population estimates are revised regularly.

Secondary Grades 9–12

Projections of secondary enrollment rates were considered for ages 12 through 34. Secondary enrollments are negligible for the remaining ages. Secondary enrollment rates have fluctuated within a narrow range from 1972 to 1991. Therefore, alternative enrollment rate projections were not calculated. The only set of projections computed was based on constant enrollment rates (table A1.2).

College Full-Time and Part-Time Enrollment

Projections of full-time and part-time college enrollments were considered only for ages 16 and over. (College enrollment is negligible for earlier ages.) Three alternative projections were made using various assumptions. Table A1.3 shows enrollment rates for 1991 and low, middle, and high alternative projected enrollment rates for 1999 and 2004.

Table A1.4 shows the equations used to project enrollment rates for 18-year-old men enrolled part-time and 20-year-old men enrolled part-time. Table A1.5 shows the equation used to project enrollment rates for 18-year-old women enrolled part-time.

Enrollment in Public Elementary and Secondary Schools, by Grade Group and Organizational Level

The third stage of IFMOD projects public enrollment in elementary and secondary schools by grade group and by organizational level. Public enrollments by age were based on enrollment rate projections for nursery and kindergarten, grade 1, elementary ungraded and special, secondary ungraded and special, and postgraduate enrollment. Grade retention rate projections were used for grades 2 through 12. Table A1.6 shows the public school enrollment rates and table A1.7 shows the public grade-retention rates for 1991 and projections for 1999 and 2004. The projected rates in tables A1.6 and A1.7 were used to compute the projections of enrollments in elementary and secondary schools, by grade, shown in table 1.

College Enrollment, by Sex, Attendance Status, and Level Enrolled; and by Type and Control of Institution

The fourth stage of IFMOD projects enrollments in institutions of higher education, by sex, attendance status, and level enrolled by student and by type and control of institution. For each age group, the percent that enrollment by age, attendance status, level enrolled, and by type of institution was of total enrollment was projected. These projections are shown in tables A1.8 and A1.9, along with actual values for 1991. For all projections, it was assumed that there was no enrollment in 2-year institutions at the postbaccalaureate level (graduate and first-professional).

The projected rates in tables A1.8 and A1.9 were then adjusted to agree with the projected age-specific enrollment rates in the first stage of IFMOD. The adjusted rates were then applied to the projected enrollments by age group, sex, and attendance status from the first stage of IFMOD to obtain projections by age group, sex, attendance status, level enrolled, and type of institution.

For each enrollment category—sex, attendance status, level enrolled, and type of institution—the percent that public enrollment was of total enrollment was projected. These projections are shown in table A1.10, along with actual percent for 1991 and projections for 1999 and 2004. The projected rates shown were then applied to the projected enrollments in each enrollment category to obtain projections by control of institution.

For each enrollment category by sex and enrollment level, and by type and control of institution, the percent that graduate enrollment was of postbaccalaureate enrollment was projected. Actual rates for 1991 and projections for 1999 and 2004 are shown in table A1.11. The projected rates in table A1.11 were then applied to projections of postbaccalaureate enrollment to obtain graduate and first-professional enrollment projections by sex and attendance status, and by type and control of institution.

Full-Time-Equivalent Enrollment, by Type and Control of Institution and by Level Enrolled

The fifth stage of IFMOD projects full-time-equivalent enrollment, by type and control of institution and by level enrolled. For each enrollment category by level enrolled and by type and control of institution, the percent that the full-time-equivalent of part-time enrollment was of part-time enrollment was projected. Actual percents for 1991 and projections for 1999 and 2004 are shown in table A1.12.

These projected percents were applied to projections of enrollment by level enrolled and by type and control of institution from the fourth stage of IFMOD. The projections of the full-time-equivalent of part-time enrollment were added to projections of full-time enrollment (from the previous stage) to obtain projections of full-time-equivalent enrollment.

Projection Accuracy

An analysis of projection errors from the past ten editions of *Projections of Education Statistics* indicates that the mean absolute percentage errors (MAPEs) for lead times of 1, 2, 5, and 10 years out for projections of public school enrollment in grades K–12 were 0.4, 0.6, 1.1, and 2.3 percent, respectively. For the 1-year-out prediction, this means that one would expect the projection to be within 0.4 percent of the actual value, on the average. For projections of public school enrollment in grades K–8, the MAPEs for lead times of 1, 2, 5, and 10 years were 0.6, 0.9, 1.1, and 3.6 percent, respectively, while those for projections of public school enrollment in grades 9–12 were 0.6, 0.6, 1.2, and 3.5 percent for the same lead times.

For projections of enrollment in higher education, an analysis of projection errors based on the past seven editions of *Projections of Education Statistics* indicates that the MAPEs for lead times of 1, 2, and 5 years were 1.8, 3.8, and 4.1 percent, respectively. For the 1-year-out prediction, this means that one would expect the projection to be within 1.8 percent of the actual value, on the average.

Basic Methodology

The notation and equations that follow describe the basic models used to project public elementary and secondary enrollment.

Public Elementary and Secondary Enrollment

Let:

i = Subscript denoting age

j = Subcript denoting grade

t = Subscript denoting time

K_t = Enrollment at the nursery and kindergarten level

G_{jt} = Enrollment in grade j

G_{1t} = Enrollment in grade 1

E_t = Enrollment in elementary special and ungraded programs

S_t = Enrollment in secondary special and ungraded programs

PG_t = Enrollment in postgraduate programs

P_{it} = Population age i

RK_t = Enrollment rate for nursery and kindergarten

RG_{1t} = Enrollment rate for grade 1

RE_t = Enrollment rate for elementary special and ungraded programs

RS_t = Enrollment rate for secondary special and ungraded programs

RPG_t = Enrollment rate for postgraduate programs

EG_t = Total enrollment in elementary grades (K–8)

SG_t = Total enrollment in secondary grades (9–12)

R_{jt} = Retention rate for grade j: the proportion that enrollment in grade j in year t is of enrollment in grade j–1 in year t–1.

Then:

$$EG_t = K_t + E_t + \sum_{j=1}^{8} G_{jt}$$

$$SG_t = S_t + PG_t + \sum_{j=9}^{12} G_{jt}$$

Where:

K_t = $RK_t(P_{5t})$

G_{jt} = $R_{jt}(G_{j-1, t--1})$

$$E_t = RE_t \left(\sum_{i=5}^{13} P_{it} \right)$$

G_{1t} = $RG_{1t}(P_{6t})$

$$S_t = RS_t \left(\sum_{i=14}^{17} P_{it} \right)$$

PG_t = $RPG_t(P_{18t})$

Higher Education Enrollment

For institutions of higher education, projections were computed separately by sex and attendance status of student. The notation and equations are:

Let:

i = Subscript denoting age except:

i = 25: ages 25–29

i = 26: ages 30–34

i = 27: ages 35 and over for enrollment (35–44 for population)

t = Subscript denoting year

E_{it} = Enrollment of students age i

P_{it} = Population age i

R_{it} = Enrollment rate for students age i

T_{it} = Total enrollment for particular subset of students: full-time men, full-time women, part-time men, part-time women

Then:

$$T_{it} = \sum_{i=16}^{27} E_{it}$$

Where:

E_{it} = $R_{it}(P_{it})$

Methodological Tables

The tables in this section give the rates used to calculate projections of enrollments, basic assumptions underlying enrollment projections (table A1.13), and methods used to estimate values for which data are not available (table A1.14).

Private School Enrollment

Projections of private school enrollment were derived in the following manner. For 1992, the ratio of private school enrollment to public school enrollment was calculated by grade level. These 1992 ratios were then held constant over the projection period. These ratios were then applied to projections of public school enrollment by grade level to yield projections of private school enrollment. This method assumes that the future pattern in the trend of private school enrollment will be the same as that in public school enrollment. The reader is cautioned that a number of factors could alter the assumptions of constant ratios over the projection period.

Figure 62

General structure and methodology of the Interactive Forecasting Model (IFMOD)

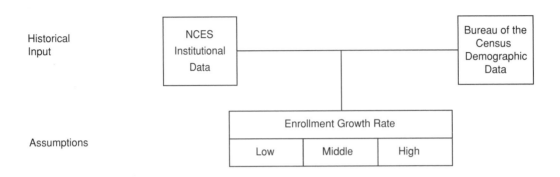

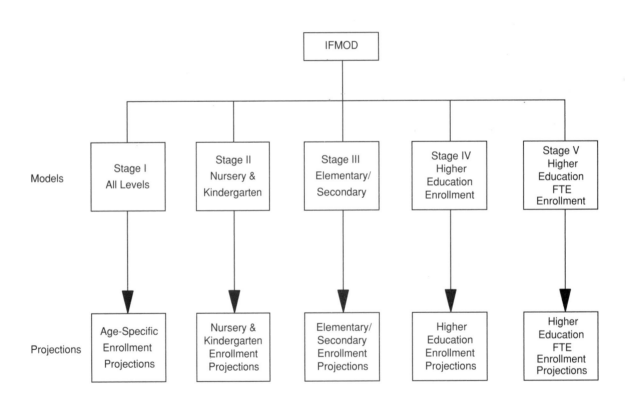

Table A1.1.—Elementary enrollment rates, by age and sex

Age	Boys		Girls	
	1991	1993–2004	1991	1993–2004
5	5.1	5.0	6.3	6.1
6	83.9	83.9	87.7	88.7
7	104.1	103.8	106.5	104.2
8	105.5	105.0	105.9	105.2
9	100.3	100.6	98.7	100.1
10	101.4	100.9	104.1	102.5
11	104.5	104.3	101.3	102.8
12	106.0	103.5	103.7	102.5
13	96.9	96.7	97.6	96.2
14	35.4	36.8	26.2	26.0
15	5.9	6.8	3.3	3.6
16	0.2	0.5	0.1	0.2
17	0.0	0.1	0.0	0.0
18	0.0	0.0	0.3	0.1

Table A1.2.—Secondary enrollment rates, by age and sex

Age	Boys		Girls	
	1991	1993–2004	1991	1993–2004
12	0.1	0.2	0.1	0.3
13	5.0	5.1	6.5	7.0
14	62.5	63.2	70.4	72.2
15	90.4	89.1	91.1	91.1
16	91.0	91.3	93.0	92.9
17	81.8	80.2	79.1	78.5
18	27.0	25.8	17.5	17.5
19	7.9	6.5	4.4	3.9
20	1.9	1.4	1.6	1.3
21	0.8	0.8	0.5	0.7
22	0.6	0.5	0.4	0.4
23	0.3	0.3	1.1	0.6
24	0.4	0.5	0.4	0.3
25–29	0.2	0.2	0.3	0.4
30–34	0.2	0.2	0.4	0.3

Table A1.3.—College enrollment rates, by age, sex, and attendance status, with alternative projections

Age, sex, and attendance status	1991	Low alternative		Middle alternative		High alternative	
		1999	2004	1999	2004	1999	2004
Men							
Full-time:							
16	0.1	0.1	0.1	0.1	0.1	0.1	0.1
17	2.0	2.5	2.5	2.8	2.8	2.8	2.8
18	27.6	26.8	26.8	28.6	28.5	28.8	28.8
19	31.2	31.9	31.9	35.2	37.4	35.2	37.4
20	25.7	24.6	24.6	27.3	27.8	28.4	28.9
21	25.8	27.1	27.1	28.9	28.9	31.9	31.9
22	19.9	22.3	22.3	23.4	23.4	23.9	23.9
23	14.0	14.1	14.1	14.6	14.6	16.3	16.3
24	9.8	9.6	9.6	9.8	9.8	10.1	10.2
25–29	4.7	4.8	4.8	5.0	5.0	5.6	5.6
30–34	1.7	1.9	1.9	1.9	1.9	2.0	2.0
35–44	1.0	1.1	1.1	1.1	1.1	1.2	1.2
Part-time:							
16	0.0	0.0	0.0	0.0	0.0	0.0	0.0
17	0.4	0.5	0.5	0.6	0.6	0.6	0.6
18	3.1	3.8	3.8	3.8	3.8	3.8	3.8
19	3.4	3.4	3.4	3.6	3.6	4.1	4.3
20	5.5	5.7	5.7	6.8	7.4	6.8	7.4
21	5.5	5.8	5.8	6.3	6.8	6.9	7.7
22	9.0	9.4	9.4	10.3	10.3	11.4	11.4
23	6.4	6.8	6.8	6.8	6.8	7.0	7.0
24	4.4	4.6	4.6	4.7	4.8	4.7	4.8
25–29	5.6	5.9	5.9	6.1	6.1	6.5	6.5
30–34	4.3	4.4	4.4	4.5	4.5	5.1	5.1
35–44	4.0	4.1	4.1	4.2	4.2	4.3	4.3
Women							
Full-time:							
16	0.2	0.2	0.2	0.2	0.2	0.3	0.3
17	4.4	4.9	4.9	4.9	4.9	5.2	5.2
18	36.3	38.2	38.2	38.2	38.2	39.3	39.3
19	38.3	40.2	40.2	41.4	41.4	43.0	43.0
20	30.7	31.0	31.0	33.9	33.9	35.1	35.1
21	31.4	30.7	30.7	31.3	31.3	33.7	33.7
22	15.3	15.5	15.5	15.8	15.8	16.4	16.4
23	10.9	11.0	11.0	12.5	13.4	14.1	14.1
24	9.8	10.6	10.6	10.6	10.6	11.9	11.9
25–29	3.6	3.6	3.6	3.6	3.6	3.9	3.9
30–34	1.9	1.9	1.9	1.9	1.9	2.0	2.0
35–44	1.7	1.6	1.6	1.7	1.7	1.7	1.7
Part-time:							
16	0.0	0.0	0.0	0.0	0.0	0.0	0.0
17	0.0	0.5	0.5	0.5	0.5	0.5	0.5
18	5.1	5.1	5.1	6.0	6.0	6.5	6.5
19	5.4	5.7	5.7	6.3	6.3	6.8	6.8
20	6.1	6.1	6.1	6.8	7.0	7.0	7.2
21	6.1	6.4	6.4	7.1	7.1	7.2	7.2
22	9.5	9.7	9.7	11.1	11.5	11.7	11.7
23	6.8	6.5	6.5	8.1	8.1	8.2	8.2
24	6.1	6.4	6.4	7.0	7.0	7.3	7.3
25–29	6.6	6.6	6.6	7.2	7.2	7.3	7.8
30–34	5.3	5.5	5.5	5.7	5.7	6.0	6.0
35–44	7.9	8.2	8.2	8.2	8.2	8.4	8.4

Table A1.4.—Equations for selected college enrollment rates of men, by age and attendance status

Equation		R^2	Durbin-Watson statistic [1]	Estimation technique
RTPT18M	= -0.019 + 0.00109UR1619 + 0.00000205PCI92 (3.3) (4.4)	0.70	2.4	OLS [2]
RTPT20M	= -0.0167 + 0.000004PCI92 (7.0)	0.68	1.7	OLS [2]

R^2 = Coefficient of determination.

[1] For an explanation of the Durbin-Watson statistic, see J. Johnston, *Econometric Methods*, New York: McGraw-Hill, 1972, pages 251–252.
[2] OLS equals Ordinary Least Squares.

Where:

RTPT18M = Enrollment rate of 18-year-old males enrolled part- time
RTPT20M = Enrollment rate of 20-year-old males enrolled part- time
UR1619 = Unemployment rate of 16- to 19-year-olds
PCI92 = Disposable income per capita in 1991–92 dollars

NOTE: Numbers in parentheses are t-statistics. The time period of observations used in the equations is from 1967 to 1991.

Table A1.5.—Equation for selected college enrollment rates of women, by age and attendance status

Equation			R^2	Durbin-Watson statistic [1]	Estimation technique
RTPT18W	=	-0.0108 + 0.0000036PCI92 (6.3)	0.63	1.7	OLS [2]

R^2 = Coefficient of determination.

[1] For an explanation of the Durbin-Watson statistic, see J. Johnston, *Econometric Methods*, New York: McGraw-Hill, 1972, pages 251–252.

[2] OLS equals Ordinary Least Squares.

Where:

RTPT18W   =Enrollment rate of 18-year-old females enrolled part- time

PCI92   =Disposable income per capita in 1991–92 dollars

NOTE: Numbers in parentheses are t-statistics. The time period of observations used in the equations is from 1967 to 1991.

Table A1.6.—Enrollment rates in public schools, by grade level

Grade level	Population base age	1991	Projected	
			1999	2004
Kindergarten	5	99.0	97.3	97.3
Grade 1	6	96.6	96.7	96.7
Elementary ungraded and special	5–13	1.7	1.7	1.7
Secondary ungraded and special	14–17	1.9	2.0	2.0
Postgraduate	18	0.4	0.3	0.3

Table A1.7.—Public school grade retention rates

Grade	1991	Projected	
		1999	2004
1 to 2	96.0	95.4	95.4
2 to 3	100.2	100.1	100.1
3 to 4	100.5	100.4	100.4
4 to 5	100.6	100.5	100.5
5 to 6	101.3	101.3	101.3
6 to 7	102.3	102.8	102.8
7 to 8	98.5	98.3	98.3
8 to 9	111.1	110.5	110.5
9 to 10	92.0	92.3	92.3
10 to 11	91.3	91.1	91.1
11 to 12	91.5	90.9	90.9

Table A1.8.—Full-time enrollment, by level enrolled and type of institution, as a percent of total enrollment, for each age and sex classification

Age	Men			Women		
	1991	1999	2004	1991	1999	2004
Undergraduate, 4-year institutions						
16–17 years old	71.9	70.8	70.8	59.7	64.6	64.6
18–19 years old	65.9	66.3	66.3	67.8	69.1	69.1
20–21 years old	79.0	79.9	79.9	82.2	82.3	82.3
22–24 years old	66.4	66.6	66.6	56.1	60.0	60.0
25–29 years old	41.0	40.5	40.5	38.7	40.2	40.2
30–34 years old	28.3	29.0	29.0	35.4	37.1	37.1
35 years and over	29.0	29.5	29.5	41.6	41.6	41.6
Undergraduate, 2-year institutions						
16–17 years old	28.1	29.0	29.0	40.4	35.4	35.4
18–19 years old	34.1	33.7	33.7	32.2	30.9	30.9
20–21 years old	21.0	20.1	20.1	17.8	17.7	17.7
22–24 years old	17.5	15.7	15.7	18.0	17.3	17.3
25–29 years old	19.8	17.3	17.3	29.1	27.4	27.4
30–34 years old	19.7	18.9	18.9	46.0	39.1	39.1
35 years and over	31.9	27.0	27.0	35.9	34.2	34.2
Postbaccalaureate, 4-year institutions						
16–17 years old	—	—	—	—	—	—
18–19 years old	—	—	—	—	—	—
20–21 years old	—	—	—	—	—	—
22–24 years old	16.1	17.7	17.7	25.9	22.7	22.7
25–29 years old	39.3	42.3	42.3	32.2	32.4	32.4
30–34 years old	52.0	52.1	52.1	18.6	23.7	23.7
35 years and over	39.2	43.5	43.5	22.5	24.3	24.3

—Not applicable.

NOTE: Projections shown for 1999 and 2004 were adjusted to add to 100 percent before computing projections shown in tables 3 through 22.

Table A1.9.—Part-time enrollment, by level enrolled and type of institution, as a percent of total enrollment, for each age and sex classification

Age	Men			Women		
	1991	1999	2004	1991	1999	2004
Undergraduate, 4-year institutions						
16–17 years old	0.0	11.5	11.5	0.0	8.9	8.9
18–19 years old	10.9	16.1	16.1	13.3	15.3	15.3
20–21 years old	18.2	20.7	20.7	23.5	24.9	24.9
22–24 years old	31.9	33.1	33.1	26.8	29.4	29.4
25–29 years old	26.9	29.6	29.6	24.4	28.3	28.3
30–34 years old	26.8	27.6	27.6	27.4	26.9	26.9
35 years and over	32.5	29.3	29.3	28.1	26.5	26.5
Undergraduate, 2-year institutions						
16–17 years old	94.6	82.8	82.8	0.0	48.3	48.3
18–19 years old	83.4	77.7	77.7	81.7	79.7	79.7
20–21 years old	74.9	73.1	73.1	71.2	69.5	69.5
22–24 years old	57.5	54.9	54.9	59.4	56.9	56.9
25–29 years old	55.7	51.9	51.9	57.1	52.9	52.9
30–34 years old	51.0	50.5	50.5	57.1	56.6	56.6
35 years and over	42.4	45.0	45.0	51.8	53.0	53.0
Postbaccalaureate, 4-year institutions						
16–17 years old	5.4	5.7	5.7	0.0	2.8	2.8
18–19 years old	5.7	6.2	6.2	5.0	5.0	5.0
20–21 years old	6.9	6.2	6.2	5.4	5.6	5.6
22–24 years old	10.6	12.0	12.0	13.8	13.7	13.7
25–29 years old	17.4	18.5	18.5	18.4	18.9	18.9
30–34 years old	22.2	22.0	22.0	15.5	16.5	16.5
35 years and over	25.1	25.7	25.7	20.1	20.5	20.5

NOTE: Projections shown for 1999 and 2004 were adjusted to add to 100 percent before computing projections shown in tables 3 through 22.

Table A1.10.—Public college enrollment as a percent of total enrollment, by attendance status, sex, level enrolled, and by type of institution

Enrollment category	Men			Women		
	1991	1999	2004	1991	1999	2004
Full-time, undergraduate, 4-year institutions	69.9	69.7	69.7	69.1	69.1	69.1
Part-time, undergraduate, 4-year institutions	73.0	73.1	73.1	69.9	70.1	70.1
Full-time, undergraduate, 2-year institutions	91.7	91.5	91.5	90.2	89.8	89.8
Part-time, undergraduate, 2-year institutions	98.1	97.5	97.5	98.5	98.2	98.2
Full-time, postbaccalaureate, 4-year institutions	56.2	56.3	56.3	59.0	59.6	59.6
Part-time, postbaccalaureate, 4-year institutions	59.0	58.9	58.9	66.2	66.8	66.8

Table A1.11.—Graduate enrollment as a percent of total postbaccalaureate enrollment, by sex and attendance status, and by type and control of institution

Enrollment categoy	Men			Women		
	1991	1999	2004	1991	1999	2004
Full-time, 4-year, public	77.6	71.1	76.1	81.4	80.6	80.6
Part-time, 4-year, public	98.8	98.9	98.9	99.5	99.5	99.5
Full-time, 4-year, private	58.3	57.1	57.1	66.5	65.1	65.1
Part-time, 4-year, private	91.6	91.7	91.7	95.5	95.6	95.6

Table A1.12.—Full-time-equivalent of part-time enrollment as a percent of part-time enrollment, by level enrolled and by type and control of institution

Enrollment category	1991	1999	2004
Public, 4-year, undergraduate	40.0	40.1	40.1
Public, 2-year, undergraduate	33.6	33.6	33.6
Private, 4-year, undergraduate	40.0	39.8	39.8
Private, 2-year, undergraduate	39.0	39.4	39.4
Public, 4-year, graduate	36.2	36.2	36.2
Private, 4-year, graduate	38.1	38.1	38.1
Public, 4-year, first-professional	60.0	57.1	57.1
Private, 4-year, first-professional	54.2	56.1	56.1

Table A1.13.—Enrollment (assumptions)

Variables	Assumptions	Alternatives	Tables
Elementary and Secondary enrollment	Age-specific enrollment rates will remain constant at levels consistent with the most recent rates.	Middle (no alternatives)	1, 2
	Public enrollment rates and public grade retention rates will remain constant at levels consistent with the most recent rates.	Middle (no alternatives)	1, 2
	The percentage of 7th and 8th grade public students enrolled in school organized as secondary schools will remain constant at levels consistent with the most recent rates.	Middle (no alternatives)	2
College full-time and part-time enrollment, by age			
Men	Age-specific enrollment rates for the younger age cohorts will increase over the projection period, while those for the older age groups are expected to remain constant at levels consistent with the most recent rates or increase slightly.	Middle	3–5 9–16
	Age-specific enrollment rates will equal the middle alternative rate or change at a slower rate.	Low	3–5 9–16
	Age-specific enrollment rates will either equal the middle alternative or increase at a faster rate, based on past trends.	High	3–5 9–16
Women	Age-specific enrollment rates for the younger age cohorts will increase over the projection period, while those for the older age groups are expected to increase slightly.	Middle	3–5 9–16
	Age-specific enrollment rates will equal the middle alternative rate or change at a slower rate.	Low	3–5 9–16
	Age-specific enrollment rates will either equal the middle alternative or increase at a faster rate, based on past trends.	High	3–5 9–16
College enrollment, by sex, attendance status, and level enrolled by student, and by type of institution	For each group and for each attendance status separately, enrollment by sex and level enrolled by student, and by type of institution as a percent of total enrollment, will follow past trends through 2004. For each age group and attendance status category, the restriction that the sum of the percentages must equal 100 percent was applied.	High, middle, and low	3–5 9–16
College enrollment, by control of institution	For each enrollment category, by sex, attendance status, and level enrolled by student, and by type of institution, public enrollment as a percent of total enrollment will remain constant at levels consistent with the most recent rates.	High, middle, and low	3–5 9–16
Graduate enrollment	For each enrollment category, by sex and attendance status of student, and by type and control of institution, graduate enrollment as a percent of postbaccalaureate enrollment will remain constant at levels consistent with the most recent rates.	High, middle, and low	17
Full-time-equivalent of part-time enrollment	For each enrollment category, by type and control of institution and level enrolled by student, the percent that full-time-equivalent of part-time enrollment is of part-time enrollment will remain constant at levels consistent with the most recent rates.	High, middle, and low	23–25

Table A1.14.—Enrollment (estimation methods)

Variables	Years	Estimation method	Tables
Enrollment in private elementary and secondary schools, by level	1988 1989 1990	Grade-by-grade data for private elementary, secondary, and combined schools were aggregated to estimate private school enrollment by grade level.	1 2
Enrollment in institutions of higher education, by age and attendance status	1984 1989 1992	For each sex, enrollment data from the Bureau of Census by individual ages and by attendance status for 2-year age groups were combined by assuming that within the 2-year age groups, age and attendance status were distributed independently. The resultant enrollment estimates by age and attendance status were then adjusted to NCES enrollment counts by attendance status.	6 7 8

A2. High School Graduates

Projections of public high school graduates were developed in the following manner. The number of public high school graduates was expressed as a percent of grade 12 enrollment in public schools for 1972 to 1991. This percent was projected using single exponential smoothing and applied to projections of grade 12 enrollment to yield projections of high school graduates in public schools. (The dropout rate is not related to this percent. This percent does not make any assumptions regarding the dropout rate.) The grade 12 enrollment was projected based on grade-by-grade retention rates and population projections developed by the Bureau of the Census. This percent was assumed to remain constant at levels consistent with the most recent rates. This method assumes that past trends in factors affecting graduation will continue over the projection period.

Projections of private high school graduates were derived in the following manner. For 1991–92, the ratio of private high school graduates to public school graduates was calculated. The ratio for 1991–92 was held constant over the projection period. It was then applied to projections of public high school graduates to yield projections of private high school graduates. This method assumes that the future pattern of private high school graduates will be the same as that of public high school graduates. The reader should be aware that a number of factors could alter the assumption of a constant ratio over the projection period.

Projection Accuracy

An analysis of projections from models used in the past ten editions of *Projections of Education Statistics* indicates that the mean absolute percentage errors (MAPEs) for projections of public high school graduates were 0.6 percent for 1 year ahead, 1.1 percent for 2 years ahead, and 1.9 percent for 5 years ahead. For the 2-year-ahead prediction, this means that one would expect the projection to be within 1.1 percent of the actual value, on the average.

A3. Earned Degrees Conferred

Projections of associate and bachelor's degrees by sex and master's, doctor's, and first-professional degrees for women were based on demographic models that relate degree awards to college-age populations and college enrollment by level enrolled and attendance status. Projections of master's, doctor's, and first-professional degrees for men were based on the author's evaluation of past and most recent changes in the historical data and the likely impact these changes would have on future trends.

Associate Degrees

Associate degree projections by sex were based on undergraduate enrollment by attendance status in 2-year institutions. Results of the regression analysis used to project associate degrees by sex are shown in table A3.1.

Bachelor's Degrees

Bachelor's degree projections by sex were based on the 18- to 24-year-old population, 25- to 34-year-old population, and undergraduate enrollment by attendance status in 4-year institutions. Results of the regression analysis used to project bachelor's degrees by sex are shown in table A3.2.

Master's Degrees

Master's degree projections for women were based on the 35- to 44-year-old population and part-time graduate enrollment in 4-year institutions. Results of the regression analysis used to project master's degrees for women are shown in table A3.3. Projections of master's degrees awarded to men were calculated as the average of the low and high alternatives. (The low alternative assumes that master's degrees awarded to men will increase by 3,000 degrees through 1995–96, decrease by 3,000 degrees through 2001–2002, and then hold steady through 2003–2004. The high alternative assumes that master's degrees awarded to men will increase by 9,000 degrees through 1995–96, decrease by 9,000 degrees through 2001–2002, and then hold steady through 2003–2004.)

Doctor's Degrees

Doctor's degree projections for women were based on the 35- to 44-year-old population, graduate enrollment by attendance status in 4-year institutions, and a time trend variable. Results of the regression analysis used to project doctor's degrees for women are shown in table A3.4. Projections of doctor's degrees awarded to men were cal-culated as the average of the low and high alternatives. (The low alternative assumes that doctor's degrees awarded to men will decrease by 1,400 degrees per year through 2003–2004. The high alternative assumes that doctor's degrees awarded to men will remain around 27,000 degrees over the projection period.)

First-Professional Degrees

First-professional degree projections for women were based on first-professional enrollment by attendance status in 4-year institutions. Results of the regression analysis used to project first-professional degrees for women are shown in table A3.5. Projections of first-professional degrees awarded to men were calculated as the average of the low and high alternatives. (The low alternative assumes that first-professional degrees awarded to men will decrease by 100 degrees through 1998–99 and hold steady through 2003–2004. The high alternative assumes that first-professional degrees awarded to men will increase by 300 degrees through 1995–96, fall by 100 degrees through 1998–99, and then decrease by 200 degrees through 2003–2004.)

Methodological Tables

These tables describe equations used to calculate projections (tables A3.1 through A3.5), and basic assumptions underlying projections (table A3.6).

Projection Accuracy

An analysis of projection errors from similar models used in the past eight editions of *Projections of Education Statistics* indicates that mean absolute percentage errors (MAPEs) for bachelor's degree projections were 2.2 percent for 1 year out, 3.5 percent for 2 years out, and 4.2 percent for 5 years out. For the 1-year-out prediction, this means that one would expect the projection to be within 2.2 percent of the actual value, on the average. For first-professional degrees, the MAPEs were 2.6, 2.6, and 1.6 percent, respectively. For doctor's degrees, based on the past seven editions of *Projections of Education Statistics*, the MAPEs were 2.8, 4.6, and 3.3 percent, respectively. MAPEs for master's degrees, based on the past six editions of *Projections of Education Statistics*, were 2.7, 5.0, and 4.7, respectively. MAPEs for associate degrees, based on the past four editions of *Projections of Education Statistics*, were 1.5 percent for 1 year out, 2.7 percent for 2 years out, and 5.6 percent for 3 years out.

Table A3.1.—Equations for associate degrees

			Equation	R^2	Durbin-Watson statistic [1]	Estimation technique
Men	ASSOCM	=	$16{,}056.2 + 180.2\text{UGFTM2} + 21.4\text{UGPTM2}$ $(6.0)\qquad\quad (2.2)$	0.86	1.7	OLS [2]
Women	ASSOCW	=	$-1{,}773.3 + 281.9\text{UGFTW2}$ (42.6)	0.99	1.3	OLS [2]

$R^2 =$ Coefficient of determination.

[1] For an explanation of the Durbin-Watson statistic, see J. Johnston, *Econometric Methods*, New York: McGraw-Hill, 1972, pages 251–252.
[2] OLS equals Ordinary Least Squares.

Where:

ASSOCM	=Number of associate degrees awarded to men
ASSOCW	=Number of associate degrees awarded to women

UGFTM2	=Full-time male undergraduate enrollment in 2-year institutions lagged 2 years
UGPTM2	=Part-time male undergraduate enrollment in 2-year institutions lagged 2 years
UGFTW2	=Full-time female undergraduate enrollment in 2-year institutions lagged 2 years

NOTE: Numbers in parentheses are t-statistics. The time period of observations used in the equations is from 1969–70 to 1990–91.

Table A3.2.—Equations for bachelor's degrees

		Equation	R^2	Durbin-Watson statistic [1]	Estimation technique
Men	BACHM	$= 60{,}668.4 - 6.4 P1824M - 4.65 P2534M$ $\phantom{= 60{,}668.4 - }(-2.2)(-3.9)$ $+\ 218.1 UGFT4M\ +\ 154.6 UGPT4M$ $(7.8)(1.9)$	0.82	1.8	OLS [2]
Women	BACHW	$= 169{,}712.9 - 16.6 P1824W + 289.0 UGFT4W$ $\phantom{= 169{,}712.9 - }(-4.9)(11.9)$ $-\ 109.3 UGPT4W$ (-2.4)	0.99	1.7	AR1 [3]

$R^2 =$ Coefficient of determination.

[1] For an explanation of the Durbin-Watson statistic, see J. Johnston, *Econometric Methods*, New York: McGraw-Hill, 1972, pages 251–252.

[2] OLS equals Ordinary Least Squares.

[1] For an explanation of the Durbin-Watson statistic, see J. Johnston, *Econometric Methods*, New York: McGraw-Hill, 1972, pages 251–252.

[2] OLS equals Ordinary Least Squares.

[3] AR1 equals an estimation procedure for correcting the problem of first-order autocorrelation. Specifically, the maximum likelihood procedure of the statistical program RATS was used to estimate rho. In this equation, rho is equal to 0.68 with a t-statistic of (3.5). For a general discussion of the problem of autocorrelation, and the method used to forecast in the presence of autocorrelation, see G. Judge, W. Hill, R. Griffiths, H. Lutkepohl, and T. Lee, *The Theory and Practice of Econometrics*, New York: John Wiley and Sons, 1985, pages 315-318.

Where:

BACHM	=Number of bachelor's degrees awarded to men
BACHW	=Number of bachelor's degrees awarded to women
P1824M	=Population of 18- to 24-year-old males
P1824W	=Population of 18- to 24-year-old females
P2534M	=Population of 25- to 34-year-old males
UGFT4M	=Full-time male undergraduate enrollment in 4-year institutions lagged 3 years
UGPT4M	=Part-time male undergraduate enrollment in 4-year institutions lagged 3 years
UGFT4W	=Full-time female undergraduate enrollment in 4-year institutions lagged 3 years
UGPT4W	=Part-time female undergraduate enrollment in 4-year institutions lagged 3 years

NOTE: Numbers in parentheses are t-statistics. The time period of observations used in the equations is from 1969–70 to 1990–91.

Table A3.3.—Equation for master's degrees

	Equation			R^2	Durbin-Watson statistic[1]	Estimation technique
Women	MASTW	=	27,225.9 - 3.5P3544W + 365.5GPTW (-3.8) (12.3)	0.94	1.0	OLS[2]

R^2 = Coefficient of determination.

[1] For an explanation of the Durbin-Watson statistic, see J. Johnston, *Econometric Methods*, New York: McGraw-Hill, 1972, pages 251–252.

[2] OLS equals Ordinary Least Squares.

Where:

MASTW   =Number of master's degrees awarded to women
P3544W   =Population of 35- to 44-year-old females
GPTW   =Part-time female graduate enrollment

NOTE: Numbers in parentheses are t-statistics. The time period of observations used in the equations is from 1969–70 to 1990–91.

Table A3.4.—Equation for doctor's degrees

			Equation	R^2	Durbin-Watson statistic [1]	Estimation technique
Women	DOCW	=	2,564.2 + 5.2GPTW + 404.3TIME (1.6) (8.2)	0.99	1.6	AR1 [3]

R^2 = Coefficient of determination.

[1] For an explanation of the Durbin-Watson statistic, see J. Johnston, *Econometric Methods*, New York: McGraw-Hill, 1972, pages 251–252.

[2] OLS equals Ordinary Least Squares.

[3] AR1 equals an estimation procedure for correcting the problem of first-order autocorrelation. Specifically, the maximum likelihood procedure of the statistical program RATS was used to estimate rho. In this equation, rho is equal to 0.67 with a t-statistic of (3.7). For a general discussion of the problem of autocorrelation, and the method used to forecast in the presence of autocorrelation, see G. Judge, W. Hill, R. Griffiths, H. Lutkepohl, and T. Lee, *The Theory and Practice of Econometrics*, New York: John Wiley and Sons, 1985, pages 315-318.

Where:

DOCW   = Number of doctor's degrees awarded to women
GPTW   = Part-time female graduate enrollment lagged 1 year
TIME   = Time trend, 1969–70 equals 1

NOTE: Numbers in parentheses are t-statistics. The time period of observations used in the equations is from 1969–70 to 1990–91.

Table A3.5.—Equation for first-professional degrees

	Equation				R^2	Durbin-Watson statistic [1]	Estimation technique
Women	FPROW	=	-2,765.5 + 271.3FPFTW + 429.3FPPTW		0.99	1.2	OLS [2]
			(9.7) (1.9)				

R^2 = Coefficient of determination.

[1] For an explanation of the Durbin-Watson statistic, see J. Johnston, *Econometric Methods*, New York: McGraw-Hill, 1972, pages 251–252.

[2] OLS equals Ordinary Least Squares.

Where:

FPROW	=Number of first-professional degrees awarded to women
FPFTW	=Full-time female first-professional enrollment lagged 1 year
FPPTW	=Part-time female first-professional enrollment lagged 3 years

NOTE: Numbers in parentheses are t-statistics. The time period of observations used in the equations is from 1969–70 to 1990–91.

Table A3.6.— Earned degrees conferred (assumptions)

Variables	Assumptions	Alternatives	Tables
Associate degrees			
Men	The number of associate degrees awarded to men is a linear function of full-time and part-time undergraduate enrollment in 2-year institutions lagged 2 years. This relationship will continue through 2003–2004.	Middle	27
Women	The number of associate degrees awarded to women is a linear function of full-time undergraduate enrollment in 2-year institutions lagged 2 years. This relationship will continue through 2003–2004.	Middle	27
Bachelor's degrees			
Men	The number of bachelor's degrees awarded to men is a linear function of full-time and part-time undergraduate enrollment in 4-year institutions lagged 3 years, the 18- to 24-year-old population, and 25- to 34-year-old population. This relationship will continue through 2003–2004.	Middle	28
Women	The number of bachelor's degrees awarded to women is a linear function of full-time and part-time undergraduate enrollment in 4-year institutions lagged 3 years and the 18- to 24-year-old population. This relationship will continue through 2003–2004.	Middle	28
Master's degrees			
Men	The number of master's degrees awarded to men equals the average of the low and high alternatives.	Middle	29
Women	The number of master's degrees awarded to women is a linear function of part-time graduate enrollment and the 35- to 44-year-old population. This relationship will continue through 2003–2004.	Middle	29
Doctor's degrees			
Men	The number of doctor's degrees awarded to men equals the average of the low and high alternatives.	Middle	30
Women	The number of doctor's degrees awarded to women is a linear function of part-time graduate enrollment lagged 1 year and time. This relationship will continue through 2003–2004.	Middle	30
First-professional degrees			
Men	The number of first-professional degrees awarded to men equals the average of the low and high alternatives.	Middle	31
Women	The number of first-professional degrees awarded to women is a linear function of full-time first-professional enrollment lagged 1 year and part-time first-professional enrollment lagged 3 years. This relationship will continue through 2003–2004.	Middle	31

A4. Classroom Teachers

Public Classroom Teachers

Numbers of public elementary and secondary classroom teachers were projected using a model similar to that used in *Projections of Education Statistics to 2003*, only the coefficients were re-estimated. The number of public school teachers was projected separately for the elementary and secondary levels. The elementary teachers were modeled as a function of disposable income per capita, local education revenue receipts from state sources per capita, and elementary enrollment. Secondary teachers were modeled as a function of disposable income per capita, education revenue receipts from state sources per capita (lagged 3 years), and secondary enrollment. Both disposable income per capita and local education revenue receipts from state sources were in constant 1991–92 dollars.

The equations in this section should be viewed as forecasting rather than structural equations, as the limitations of time and available data precluded the building of a large-scale, structural teacher model. The particular equations shown were selected on the basis of their statistical properties, such as coefficients of determination (R^2s), the t-statistics of the coefficients, the Durbin-Watson statistic, and residual plots.

The multiple regression technique used yields good projections only if the relationships that existed among the variables in the past continue throughout the projection period.

The public elementary classroom teacher model is:

$$\text{ELTCH} = b_0 + b_1\text{PCI92} + b_2\text{SGRANT} + b_3\text{ELENR}$$

where:

ELTCH is the number of public elementary classroom teachers.

PCI92 is disposable income per capita in 1991–92 dollars;

SGRANT is the level of education revenue receipts from state sources per capita in 1991–92 dollars; and

ELENR is the number of students enrolled in public elementary schools.

Each variable affects the number of teachers in the expected way. As people receive more income, the state spends more money on education, and as enrollment increases, the number of elementary teachers hired increases.

The public secondary classroom teacher model is:

$$\text{SCTCH} = b_0 + b_1\text{PCI92} + b_2\text{SGRANT3} + b_3\text{SCENR}$$

where:

SCTCH is the number of public secondary classroom teachers;

PCI92 is disposable income per capita in 1991–92 dollars;

SGRANT3 is the level of education revenue receipts from state sources per capita in 1991–92 dollars, lagged 3 years, and;

SCENR is the number of students enrolled in public secondary schools.

Each variable affects the number of teachers in the expected way. As people receive more income, the state spends more money on education, and as enrollment increases, the number of secondary teachers hired increases.

Table A4.1 summarizes the results for the elementary and secondary public teacher models.

Enrollment is by organizational level, not by grade level. Thus, secondary enrollment is not the same as grade 9–12 enrollment because some states count some grade 7 and 8 enrollment as secondary. The distribution of the number of teachers is by organizational level, not by grade span.

Private Classroom Teachers

Projections of private classroom teachers were derived in the following manner. For 1992, the ratio of private school teachers to public school teachers was calculated by organizational level. These 1992 ratios were held constant over the projection period. The ratios were then applied to projections of public school teachers by organizational level to yield projections of private school teachers. This method assumes that the future pattern in the trend of private school teachers will be the same as that for public school teachers. The reader is cautioned that a number of factors could alter the assumption of constant ratios over the projection period.

The total number of public school teachers, enrollment by organizational level, and education revenue receipts from state sources used in these projections were from the Common Core of Data (CCD) survey conducted by NCES. The proportion of teachers by organizational level was taken from the National Education Association and then applied to the total number of teachers from CCD to produce the number of teachers by organizational level. The number of private classroom teachers was obtained from "Public and Private Elementary and Secondary Education Statistics: School Year 1992–93," *Early Estimates*.

Disposable income was obtained from DRI/McGraw-Hill and population data were from the Bureau of the Census.

Projection Accuracy

An analysis of projection errors from the past ten editions of *Projections of Education Statistics* indicated that the mean absolute percentage errors (MAPEs) for projections of classroom teachers in public elementary and secondary schools were 0.9 percent for 1 year out, 1.4 percent for 2 years out, 3.2 percent for 5 years out, and 2.6 percent for 10 years out. For the 2-year-ahead prediction, this means that one would expect the projection to be within 1.4 percent of the actual value, on the average.

Table A4.1.—Equations for public elementary and secondary classroom teachers

		Equation	R^2	Durbin-Watson statistic [1]	Estimation technique
Elementary	ELTCH	$= -312.3 + 0.044PCI92 + 0.5SGRANT$ $(7.1)\quad\quad(2.6)$ $+ 0.03ELENR$ (10.6)	0.99	1.0	OLS [2]
Secondary	SCTCH	$= -221.3 + 0.03PCI92 + 0.2SGRANT3$ $(8.7)\quad\quad(2.2)$ $+ 0.04SCENR$ (21.9)	0.98	1.7	OLS [2]

$R^2 =$ Coefficient of determination.

[1] For an explanation of the Durbin-Watson statistic, see J. Johnston, *Econometric Methods*, New York: McGraw-Hill, 1972, pages 251–252.

[2] OLS equals Ordinary Least Squares.

Where:

ELTCH = Number of public elementary classroom teachers
SCTCH = Number of public secondary classroom teachers
PCI92 = Disposable income per capita in 1991–92 dollars

SGRANT = Education revenue receipts from state sources per capita
SGRANT3 = Education revenue receipts from state sources per capita lagged 3 years
ELENR = Number of students enrolled in public elementary schools
SCENR = Number of students enrolled in public secondary schools

NOTE: Numbers in parentheses are t-statistics. The time period of observations used in the equation for elementary teachers is from 1960 to 1992. The time period used in the equation for secondary teachers is from 1965 to 1992.

A5. Expenditures of Public Elementary and Secondary Schools

Econometric techniques were used to produce the projections for current expenditures and average teacher salaries. The equations in this chapter should be viewed as forecasting, rather than structural, equations. The limitations of time and available data precluded the building of large-scale, structural, models. The particular equations shown were selected on the basis of their statistical properties, such as coefficients of determination (R^2's), the t-statistics of the variables, the Durbin-Watson statistic, and residual plots.

The multiple regression technique used yields good forecasting results only if the relationships that existed among the variables in the past continue throughout the projection period.

The Elementary and Secondary School Current Expenditure Model

There has been a large body of work, both theoretical and empirical, on the demand for local public services such as education. The elementary and secondary school current expenditure model is based on this work.

The model that is the basis for the elementary and secondary school current expenditure model has been called the median voter model. In brief, the theory states that spending for each public good in the community (in this case, education), reflects the preferences of the "median voter" in the community. This individual is identified as the voter in the community with the median income and median property value. Hence, the amount of spending in the community reflects the price of education facing the voter with the median income, as well as his income and tastes. There are competing models in which the level of spending reflects the choices of others in the community, such as the "bureaucrats." The median voter model was chosen as the basis of the elementary and secondary school current expenditure model as it has been the one most thoroughly studied.

There have been many empirical studies of the demand for education expenditures using the median voter model. In most instances, researchers have used cross-sectional data. The elementary and secondary school current expenditure model was built on the knowledge gained from these cross-sectional studies and was adapted from them for use in a time series study.

In a median voter model, the demand for education expenditures is typically linked to four different types of variables: 1) measures of the income on the median voter; 2) measures of intergovernmental aid for education going indirectly to the median voter; 3) measures of the price to the median voter of providing one more dollar of education expenditures per pupil; and 4) any other variables that may affect one's tastes for education. The elementary and secondary school current expenditure model contains variables reflecting the first three types of variables. The model is:

$$\ln(CUREXP) = b_0 + b_1\ln(PCI) + b_2\ln(SGRANT) + b_3\ln(ADAPOP)$$

where:

ln indicates the natural log;

CUREXP equals current expenditures of public elementary and secondary schools per pupil in average daily attendance in constant 1991–92 dollars;

PCI equals disposable income per capita in constant 1991–92 dollars;

SGRANT equals local governments' education revenue receipts from state sources, per capita, in constant 1991–92 dollars; and

ADAPOP equals the ratio of average daily attendance to the population.

The model was estimated using a method for correcting for autocorrelation —the maximum likelihood search procedure of the program Regression Analysis of Time Series (RATS). This was done because the test statistics were significantly better than those from the ordinary least squares (OLS) estimation, and the Durbin-Watson statistic was in the inconclusive region when the model was estimated using OLS. This is the second edition of *Projections of Education Statistics* in which this method of estimation, rather than OLS, was used. Ordinary least squares was used in the previous four editions of *Projections of Education Statistics*. The sample period was from 1959–60 to 1990–91. All variables were placed in log form, as the test statistics were superior for that form and there is some evidence from the cross-sectional studies that the log form is superior.

There are potential problems with using a model for local government education expenditures for the nation as a whole. Two such problems concern the variable SGRANT. First, the amount of money which local governments receive for education from state government varies substantially by state. Second, the formulas used to apportion state moneys for education among local governments vary by state.

Beginning in 1988–89, there was a major change in the survey form used to collect data on current expenditures.

131

This new survey form produces a more complete measure of current expenditures; therefore, the values for current expenditures are not completely comparable to the previously collected numbers. In a crosswalk study, data for a majority of states were also collected for 1986–87 and 1987–88 that were comparable to data from the new survey form. A comparison of these data with those from the old survey form suggests that the use of the new survey form may have increased the national figure for current expenditures by approximately 1.4 percent over what it would have been if the survey form had not been changed. When the model was estimated, all values for current expenditures before 1988–89 were increased by 1.4 percent.

The results for the model are shown in table A5.1. Each variable affects current expenditures in the direction that would be expected. As people receive more income, either directly (PCI) or from the state government (SGRANT), the level of spending increases. As the number of pupils increases relative to the population (that is, as ADAPOP increases), the level of spending per pupil falls.

From the cross-sectional studies of the demand for education expenditures, we have an estimate of how sensitive current expenditures are to changes in PCI and ADAPOP. We can compare the results from this model with those from the cross-sectional studies. For this model, an increase in PCI of 1 percent, with SGRANT and ADAPOP held constant, would result in an increase of current expenditures per pupil in average daily attendance of approximately 0.52 percent. With PCI and SGRANT held constant, an increase of 1 percent in ADAPOP would result in a decrease in current expenditures per pupil in average daily attendance of approximately 0.37 percent. Both numbers are well within the range of what has been found in other studies.

The results from this model are not completely comparable with those from the previous editions of *Projections of Education Statistics*. That is because there was a change in the definition of the disposable income.

Projections for total current expenditures were made by multiplying the projections for current expenditures per pupil in average daily attendance by projections for average daily attendance. The projections for total current expenditures were divided by projections for fall enrollment to produce projections of current expenditures per pupil in fall enrollment. Current-dollar projections were produced by multiplying the constant-dollar projections by projections for the Consumer Price Index.

Three alternative sets of projections for current expenditures are presented: the middle alternative projections; the low alternative projections; and the high alternative projections. The alternative sets of projections differ because of varying assumptions about the growth paths for disposable income and revenue receipts from state sources.

The alternative sets of projections for the economic variables including disposable income were developed using variations of three economic scenarios developed by DRI for use on its U.S. Quarterly Model. The U.S. Quarterly model is an econometric model of the U.S.

economy developed by DRI for the personal computer which projects more than 1,200 economic concepts. Periodically, DRI supplies alternative economic scenarios of the economy, including long-term scenarios. Users have the option of either producing projections directly from the scenarios supplied by DRI or first altering some of the underlying assumptions of the scenarios and then producing the projections. The most recent series of long-term scenarios (February 1993) was used as bases for the three sets of alternative economic projections used here, although there were some changes in the underlying assumptions.

DRI's trend scenario was used as a base for the middle alternative projections of the economic variables. DRI's trend scenario depicts a mean of possible paths that the economy could take over the forecast period, barring major shocks. The economy, in this scenario, evolves smoothly, if unspectacularly. The only change from DRI's trend scenario was that the most recent middle set of population projections as developed by the Bureau of the Census was substituted for DRI's population projections.

DRI's pessimistic scenario was used as a base for the low alternative projections. As with the middle set of projections, the Bureau of the Census' recent middle set of population projections was substituted for DRI's population projections. For the low alternative projections, some changes were made in some of DRI's assumptions concerning personal income that resulted in lower projections for disposable income.

Similarly, DRI's optimistic scenario was used as a base for the high alternative projections. The Bureau of the Census' recent middle set of population projection was substituted for DRI's population projections and some changes were made in some of DRI's assumptions concerning personal income that resulted in higher projections for disposable income.

Hence, using DRI's U.S. Quarterly Model and their February 1993 long-term scenarios, three sets of projections, the middle alternative projections, the low alternative projections, and the high alternative projections, were developed for the economic variables.

In the middle alternative projections, disposable income per capita rises each year from 1993–94 to 2003–2004 at rates between 0.7 and 1.4 percent. In the low alternative projections, disposable income per capita ranging between -1.3 and 1.2 percent and in the high alternative projections disposable income per capita rises at rates between 0.7 and 3.9 percent.

Projections for revenue receipts from state sources were produced using two different methods. For the middle alternative projections and high alternative projections, projections for revenue receipts from state sources were produced using an econometric model. The low alternative projections were produced by using the same method used to produce the low projections presented in the previous edition of *Projections of Education Statistics*.

The model for revenue receipts from state sources is:

$$\text{SGRANT} = b_0 + b_1 \text{PERTAX1} + b_2 \text{BUSTAX1} + b_3 \text{ADAPOP} + b_4 \text{ININCR}$$

where:

SGRANT equals local governments' education revenue receipts from state sources, per capita, in constant 1991–92 dollars;

PERTAX1 equals personal taxes and nontax receipts to state and local governments, per capita, in constant 1991–92 dollars lagged one period;

BUSTAX1 equals indirect business taxes and tax accruals, excluding property taxes, to state and local governments, per capita, in constant 1991–92 dollars lagged one period;

ADAPOP equals the ratio of average daily attendance to the population; and

ININCR equals the rate of change in the inflation rate measured by the Consumer Price Index.

This equation was estimated using ordinary least squares for the sample period from 1960–61 to 1990–91. The results for the model are shown in table A5.1.

The values of the coefficients in this model follow expectations. As state governments receive more revenue (higher PERTAX1 and BUSTAX1), they have more money to send to local governments for education. As the enrollment increases relative to the population (higher ADAPOP), so does the amount of aid going to education. Finally, in years with rapidly increasing inflation (higher ININCR), the real dollar values of revenue receipts from state governments to local governments would fall, other things being equal.

Two alternative projections were produced for SGRANT using this model. Each is based on a different set of projections for personal taxes, business taxes, and the rate of change in the inflation rate. The middle set of projections was produced using the values for these variables from the middle set of alternative projections. The high set of projections was produced using the values from the high set of alternative projections. In the middle set of projections, personal taxes and nontax receipts increase at rates between 1.3 and 5.3 percent and indirect business taxes and tax accruals increase at rates between -0.1 and 3.0 percent. In the high set of projections, personal taxes and nontax receipts increase at rates between 1.5 and 8.7 percent, and indirect business taxes and tax accruals increase at rates between 0.0 and 3.9 percent.

A third scenario was produced using an alternative method: revenue receipts from state sources are assumed to increase at a rate equal to the growth rate of state and local purchases of goods and services as forecast by the low set of alternative projections. As elementary and secondary education's share of all state and local government expenditures has been steadily increasing, this method may result in an underestimate.

In the middle set of projections, revenue receipts from state sources increase at rates between 0.7 and 4.4 percent

for the period from 1993–94 to 2003–2004. In the low set of projections, they increase at rates between 0.0 and 2.4 percent. In the high set of projections, they increase at rates between 0.8 and 5.4 percent.

The Elementary and Secondary Teacher Salary Model

Most studies conducted on teacher salaries, like those on current expenditures, have used cross-sectional data. Unlike current expenditures models, however, the models for teacher salaries from these existing cross-sectional studies cannot easily be reformulated for use with time-series data. One problem is that we do not have sufficient information concerning the supply of qualified teachers who are not presently teaching. Hence, the elementary and secondary salary model contains terms that measure the demand for teachers in the economy.

The elementary and secondary teacher salary model is:

$$SALARY = b_0 + b_1 CUREXP + b_2 ADAPOP + b_3 DIFADA1$$

where:

SALARY equals the average annual salary of teachers in public elementary and secondary schools in constant 1991–92 dollars;

CUREXP equals current expenditures of public elementary and secondary schools per pupil in average daily attendance in constant 1991–92 dollars;

ADAPOP equals the ratio of average daily attendance to the population; and

DIFADA1 equals the change in average daily attendance lagged 1 period.

The model was estimated using the period from 1959–60 to 1990–91 as a sample period. To estimate the elementary and secondary teacher salary model, a method for correcting for autocorrelation—the maximum likelihood search procedure of the program RATS—was used. This was done because the test statistics were significantly better than those from the OLS estimations, and the Durbin-Watson statistic was in the inconclusive region when the model was estimated using OLS. The Durbin-Watson statistic, however, is still in the inconclusive range, suggesting that there still maybe a problem with autocorrelation.

Due to the effects caused by the change shown in survey forms, the values for current expenditures for 1959–60 to 1987–88 were increased by 1.4 percent.

The results for this model are also shown in table A5.1.

There is no literature for comparing the sizes of the coefficients. However, the direction of the impact each variable has on salaries is as expected: As the level of spending per pupil increases (higher CUREXP), more teachers can be hired, so demand for teachers increases and salaries increase; as the number of students increases (higher ADAPOP and DIFADA1), demand for teachers increases, so salaries increase.

As for current expenditures, three different scenarios are presented for teacher salaries. The same projections for ADAPOP and DIFADA1 are used for each alternative projection; the sole difference between the projections is in the projection for current expenditures. The middle alternative projection for salaries uses the middle alternative projection for current expenditures. The low alternative projection for salaries uses the low alternative projection for current expenditures. The high alternative projection for salaries uses the high alternative projection for current expenditures.

Current expenditures, average teacher salaries, and the number of teachers are interrelated. Hence, an exercise was conducted to see whether the projections of these three time series were consistent.

The number of teachers was multiplied by the average salary and then divided by current expenditures for every school year from 1978–79 until 2003–2004 (using the middle alternative projection for teachers, salaries, and current expenditures). The resulting value shows the portion of current expenditures that is spent on teacher salaries. The portion of current expenditures that goes toward teacher salaries has been in a slow downward trend, with the teacher salary share falling from 42.0 percent in 1978–79 to 39.4 percent in 1990–91. With the projected values, the portion of current expenditures that go toward teacher salaries continues to fall slowly, falling to 39.4 percent in 2003–2004.

The results of this exercise indicate that the projections of these three time series are consistent.

Projection Accuracy

This is the sixth consecutive year in which *Projections of Education Statistics* has contained projections of current expenditures and teacher salaries. The actual values of current expenditures and teacher salaries can be compared with the projected values in the previous editions to examine the accuracy of the models.

The projections from the various editions of *Projections of Education Statistics* were placed in 1981–82 dollars using the Consumer Price Indices that appeared in each edition.

The projections for current expenditures presented in *Projections of Education Statistics to 1997–98* were produced by a model slightly different from the model used for the projections presented in this edition: calendar year data, rather than school year data, were used for disposable income, the population, and the Consumer Price Index. The independent variables used in *Projections of Education Statistics to 2000*, *Projections of Education Statistics to 2001: An Update*, *Projections of Education Statistics to 2002*, and *Projections of Education Statistics to 2003* were the same as those used in this edition. With this edition,

however, there was a change in the definition of disposable income. In *Projections of Education Statistics to 2003* and in the present edition, a method for correcting for autocorrelation was used to estimate the model. In the earlier four editions, ordinary least squares was used to estimate the model.

Mean absolute percentage errors (MAPEs) were calculated for current expenditures and current expenditures per pupil. The MAPEs for projections of current expenditures were 1.7 percent for the 1-year-ahead projections, 2.6 percent for the 2-years-ahead projections, 2.5 percent for the 3-years-ahead projection, 2.1 percent for the 4-years-ahead projection, and 0.6 percent for the 5-years-ahead projection. The MAPEs for current expenditures per pupil were 1.3 percent (1-year-ahead), 1.9 percent (2-years-ahead), 1.7 percent (3-years-ahead), 1.5 percent (4-years-ahead), and 0.8 percent (5-years-ahead).

Some of the differences between the actual values and the projected values for current expenditures and current expenditures per pupil are due to the change in the survey form for current expenditures that took place in 1988–89. The results of the crosswalk study suggest that values for current expenditures as presently collected are approximately 1.4 percent higher than they would have been if no change had been made. If the projections for 1988–89, 1989–90, and 1990–91 which appeared in *Projections of Education Statistics to 1997–98*, *Projections of Education Statistics to 2000*, *Projections of Education Statistics to 2001: An Update*, are increased by 1.4 percent, the MAPEs decrease. When this adjustment was made, the MAPEs for current expenditures were 1.0 percent (1-year-ahead), 1.6 percent (2-years-ahead), 1.2 percent (3-years-ahead), 0.7 percent (4-years-ahead), and 0.8 percent (5-years-ahead), and the MAPEs for current expenditures per pupil were 0.6 percent (1-year-ahead), 1.1 percent (2-years-ahead), 1.2 percent (3-years-ahead), 0.3 percent (4-years-ahead), and 0.6 percent (5-years-ahead).

Projections for teacher salaries also appeared in the four most recent editions of *Projections of Education Statistics.*

The projections of teacher salaries presented in the earlier editions were produced using a similar set of independent variables. The same set of independent variables was used to produce the projections in *Projections of Education Statistics to 2000*. In the other three editions of *Projections of Education Statistics* in which projections of teacher salaries appear, an additional variable, the change in average daily attendance lagged two periods, was also included. The projections presented in *Projections of Education Statistics to 1997–98* were produced by using calendar year data, rather than school year data, for the population and the Consumer Price Index.

The MAPEs for projections of teacher salaries were 1.2 percent (1-year-ahead), 2.0 percent (2-years-ahead), 2.4 percent (3-years-ahead), 4.0 (4-years-ahead), and 6.8 (5-years-ahead).

Sources of Past and Projected Data

Numbers from several different sources were used to produce these projections. In some instances, the time series used were made by either combining numbers from various sources or manipulating the available numbers. The sources and the methods of manipulation are described here.

The time series used for current expenditures was compiled from several different sources. For the school years ending in even numbers from 1959–60 to 1975–76, the numbers for current expenditures were taken from various issues of *Statistics of State School Systems*, published by NCES. The numbers for the school years ending in odd numbers during the 1960s were taken from various issues of the National Education Association's *Estimates of School Statistics*. For the school years ending in odd numbers during the 1970s, up to and including 1976–77, the numbers were taken from various issues of *Revenues and Expenditures for Public Elementary and Secondary Education*, published by NCES. For the school years from 1977–78 until 1990–91, the numbers were taken from the NCES Common Core of Data survey and unpublished data.

For 1974–75 and 1976–77, expenditures for summer schools were subtracted from the published figures for current expenditures. The value for 1972–73 was the sum of current expenditures at the local level, expenditures for administration by state boards of education and state departments of education, and expenditures for administration by intermediate administrative units.

Note that although the data from the different sources are similar, they are not entirely consistent. Also, the NCES numbers beginning with 1980–81 are not entirely consistent with the earlier NCES numbers, due to differing treatments of items such as expenditures for administration by state governments and expenditures for community services.

For most years, the sources for the past values of average daily attendance were identical to the sources for current expenditures. For 1978–79, the number was taken from *Revenues and Expenditures for Public Elementary and Secondary Education*.

Projections for average daily attendance for the period from 1991–92 to 2003–2004 were made by multiplying the projections for enrollment by the average value of the ratios of average daily attendance to the enrollment

from 1981–82 to 1990–91; this average value was approximately 0.93.

The values for fall enrollment from 1959–60 to 1977–78 were taken from issues of the NCES publication *Statistics of Public Elementary and Secondary Schools*. The 1978–79 value was taken from the *NCES Bulletin* of October 23, 1979, ''Selected Public and Private Elementary and Secondary Education Statistics.'' The values from 1979–80 to 1991–92 were taken from the NCES Common Core of Data survey. The number for 1992–93 was taken from the 1992–93 *Early Estimates*. The projections for fall enrollment are those presented in Chapter 1.

For 1959–60 to 1990–91, the sources for revenue receipts from state sources were the two NCES publications *Statistics of State School Systems* and *Revenues and Expenditures for Public Elementary and Secondary Education* and the NCES Common Core of Data survey. The methods for producing the alternative projections for revenue receipts from state sources are outlined above.

The numbers for average teacher salaries were taken from various issues of the National Education Association's *Estimates of School Statistics*.

The projected values for disposable income, personal taxes and nontax receipts to state and local governments, and indirect business taxes and tax accruals to state and local governments, were developed using DRI/McGraw-Hill's U.S. Quarterly Model. Projected values of the Bureau of Labor Statistic's Consumer Price Index for all urban consumers, which was used for adjusting current expenditures, teacher salaries, revenue receipts from state sources, and the state revenue variables, were also developed using the U.S. Quarterly Model. DRI/McGraw-Hill supplied the historic values for these variables.

Both the historic and projected values for the population were supplied by the U.S. Bureau of the Census.

The values of all the variables from DRI were placed in school-year terms. The school-year numbers were calculated by taking the average of the last two quarters of 1 year and the first two quarters of the next year.

The Elementary and Secondary School Price Index was considered as a replacement for the Consumer Price Index for placing current expenditures and teacher salaries in constant dollars. As projections of the price index are required for placing the forecasts into current dollars, and as there are no projections of the Elementary and Secondary School Price Index, the Consumer Price Index was used.

Table A5.1.—Equations for current expenditures per pupil in average daily attendance, average annual salaries of teachers, and education revenue receipts from state sources

Dependent variable	Equation	$\bar{R}^2$	Durbin-Watson statistic	Estimation technique [*]	Rho
Current expenditures per pupil	ln(CUREXP) = - 1.145 + 0.521ln(PCI) + 0.651ln(SGRANT) (-0.83) (2.11) (4.75) - 0.374ln(ADAPOP) (-2.91)	0.997	1.886	AR1	0.368 (1.97)
Average annual salaries	SALARY = - 9429.4 + 4.22CUREXP + 134308ADAPOP (-3.17) (17.82) (10.27) + 0.00082DIFADA1 (4.06)	0.984	1.490	AR1	0.721 (4.71)
Education revenue receipts from state sources per capita	SGRANT = - 126.1 + 0.27PERTAX1 + 0.31BUSTAX1 (-4.35) (3.09) (1.93) + 688ADAPOP - 13.6ININCR (3.11) (-3.49)	0.992	1.965	OLS	

[*] OLS = Ordinary Least Squares. AR1 is an estimation procedure for correcting the problem of first-order autocorrelation. Specifically, the maximum likelihood procedure of the statistical program RATS was used to estimate rho. For a general discussion of the problem of autocorrelation, and the methods to correct it, see Johnston (1972), chapter 8. For a discussion of the method used to forecast in the presence of autocorrelation, see G. Judge, W. Hill, R. Griffiths, H. Lutkepohl, and T. Lee, *The Theory and Practice of Econometrics*, New York: John Wiley and Sons, 1985, pages 315–318.

NOTES: The sample size for revenue receipts from state sources is 31. The sample size for current expenditures and teacher salaries is 32. Numbers in parentheses are t-statistics. $\bar{R}^2$ = Coefficient of determination, adjusted for degrees of freedom. For an explanation of the Durbin-Watson statistic, see J. Johnston, *Econometric Methods*, New York: McGraw-Hill, 1972, pages 251–252. (This table was prepared June 1993.)

A6. Expenditures of Institutions of Higher Education

A total of eight higher education expenditure models was estimated: one current-fund expenditure model and one educational and general expenditure model for each of the four types of higher education institutions—public 4-year; public 2-year; private 4-year; and private 2-year. For all the sectors, except private 2-year, econometric techniques were used. Due to the lack of a consistent database for private 2-year schools, exponential smoothing, which requires fewer observations, was used.

The higher education econometric models were selected on the basis of their statistical properties, such as the coefficients of determination (R^2), the t-statistics of the variables, the Durbin-Watson statistic, and residual plots. These econometric models will yield good forecasting results only if the relationships that existed among the variables in the past continue throughout the projection period.

Higher Education Institutions Expenditure Models

Similar econometric models were developed for three types of institutions. While there has been significantly less work by economists studying the factors influencing higher education finance data than those influencing elementary and secondary finance data, there have been some valuable studies. This body of work was used in building these models.

In Chapter 7, some of the factors that are historically associated with the level of expenditures were discussed. These were: (1) the state of the economy; (2) the inflation rate; and (3) enrollments. Each of the models presented here contains variables measuring at least two of these three factors. Either disposable income per capita or revenues of state and local governments per capita was used to measure the state of the economy. Two measures of the inflation rate were considered: the rate of change in the inflation rate; or a dummy for years with inflation rates greater than 8 percent. In each equation, an enrollment variable was included.

For each dependent variable, a number of alternative specifications were examined. In each case, the choice of the final specification was made after considering such factors as the coefficients of determination, the t-statistics of the variables, residual plots, and ex-post mean absolute percent errors. The final specification of each model has the dependent variables and some of the independent variables as first differences. Linear and log-linear specifications were also examined.

The Public 4-Year Institutions Expenditure Models

The public 4-year institutions current-fund expenditure model is:

$$DPUTCUR4 = b_0 + b_1 DSTREV1 + b_2 DPUFTE4 + b_3 DUMMY$$

where:

DPUTCUR4 is the change in current-fund expenditures per student in full-time-equivalent (FTE) enrollment in public 4-year institutions in constant 1991–92 dollars;

DSTREV1 is the change in the sum of personal tax and nontax receipts to state and local governments and indirect business taxes and tax accruals, excluding property taxes, to state and local governments, per capita, in constant 1991–92 dollars lagged one year;

DPUFTE4 is the change in FTE enrollment in public 4-year institutions; and

DUMMY is a dummy variable equaling 1 when the inflation rate is greater than 8 percent and 0 otherwise.

This model and the other econometric models were estimated using a sample period from 1968–69 to 1990–91. Ordinary least squares was used to estimate all the public institution models.

The results for this model are on table A6.1. Each variable affects current-fund expenditures in a logical fashion. The more revenues that state and local governments receive, the more expenditures they can make for public institutions of higher education. In a year with high inflation (DUMMY equals 1), current-fund expenditures in constant dollars are lower than they would have been otherwise. The more students in public 4-year institutions, the less money to be spent per student.

Three projections were produced: the middle alternative set of projections, the low alternative set of projections, and the high alternative set of projections. Each set of projections was based on a different set of assumptions for the revenues of state and local governments per capita. The projections for revenues of state and local governments per capita and the other economic variables used to produced the higher education expenditure projections were produced using the U.S. Quarterly Model of DRI/McGraw–Hill's (DRI). The development of these alternative sets of projections is discussed in Appendix A5.

In the middle set of alternative projections, the revenues of state and local governments per capita increase at rates between 0.6 and 3.9 percent. In the low set of alternative projections, the revenues of state and local governments per capita increase at rates between 0.2 and 3.1 percent. In the high set of alternative projections, the revenues of state and local governments per capita increase at rates between 0.7 and 5.7 percent.

Projections for total current-fund expenditures were made by multiplying the projections for current-fund expenditures per student in FTE enrollment by projections for FTE enrollment. Current dollar projections were produced by multiplying the constant dollar projections by projections for the Consumer Price Index. All the higher education total expenditure projections and all the current dollar projections were calculated in similar fashion.

A model for educational and general expenditures of public 4-year institutions was developed using the same variables as the current-fund expenditure model. The model is:

$$DPUED4 = b_0 + b_1 DSTREV1 + b_2 DPUFTE4 + b_3 DUMMY$$

where:

DPUED4 is the change in educational and general expenditures per student in FTE enrollment in public 4-year institutions in constant 1991–92 dollars.

As with current-fund expenditures, each variable affects expenditures in the expected way.

The Public 2-Year Institutions Expenditure Models

The public 2-year institutions current-fund expenditure model has a form similar to the public 4-year institutions current-fund expenditure model except that the public 2-year institutions model does not contain any inflation variables. The model is:

$$DPUTCUR2 = b_0 + b_1 DSTREV1 + b_2 DPUFTE2$$

where:

DPUTCUR2 is the change in current-fund expenditures per student in FTE enrollment in public 2-year institutions in constant 1991–92 dollars; and

DPUFTE2 is the change in FTE enrollment in public 2-year institutions.

The results for this model are on table A6.1. Again, the DSTREV1 has the expected positive effect on expenditures and the FTE enrollment variable has the expected negative impact.

The public 2-year institutions educational and general expenditure model is virtually identical to its current-fund expenditures counterpart. It is:

$$DPUED2 = b_0 + b_1 DSTREV1 + b_2 DPUFTE2$$

where:

DPUED2 is the change in educational and general expenditures per student in FTE enrollment in public 2-year institutions in constant 1991–92 dollars.

The Private 4-Year Institutions Expenditure Models

The private 4-year institutions current-fund expenditure model is:

$$DPRTCUR4 = b_0 + b_1 DPCI + b_2 DPRFTE4 + b_3 ININCR$$

where:

DPRTCUR4 is the change in current-fund expenditures per student in FTE enrollment in private 4-year institutions in constant 1991–92 dollars;

DPRFTE4 is the change in FTE enrollment in private 4-year institutions to the population; and

ININCR is the rate of change in the inflation rate measured by the Consumer Price Index.

The model was estimated using a method for correcting for autocorrelation—the maximum likelihood search procedure of the program Regression Analysis of Time Series (RATS).

The three alternative sets of projections for current-fund expenditures were produced using varying assumptions about the growth paths for disposable income and the rate of change in the inflation rate measured by the Consumer Price Index. These disposable income and inflation rate projections were also developed using the U.S. Quarterly Model of DRI/McGraw-Hill.

In the middle set of projections, disposable income per capita rises each year from 1993–94 to 2003–2004 at rates between 0.7 and 1.4 percent. In the low set of projections, disposable income per capita increases at rates between -1.3 and 1.2 percent. In the high set of projections, disposable income per capita increases at rates between 0.7 and 3.9 percent.

In the middle set of projections, the inflation rate varies between 2.9 percent and 4.0 percent. In low set of projections, it varies between 4.0 percent and 5.2 percent, and in the high set of projections, it varies between 2.5 percent and 3.7 percent for the high alternative.

The private 4-year institutions educational and general expenditure model is:

$$DPRIED4 = b_0 + b_1 DPCI + b_2 DPRFTE4 + b_3 ININCR$$

where:

DPRIED4 is the change in educational and general expenditures per student in FTE enrollment in private 4-year institutions in constant 1991–92 dollars.

The Private 2-Year Institutions Expenditure Models

Unlike the other higher education variables, econometric methods were not used for either private 2-year current-fund expenditures or private 2-year educational and general expenditures. This was due to a change in the sample universe for private 2-year institutions. The period for which the private 2-year universe is relatively consistent, from 1982–83 to 1990–91, has only nine observations. This is too short a period for econometric techniques, so another means of projecting private 2-year institution expenditures was required. Hence, exponential smoothing, which can operate with only nine observations, was used.

Both current-fund expenditures per student and educational and general expenditures per student were modeled using single exponential smoothing. To do this, the forecasting package Forecast Pro was used. For current-fund expenditures per student, a smoothing constant of 0.97 was used and for educational and general expenditures per student a smoothing constant of 1.00 was used.

Projection Accuracy

This is the third time in the past ten years that *Projections of Education Statistics* has contained projections of higher education expenditure data. The other two editions were the *Projections of Education Statistics to 2003* and *Projections of Education Statistics to 2000*. The projected values for 1990–91 that appeared in *Projections of Education Statistics to 2003* and the projected values for 1986–87 through 1990–91 which appeared in *Projections of Education Statistics to 2000* can be compared to the actual values. The projections that appeared in *Projections of Education Statistics to 2003* were developed using the same methodology as those presented here. Those that appeared in *Projections of Education Statistics to 2000* were produced using different models.

The projections for 1990–91 that appeared in *Projections of Education Statistics to 2003* were within one percent of the actual values. For total current-fund expenditures, the projected value was 0.1 percent higher than the actual value. For public 4-year institutions, the projection for current-fund expenditures was 0.6 percent higher than the actual value. For public 2-year institutions, the projection was 0.8 percent lower than the actual value. For private 4-year institutions, the projection was 0.5 percent lower than the actual value.

The projections that appeared in *Projections of Education Statistics to 2000* were not as close to the actual values as those that appeared in the more recent edition.

For all institutions in total, the projection for current-fund expenditures that appeared in *Projections of Education Statistics to 2000* was 3.6 percent lower than the actual

value for 1986–87, 3.5 percent lower than the actual value for 1987–88, 2.5 percent lower than the actual value for 1988–89, 5.6 percent lower than the actual value for 1989–90, and 6.5 percent lower than the actual value for 1990–91.

For public 4-year institutions, the projection for current-fund expenditures was 3.6 percent lower than the actual value for 1986–87, 2.2 percent lower than the actual value for 1987–88, 1.1 percent lower than the actual value for 1988–89, 4.4 percent lower than the actual value for 1989–90, and 5.2 percent lower than the actual value for 1990–91.

For public 2-year institutions, the projection for current-fund expenditures was 2.1 percent higher than the actual value for 1986–87, 5.2 percent higher than the actual value for 1987–88, 4.3 percent higher than the actual value for 1988–89, 0.8 percent higher than the actual value for 1989–90, and 0.4 percent lower than the actual value for 1990–91.

For private 4-year institutions, the projection for current-fund expenditures was 5.0 percent lower than the actual value for 1986–87, 7.7 percent lower than the actual value for 1987–88, 6.6 percent lower than the actual value for 1988–89, 9.4 percent lower than the actual value for 1989–90, and 10.4 percent lower than the actual value for 1990–91.

Sources of Data

The current-fund expenditure data and the educational and general expenditure data are from the "Financial Statistics of Institutions of Higher Education" and the Integrated Postsecondary Education Data System (IPEDS), "Finance" surveys of the National Center for Education Statistics (NCES). One manipulation of the educational and general expenditures numbers was required. From 1968–69 to 1973–74, student-aid expenditures were a separate component of current-fund expenditures. From 1974–75 on, scholarships and fellowships have been a component of educational and general expenditures. Hence, for the period 1968–69 to 1973–74, student aid was added to the published numbers for educational and general expenditures.

The full-time-equivalent (FTE) enrollment data are from the "Fall Enrollment in Colleges and Universities" surveys of NCES. The FTE enrollment figures for 1968–69, 1969–70, and 1970–71 were estimated using part-time and full-time enrollment data. Full-time equivalent enrollment was derived by adding one-third of the part-time students to the number of full-time students.

The projected values for disposable income and the revenues of state and local governments per capita were developed using DRI/McGraw-Hill's U.S. Quarterly Model. Projected values of the Bureau of Labor Statistic's Consumer Price Index for all urban consumers, which were used for adjusting the higher education finance data, and the implicit price deflator for personal consumption expenditures, which was used for adjusting disposable income per capita, were also developed using the U.S.

Quarterly Model. DRI/McGraw-Hill supplied the historic values for these variables.

Both the historic and projected values for the population were supplied by the U.S. Bureau of the Census.

The Higher Education Price Index was considered as a replacement for the Consumer Price Index for placing the higher education expenditures in constant dollars. As projections of the price index are required for placing the forecasts into current dollars, and as there are no projections of the Higher Education Price Index, the Consumer Price Index was used.

The values of all of the variables from DRI were placed in academic-year terms. The data were available in quarterly format so the academic-year numbers were calculated by taking the average of the last 2 quarters of 1 year with the first 2 of the next year.

Table A6.1.—Equations for current-fund expenditures per student in full-time equivalent enrollment and educational and general expenditures per student in full-time equivalent enrollment in public 4-year institutions, public 2-year institutions, and private 4-year institutions

Dependent variable		Equation	$\bar{R}^2$	Durbin-Watson statistic	Estimation technique[*]	Rho
Current-fund expenditures per student in public 4-year institutions	DPUTCUR4	$=$ 412 + 2.18DSTREV1 - 0.003DPUFTE4 (4.26) (1.83) (-5.00) - 331DUMMY (-3.02)	0.670	1.82	OLS	
Current-fund expenditures per student in public 2-year institutions	DPUTCUR2	$=$ 24.4 + 3.40DSTREV1 - 0.001DPUFTE2 (0.46) (4.06) (-3.60)	0.674	2.27	OLS	
Current-fund expenditures per student in private 4-year institutions	DPRTCUR4	$=$ 697 + 0.42DPCI - 0.012DPRFTE4 (3.51) (1.83) (-5.95) - 646.3ININCR (-5.13)	0.770	2.01	AR1	0.74 (4.7)
Educational and general expenditures per student in public 4-year institutions	DPUED4	$=$ 374 + 1.64DSTREV1 - 0.003DPUFTE4 (3.91) (1.40) (-5.52) - 341DUMMY (-3.14)	0.683	1.69	OLS	
Educational and general expenditures per student in public 2-year institutions	DPUED2	$=$ 10.64 + 3.53DSTREV1 - 0.0008DPUFTE2 (0.18) (3.93) (-2.66)	0.605	2.20	OLS	
Educational and general expenditures per student in private 4-year institutions	DPRIED4	$=$ 257.8 + 0.50DPCI - 0.006DPRFTE4 (1.31) (1.47) (-1.84) - 573.8ININCR (-3.0)	0.455	2.28	AR1	0.57 (2.77)

[*]OLS = Ordinary Least Squares. AR1 is an estimation procedure for correcting the problem of first-order autocorrelation. Specifically, the maximum likelihood procedure of the statistical program RATS was used to estimate rho. For a general discussion of the problem of autocorrelation, and the methods to correct it, see Johnston (1972), chapter 8. For a discussion of the method used to forecast in the presence of autocorrelation, see G. Judge, W. Hill, R. Griffiths, H. Lutkepohl, and T. Lee, *The Theory and Practice of Econometrics*, New York: John Wiley and Sons, 1985, pages 315–318.

NOTES: The sample size in for each case is 23. Numbers in parentheses are t-statistics. $\bar{R}^2$ = Coefficient of determination, adjusted for degrees of freedom. For an explanation of the Durbin-Watson statistic, see J. Johnston, *Econometric Methods*, New York: McGraw-Hill, 1972, pages 251–252. (This table was prepared June 1993.)

Appendix B

Supplementary Tables

Table B1.—Annual number of births (U.S. Census Projections, Middle Series): 50 States and D.C., 1946 to 2004

(In thousands)

Calendar Year	Number of Births
1946	3,426
1947	3,834
1948	3,655
1949	3,667
1950	3,645
1951	3,845
1952	3,933
1953	3,989
1954	4,102
1955	4,128
1956	4,244
1957	4,332
1958	4,279
1959	4,313
1960	4,307
1961	4,317
1962	4,213
1963	4,142
1964	4,070
1965	3,801
1966	3,642
1967	3,555
1968	3,535
1969	3,626
1970	3,739
1971	3,556
1972	3,258
1973	3,137
1974	3,160
1975	3,144
1976	3,168
1977	3,327
1978	3,333
1979	3,494
1980	3,612
1981	3,629
1982	3,681
1983	3,639
1984	3,669
1985	3,761

Table B1.—Annual number of births (U.S. Census Projections, Middle Series):—Continued 50 States and D.C., 1946 to 2004

(In thousands)

Calendar Year	Number of Births
1986	3,757
1987	3,809
1988	3,910
1989	4,041
1990	4,179
1991	4,094
1992	4,038
Projected	
1993	4,086
1994	4,055
1995	4,024
1996	3,995
1997	3,971
1998	3,953
1999	3,941
2000	3,934
2001	3,933
2002	3,937
2003	3,948
2004	3,965

SOURCE: U.S. Department of Commerce, Bureau of the Census, "U.S. Population Estimates, by Age, Sex, Race, and Hispanic Origin: 1980 to 1991," *Current Population Reports*, Series P-25, No. 1095, February 1993 and unpublished tabulations. (This table was prepared May 1993.)

Table B2.—Preprimary school-age populations (U.S. Census projections, Middle Series): 50 States and D.C., 1979 to 2004

(In thousands)

Year (July 1)	3 years old	4 years old	5 years old	3-5 years old
1979	3,077	3,175	3,092	9,344
1980	3,238	3,128	3,180	9,546
1981	3,261	3,274	3,129	9,664
1982	3,361	3,297	3,274	9,932
1983	3,479	3,398	3,296	10,173
1984	3,527	3,518	3,397	10,442
1985	3,566	3,568	3,518	10,652
1986	3,578	3,609	3,568	10,755
1987	3,509	3,623	3,610	10,742
1988	3,620	3,556	3,627	10,803
1989	3,646	3,669	3,559	11,036
1990	3,659	3,698	3,679	11,036
1991	3,718	3,717	3,702	11,137
1992	3,813	3,778	3,722	11,313
Projected				
1993	3,894	3,829	3,781	11,504
1994	4,084	3,958	3,836	11,878
1995	4,114	4,150	3,963	12,227
1996	4,007	4,181	4,156	12,344
1997	3,976	4,070	4,185	12,231
1998	3,946	4,040	4,075	12,061
1999	3,917	4,010	4,046	11,974
2000	3,891	3,980	4,016	11,887
2001	3,871	3,954	3,986	11,811
2002	3,856	3,934	3,961	11,751
2003	3,848	3,920	3,941	11,709
2004	3,844	3,912	3,927	11,683

SOURCE: U.S. Department of Commerce, Bureau of the Census, "U.S. Population Estimates, by Age, Sex, Race, and Hispanic Origin: 1980 to 1991," *Current Population Reports*, Series P-25, No. 1095, February 1993 and unpublished tabulations. (This table was prepared May 1993.)

Table B3.—School-age populations (U.S. Census projections, Middle Series), ages 5, 6, 5–13, and 14–17 years: 50 States and D.C., 1979 to 2004

(In thousands)

Year (July 1)	5 years old	6 years old	5–13 years old	14–17 years old
1979	3,092	3,164	31,431	16,611
1980	3,180	3,111	31,091	16,144
1981	3,129	3,186	30,711	15,610
1982	3,274	3,133	30,528	15,057
1983	3,296	3,276	30,279	14,741
1984	3,397	3,297	30,061	14,726
1985	3,518	3,398	29,892	14,888
1986	3,568	3,518	30,078	14,824
1987	3,610	3,568	30,503	14,502
1988	3,627	3,611	31,029	14,023
1989	3,559	3,625	31,413	13,536
1990	3,679	3,561	31,999	13,312
1991	3,702	3,681	32,500	13,424
1992	3,722	3,705	33,006	13,649
			Projected	
1993	3,781	3,747	33,424	13,802
1994	3,836	3,785	33,870	14,088
1995	3,963	3,838	34,263	14,591
1996	4,156	3,966	34,868	14,933
1997	4,185	4,156	35,387	15,333
1998	4,075	4,186	35,808	15,600
1999	4,046	4,077	36,253	15,639
2000	4,016	4,047	36,547	15,811
2001	3,986	4,017	36,805	15,900
2002	3,961	3,987	36,991	16,034
2003	3,941	3,962	37,107	16,277
2004	3,927	3,943	37,080	16,522

SOURCE: U.S. Department of Commerce, Bureau of the Census, "U.S. Population Estimates, by Age, Sex, Race, and Hispanic Origin: 1980 to 1991," *Current Population Reports*, Series P-25, No. 1095, February 1993 and unpublished tabulations. (This table was prepared May 1993.)

Table B4.—College-age populations (U.S. Census projections, Middle Series), ages 18, 18–24, 25–29, 30–34, and 35–44 years: 50 States and D.C., 1979 to 2004

(In thousands)

Year (July 1)	18 years old	18–24 years old	25–29 years old	30–34 years old	35–44 years old
1979	4,316	30,048	19,178	17,025	25,176
1980	4,245	30,360	19,792	17,810	25,868
1981	4,186	30,505	20,275	18,798	26,454
1982	4,136	30,433	20,816	18,781	28,095
1983	3,978	30,174	21,259	19,137	29,336
1984	3,774	29,706	21,584	19,576	30,575
1985	3,686	29,151	21,804	20,102	31,767
1986	3,623	28,467	22,018	20,552	33,081
1987	3,703	27,928	21,982	21,058	34,299
1988	3,803	27,585	21,868	21,470	35,258
1989	3,889	27,379	21,690	21,758	36,494
1990	3,603	27,038	21,356	21,990	37,845
1991	3,391	26,599	20,844	22,242	39,352
1992	3,307	26,063	20,278	22,343	39,973
Projected					
1993	3,349	26,278	20,402	22,579	40,440
1994	3,422	25,990	19,830	22,552	41,333
1995	3,385	25,609	19,382	22,446	42,219
1996	3,540	25,261	19,216	22,119	43,087
1997	3,574	24,950	19,262	21,604	43,879
1998	3,703	25,029	19,138	20,981	44,499
1999	3,883	25,524	18,852	20,399	44,946
2000	3,873	26,055	18,459	19,937	45,192
2001	3,971	26,607	18,012	19,761	45,164
2002	3,964	27,186	17,524	19,805	44,891
2003	3,918	27,563	17,431	19,684	44,336
2004	4,044	28,026	17,594	19,405	43,714

SOURCE: U.S. Department of Commerce, Bureau of the Census, "U.S. Population Estimates, by Age, Sex, Race, and Hispanic Origin: 1980 to 1991," *Current Population Reports*, Series P-25, No. 1095, February 1993 and unpublished tabulations. (This table was prepared May 1993.)

Table B5.—Average daily attendance (ADA) in public elementary and secondary schools, change in ADA, the population, and ADA as a proportion of the population: 50 States and D.C., 1978–79 to 2003–2004

Year ending	ADA [1] (in thousands)	Change in ADA	Population (in millions)	ADA as a proportion of the the population
1979	39,076	-1,003,590	223.8	0.175
1980	38,289	-787,089	226.4	0.169
1981	37,704	-585,167	228.8	0.165
1982	37,095	-609,092	231.1	0.161
1983	36,636	-458,784	233.2	0.157
1984	36,363	-272,890	235.3	0.155
1985	36,404	41,283	237.4	0.153
1986	36,523	118,842	239.6	0.152
1987	36,864	340,764	241.7	0.153
1988	37,051	186,840	243.9	0.152
1989	37,268	217,365	246.2	0.151
1990	37,799	531,224	248.6	0.152
1991	38,427	627,247	251.3	0.153
1992 [2]	38,972	545,677	254.1	0.153
1993 [3]	39,594	621,376	256.9	0.154
Projected				
1994	40,321	727,476	259.7	0.155
1995	41,063	742,322	262.5	0.156
1996	41,801	737,682	265.1	0.158
1997	42,672	871,300	267.8	0.159
1998	43,458	785,933	270.4	0.161
1999	44,010	552,102	272.9	0.161
2000	44,472	461,168	275.4	0.161
2001	44,859	387,863	277.8	0.161
2002	45,193	334,045	280.3	0.161
2003	45,480	286,722	282.7	0.161
2004	45,727	246,822	285.1	0.160

[1] Projections of average daily attendance were made by multiplying the forecasts for enrollment reported earlier in this publication by the average value of the ratio average daily attendance to the enrollment from 1982 to 1991, approximately 0.93 percent.

[2] Average daily attendance is estimated on the basis of past data.

[3] Projected.

SOURCE: U.S. Department of Commerce, Bureau of the Census, "U.S. Population Estimates, by Age, Sex, Race, and Hispanic Origin: 1980 to 1991," Series P-25, No. 1095, February 1993 and unpublished tabulations; U.S. Department of Education, National Center for Education Statistics, *Statistics of State School Systems*; Common Core of Data survey; and the Early Estimates survey; DRI/McGraw–Hill, 'U.S. Quarterly Model.' (This table was prepared June 1993.)

**Table B6.—Disposable income per capita (in constant 1991–92 dollars), [1] with alternative projections:
50 states and D.C., 1978–79 to 2003–2004**

Year ending	Disposable income per capita		
1979	$14,612	—	—
1980	14,643	—	—
1981	14,725	—	—
1982	14,828	—	—
1983	14,860	—	—
1984	15,493	—	—
1985	16,086	—	—
1986	16,337	—	—
1987	16,478	—	—
1988	16,725	—	—
1989	17,050	—	—
1990	17,129	—	—
1991	16,995	—	—
1992	17,008	—	—
1993 [2]	17,185	—	—
	Middle alternative projections	**Low alternative projections**	**High alternative projections**
1994	17,385	$16,956	$17,851
1995	17,629	17,124	18,190
1996	17,863	17,328	18,459
1997	18,003	17,454	18,627
1998	18,123	17,563	18,767
1999	18,246	17,663	18,923
2000	18,395	17,806	19,090
2001	18,560	17,986	19,257
2002	18,717	18,160	19,416
2003	18,850	18,290	19,578
2004	18,994	18,417	19,759

[1] Based on the price deflator for personal consumption expenditures, Bureau of Labor Statistics, U.S. Department of Labor.

[2] Projected.

SOURCE: DRI/McGraw-Hill, "U.S. Quarterly Model." (This table was prepared June 1993.)

Table B7.—Education revenue receipts from state source per capita (in constant 1991–92 dollars),[1] with alternative projections: 50 states and D.C. 1978–79 to 2003–2004

Year ending	Education revenue receipts from state sources per capita		
1979	$362	—	—
1980	357	—	—
1981	350	—	—
1982	333	—	—
1983	340	—	—
1984	348	—	—
1985	370	—	—
1986	390	—	—
1987	405	—	—
1988	411	—	—
1989	425	—	—
1990	430	—	—
1991	433	—	—
1992[2]	435	—	—
1993[2]	434	—	—
	Middle alternative projections	**Low alternative projections**	**High alternative projections**
1994	438	$444	$442
1995	450	448	464
1996	470	458	489
1997	485	466	504
1998	492	473	513
1999	495	474	518
2000	499	476	522
2001	503	476	527
2002	508	480	532
2003	513	483	537
2004	517	486	542

[1] Based on the Consumer Price Index for all urban consumers, Bureau of Labor Statistics, U.S. Department of Labor.

[2] Projected.

SOURCE: U.S. Department of Education, National Center for Education Statistics, *Statistics of State School Systems*; Common Core of Data survey; and Early Estimates survey; and National Education Association, annual *Estimates of State School Statistics*. (Latest edition 1992–93. Copyright 1993 by the National Education Association. All rights reserved.) (This table was prepared June 1993.)

Table B8.—Consumer Price Index (base year = 1991–92), with alternative projections:
50 States and D.C., 1978–79 to 2003–2004

Year ending	Consumer Price Index		
1979	0.495	—	—
1980	0.561	—	—
1981	0.626	—	—
1982	0.681	—	—
1983	0.710	—	—
1984	0.736	—	—
1985	0.765	—	—
1986	0.787	—	—
1987	0.805	—	—
1988	0.838	—	—
1989	0.877	—	—
1990	0.918	—	—
1991	0.969	—	—
1992	1.000	—	—
1993 *	1.030	—	—
	Middle alternative projections	**Low alternative projections**	**High alternative projections**
1994	1.060	1.072	1.055
1995	1.094	1.123	1.082
1996	1.131	1.180	1.110
1997	1.168	1.238	1.140
1998	1.209	1.300	1.175
1999	1.254	1.365	1.214
2000	1.301	1.435	1.255
2001	1.352	1.509	1.298
2002	1.404	1.587	1.344
2003	1.460	1.668	1.393
2004	1.518	1.753	1.444

* Projected.

SOURCE: DRI/McGraw-Hill "U.S. Quarterly Model." (This table was prepared June 1993.)

Table B9.—Rate of change for the inflation rate based on the Consumer Price Index, with alternative projections: 50 States and D.C., 1978–79 to 2003–2004

Year ending	Rate of change for the inflation rate		
1979	0.394	—	—
1980	0.412	—	—
1981	−0.122	—	—
1982	−0.251	—	—
1983	−0.516	—	—
1984	−0.119	—	—
1985	0.057	—	—
1986	−0.260	—	—
1987	−0.228	—	—
1988	0.839	—	—
1989	0.122	—	—
1990	0.024	—	—
1991	0.162	—	—
1992	−0.420	—	—
1993 *	−0.071	—	—
	Middle alternative projections	**Low alternative projections**	**High alternative projections**
1994	−0.006	0.281	−0.135
1995	0.100	0.217	0.024
1996	0.024	0.055	−0.013
1997	−0.002	−0.035	0.063
1998	0.062	0.009	0.131
1999	0.046	0.020	0.071
2000	0.022	0.009	0.027
2001	0.030	0.013	0.034
2002	0.007	−0.004	0.012
2003	0.011	−0.004	0.020
2004	0.013	0.000	0.019

* Projected.

SOURCE: DRI/McGraw–Hill ''U.S. Quarterly Model.'' (This table was prepared June 1993.)

Table B10.—Personal tax and nontax payments to state and local governments, per capita (in constant 1991–92 dollars), [1] with alternative projections: 50 States and D.C. 1978–79 to 2003–2004

Year ending	Personal tax and nontax payments per capita		
1979	$432	—	—
1980	421	—	—
1981	416	—	—
1982	418	—	—
1983	432	—	—
1984	476	—	—
1985	499	—	—
1986	515	—	—
1987	557	—	—
1988	554	—	—
1989	577	—	—
1990	592	—	—
1991	583	—	—
1992	590	—	—
1993 [2]	594	—	—
	Middle alternative projections	**Low alternative projections**	**High alternative projections**
1994	626	$609	$646
1995	659	631	691
1996	685	657	719
1997	704	675	741
1998	716	687	756
1999	725	697	768
2000	737	711	780
2001	750	727	793
2002	763	743	806
2003	775	757	820
2004	788	772	834

[1] Based on the Consumer Price Index for all urban consumers, Bureau of Labor Statistics, U.S. Department of Labor.

[2] Projected.

SOURCE: DRI/McGraw–Hill ''U.S. Quarterly Model.'' (This table was prepared June 1993.)

Table B11.—Indirect business taxes and nontax accruals, excluding property taxes, for state and local governments, per capita (in constant 1991–92 dollars),[1] with alternative projections: 50 States and D.C., 1978–79 to 2003–2004

Year ending	Indirect business taxes and nontax accruals per capita		
1979	$809	—	—
1980	777	—	—
1981	765	—	—
1982	750	—	—
1983	766	—	—
1984	832	—	—
1985	871	—	—
1986	913	—	—
1987	926	—	—
1988	938	—	—
1989	938	—	—
1990	946	—	—
1991	927	—	—
1992	930	—	—
1993[2]	941	—	—
	Middle alternative projections	**Low alternative projections**	**High alternative projections**
1994	953	$930	$978
1995	982	954	1,014
1996	1,002	973	1,038
1997	1,007	977	1,044
1998	1,006	972	1,044
1999	1,007	971	1,046
2000	1,011	974	1,050
2001	1,016	979	1,055
2002	1,021	986	1,060
2003	1,026	990	1,065
2004	1,033	996	1,074

[1] Based on the Consumer Price Index for all urban consumers, Bureau of Labor Statistics, U.S. Department of Labor.

[2] Projected.

SOURCE: DRI/McGraw-Hill, "U.S. Quarterly Model." (This table was prepared June 1993.)

**Table B12.— Property taxes for state and local governments per capita (constant 1991–92 dollars), [1]
with alternative projections: 50 States and D.C., 1978–79 to 2003–2004**

Year ending	Property taxes per capita		
1979	$1,241	—	—
1980	1,198	—	—
1981	1,181	—	—
1982	1,168	—	—
1983	1,199	—	—
1984	1,308	—	—
1985	1,370	—	—
1986	1,428	—	—
1987	1,483	—	—
1988	1,492	—	—
1989	1,515	—	—
1990	1,539	—	—
1991	1,510	—	—
1992	1,520	—	—
1993 [2]	1,536	—	—
	Middle alternative projections	**Low alternative projections**	**High alternative projections**
1994	1,579	$1,538	$1,624
1995	1,641	1,586	1,706
1996	1,687	1,630	1,756
1997	1,711	1,652	1,785
1998	1,722	1,660	1,800
1999	1,733	1,668	1,814
2000	1,747	1,685	1,829
2001	1,765	1,706	1,847
2002	1,784	1,729	1,866
2003	1,801	1,747	1,885
2004	1,821	1,768	1,908

[1] Based on the Consumer Price Index for all urban consumers, Bureau of Labor Statistics, U.S. Department of Labor.

[2] Projected.

SOURCE: DRI/McGraw–Hill "U.S. Quarterly Model." (This table was prepared June 1993.)

Appendix C

Data Sources

Sources and Comparability of Data

The information in this report was obtained from many sources, including Federal and state agencies, private research organizations, and professional associations. The data were collected by many methods, including surveys of a universe (such as all colleges) or of a sample, and compilations of administrative records. Care should be used when comparing data from different sources. Differences in procedures, such as timing, phrasing of questions, and interviewer training mean that the results from the different sources are not strictly comparable. More extensive documentation of one survey's procedures than of another's does not imply more problems with the data, only that more information is available.

Accuracy of Data

The accuracy of any statistic is determined by the joint effects of "sampling" and "nonsampling" errors. Estimates based on a sample will differ from the figures that would have been obtained if a complete census had been taken using the same survey instruments, instructions, and procedures. Besides sampling errors, both surveys, universe and sample, are subject to errors of design, reporting, processing, and errors due to nonresponse. To the extent possible, these nonsampling errors are kept to a minimum by methods built into the survey procedures. In general, however, the effects of nonsampling errors are more difficult to gauge than those produced by sampling variability.

Sampling Errors

The standard error is the primary measure of sampling variability. It provides a specific range—with a stated confidence—within which a given estimate would lie if a complete census had been conducted. The chances that a complete census would differ from the sample by less than the standard error are about 68 out of 100. The chances that the difference would be less than 1.65 times the standard error are about 90 out of 100. The chances that the difference would be less than 1.96 times the standard error are about 95 out of 100. The chances that it would be less than 2.58 times as large are about 99 out of 100.

The standard error can help assess how valid a comparison between two estimates might be. The standard error of a difference between two sample estimates that are uncorrelated is approximately equal to the square root of the sum of the squared standard errors of the estimates. The standard error (se) of the difference between sample estimate "a" and sample estimate "b" is:

$$se_{a-b} = (se_a^2 + se_b^2)^{1/2}$$

Note that most of the standard errors in subsequent sections and in the original documents are approximations. That is, to derive estimates of standard errors that would be applicable to a wide variety of items and could be prepared at a moderate cost, a number of approximations were required. As a result, most of the standard errors presented provide a general order of magnitude rather than the exact standard error for any specific item.

Nonsampling Errors

Both universe and sample surveys are subject to nonsampling errors. Nonsampling errors are of two kinds—random and nonrandom. Random nonsampling errors may arise when respondents or interviewers interpret questions differently, when respondents must estimate values, or when coders, keyers, and other processors handle answers differently. Nonrandom nonsampling errors result from total nonresponse (no usable data obtained for a sampled unit), partial or item nonresponse (only a portion of a response may be usable), inability or unwillingness on the part of respondents to provide information, difficulty interpreting questions, mistakes in recording or keying data, errors of collection or processing, and overcoverage or undercoverage of the target universe. Random nonresponse errors usually, but not always, result in an understatement of sampling errors and thus an overstatement of the precision of survey estimates. Because estimating the magnitude of nonsampling errors would require special experiments or access to independent data, these magnitudes are seldom available.

To compensate for suspected nonrandom errors, adjustments of the sample estimates are often made. For example, adjustments are frequently made for nonresponse, both total and partial. An adjustment made for either type of nonresponse is often referred to as an imputation, that is, substitution of the "average" questionnaire response for the nonresponse. Imputations are usually made separately within various groups of sample members that have similar survey characteristics. Imputation for item nonresponse is usually made by substituting for a missing item the response to that item of a respondent having characteristics that are similar to those of the nonrespondent.

Although the magnitude of nonsampling errors in the data used in this *Projections of Education Statistics* is frequently unknown, idiosyncrasies that have been identified are noted on the appropriate tables.

Federal Agency Sources

National Center for Education Statistics (NCES)

Common Core of Data

NCES uses the Common Core of Data (CCD) survey to acquire and maintain statistical data on the 50 states, the District of Columbia, and the outlying areas from the universe of state-level education agencies. Information about staff and students is collected annually at the school, LEA (local education agency or school district), and state levels. Information about revenues and expenditures is also collected at the state level.

Data are collected for a particular school year (July 1 through June 30) via survey instruments sent to the states by October 15 of the subsequent school year. States have 2 years in which to modify the data originally submitted.

Since the CCD is a universe survey, the CCD information presented in this edition of *Projections of Education Statistics* is not subject to sampling errors. However, nonsampling errors could come from two sources—nonreturn and inaccurate reporting. Almost all of the states submit the six CCD survey instruments each year, but submissions are sometimes incomplete or too late for publication.

Understandably, when 57 education agencies compile and submit data for over 85,000 public schools and approximately 15,000 local school districts, misreporting can occur. Typically, this results from varying interpretation of NCES definitions and differing recordkeeping systems. NCES attempts to minimize these errors by working closely with the Council of Chief State School Officers (CCSSO) and its Committee on Evaluation and Information Systems (CEIS).

The state education agencies report data to NCES from data collected and edited in their regular reporting cycles. NCES encourages the agencies to incorporate into their own survey systems the NCES items they do not already collect so that those items will also be available for the subsequent CCD survey. Over time, this has meant fewer missing data cells in each state's response, reducing the need to impute data.

NCES subjects data from the education agencies to a comprehensive edit. Where data are determined to be inconsistent, missing, or out of range, NCES contacts the education agencies for verification. NCES-prepared state summary forms are returned to the state education agencies for verification. States are also given an opportunity to revise their state-level aggregates from the previous survey cycle.

Questions concerning the Common Core of Data can be directed to:

John Sietsema
Elementary/Secondary Education Statistics Division
National Center for Education Statistics
555 New Jersey Avenue NW
Washington, DC 20208

Early Estimates System. The early estimates system is designed to allow NCES to report selected key statistics early in the school year. The information is collected through contact with public school state education agencies and a sample of private schools. Details of the two systems follow.

The source of universe statistical information about public elementary and secondary education is the Common Core of Data (CCD)—data collected annually by NCES from state education agencies. These data are reported to NCES in March, undergo NCES and state editing, and become available for publication in September—full year after the beginning of the school year. High school graduate and fiscal data are reported a year later than student and teacher data. In contrast, the estimates included in this report are made in December of the school year to which they apply.

Forty-two states, the District of Columbia, and three outlying areas participated in the public school early estimates survey in 1992. The estimates reported here were provided by state education agencies and represent the best information on public elementary and secondary schools available to states at this early stage of the school year. They are, however, subject to revision. The estimates for the remaining eight states and three outlying areas were imputed by NCES.

The source of universe statistical information on private schools in the United States is the Private School Survey. The private school universe consists of a diverse population of schools, including those with a religious orientation (for example, Catholic, Lutheran, and Jewish) as well as nonsectarian schools that include programs ranging from regular to special emphasis and special education. The private school early estimates is one reporting component of the universe collection. The basic statistical information included in this data system is collected from all private schools in the NCES universe, and the early estimates are based on a subsample of that universe.

NCES is continuing to examine and evaluate various methodologies to obtain better estimates and improve the data collection system for public and private elementary and secondary education. In the fall of 1992, the private school early estimates data were collected using Computer Assisted Telephone Interviewing, or CATI. This technique helps reduce errors in the data due to reporting or keying error, and provides an on-line editing system that enables interviewers to verify inconsistent responses.

Questions concerning the Early Estimates System can be directed to:

Frank Johnson
Elementary/Secondary Education Statistics Division
National Center for Education Statistics
555 New Jersey Avenue NW
Washington, DC 20208

Private School Early Estimates System: 1988–89. The private school early estimates are the first reporting component of the Private School Universe data collection system. In subsequent years, the statistical information will be collected from all private schools in the NCES universe, and the early estimates will be based on a subsample of that universe.

Early in October 1988, questionnaires were mailed to a national probability sample of 1,167 private elementary and secondary schools from a universe of approximately 30,000 private schools. Telephone followup of nonrespondents was initiated in late October, and data collection was completed in late November. The overall response rate was 94 percent: 978 of the 1,035 eligible schools. Some 132 of the original 1,167 schools in the sample were determined to be out of scope. While this survey was not designed specifically to yield an estimate of the number of private schools, the number of out-of-scope schools identified in this survey resulted in a weighted estimate of approximately 26,300 private schools.

The sampling frame used for the survey was composed of two nonoverlapping frames: the NCES list frame of approximately 24,000 eligible schools, and an area frame developed by the Census Bureau for 75 Primary Sampling Units (PSUs). The area frame yielded a sample size of 523 schools for the Schools and Staffing Survey (SASS). The private school early estimates area sample was drawn from the SASS area sample. The sample from the area frame was sorted by level of school, by religious orientation class within school level, then by PSU within religious orientation class, and finally by student membership within PSU.

The sample from the list frame was stratified by level of school (elementary, secondary, combined, and other) and religious orientation (Catholic, other religious, and nonsectarian), and within strata, schools were further sorted by Office of Education regions, and by student membership size within region. Each school in the sorted frame was assigned a sampling measure of size equal to the square root of student membership, and samples were selected with probabilities proportionate to size from each orientation/level stratum.

The survey data were weighted to reflect the sampling rates (probability of selection) and were adjusted for nonresponse. Estimates of standard errors were computed using a variance estimation procedure for complex sample survey data known as jackknife. The standard errors for private school early estimates for school years 1987–88 and 1988–89 are shown in the table below.

Students (1988–89)	Teachers (1988–89)	Graduates (1987–88)
96,779.9	7,624.7	9,605.4

Nonsampling errors may include such things as differences in the respondents' interpretation of the meaning to the questions, differences related to the particular time the survey was conducted, or errors in data preparation. During the design of the survey and survey pretest, an effort was made to check for consistency of interpretation of questions and to eliminate ambiguous items. The questionnaire was pretested with respondents like those who completed the survey, and the questionnaire and instructions were extensively reviewed by NCES and representatives of private school associations attending the NCES private school data users meeting. Manual and machine editing of the questionnaires was conducted to check the data for accuracy and consistency. Extensive telephone followup was conducted for missing or inconsistent items; data were keyed with 100-percent verification.

Undercoverage in the list and area frames is another possible source of nonsampling error. The area frame was used to complement the list frame through the identification of schools missing from the list frame. As the Early Estimates System and the Private School Universe data collection system develop, efforts will be directed toward updating the universe list and identifying and minimizing sources of undercoverage in both the list and area frames.

Questions concerning the Private School Early Estimates System can be directed to:

Marilyn M. McMillen
Elementary/Secondary Education Statistics Division
National Center for Education Statistics
555 New Jersey Avenue NW
Washington, DC 20208

Private School Early Estimates System: 1989–90. This is the second in a series of early estimates for private elementary and secondary education. These early estimates are key statistics reported early in the school year and include the numbers of teachers, students, and high school graduates for private elementary and secondary schools. In subsequent years, the statistical information will be collected from all private schools in the NCES universe, and the early estimates will be based on a subsample of that universe.

Early in October 1989, questionnaires were mailed to a national probability sample of 1,169 private elementary and secondary schools from a universe of approximately 27,000 private schools. Telephone followup of nonrespondents was initiated in late October, and data collection was completed in late November. The overall response rate was 95 percent: 986 of the 1,042 eligible schools. Some 127 of the original 1,167 schools in the sample were determined to be out of scope. While this survey was not designed specifically to yield an estimate of the number of private schools, the number of out-of-scope schools identified in this survey resulted in a weighted estimate of approximately 26,645 private schools.

The sampling frame used for the survey was composed of two nonoverlapping frames: the NCES list frame of approximately 24,000 eligible schools, and an area frame developed by the Census Bureau for 75 Primary Sampling Units (PSUs). The area frame yielded a sample size of 523 schools for the Schools and Staffing Survey (SASS). The private school early estimates area sample was drawn from the SASS area sample. The sample from the area frame was sorted by level of school, by religious orientation class within school level, then by PSU within religious orientation class, and finally by student membership within PSU.

The sample from the list frame was stratified by level of school (elementary, secondary, combined, and other) and religious orientation (Catholic, other religious, and nonsectarian), and within strata, schools were further sorted by Census regions, and by student membership size within region. Each school in the sorted frame was assigned a sampling measure of size equal to the square root of student membership. The sample design for the list frame was similar, differing in two ways from the design for the area frame. First, stratification by level of school yielded four, rather than three categories: elementary, secondary, combined, and other. Second, the measure of size was simply the square root of student membership.

The survey data were weighted to reflect the sampling rates (probability of selection) and were adjusted for nonresponse. Estimates of standard errors were computed using a variance estimation procedure for complex sample survey data known as balanced repeated replication. The standard errors for private school early estimates for school years 1988–89 and 1989–90 are shown in the table below.

Students (1989–90)	Teachers (1989–90)	Graduates (1988–89)
117,830.9	8,636.1	13,305.6

Nonsampling errors may include such things as differences in the respondents' interpretations of the meaning to the questions, differences related to the particular time the survey was conducted, or errors in data preparation. The survey instrument used in the 1989–90 Early Estimates data collection was developed based on the experiences of the 1988–89 Early Estimates data collection. The form was modified as needed to accommodate one data collection instrument for both the Early Estimates and Universe components of the Private School data collection system. The content of the survey was developed in consultation with representatives of private school associations attending NCES private school data users meetings. The questionnaire and instructions were extensively reviewed by NCES staff. Manual and machine editing of the questionnaires was conducted to check the data for accuracy and consistency. Data were keyed with 100-percent verification.

Undercoverage in the list and area frames is another possible source of nonsampling error. The area frame was used to complement the list frame through the identification of schools missing from the list frame. As the Early Estimates System and the Private School Universe data collection system develop, both the list and area frames will be updated periodically. For the 1989–90 Early Estimates data collection, 1,000 private schools were added to the universe list.

Questions concerning the Private School Early Estimates System can be directed to:

Marilyn M. McMillen
Elementary/Secondary Education Statistics Division
National Center for Education Statistics
555 New Jersey Avenue NW
Washington, DC 20208

Private School Early Estimates System: 1990–91. Early in September 1990, questionnaires were mailed to a national probability sample of 1,167 private elementary and secondary schools. Telephone collection of the data began in early October and was completed in mid-October. The overall response rate was 98 percent: 1,098 of the 1,119 eligible schools. Some 48 of the original 1,167 schools in the sample were determined to be out of scope. After adjusting for out-of-scope schools, the weighted estimate of private schools is 24,553.

The sampling frame used for the survey was composed of two nonoverlapping frames: the NCES Private School Survey list of approximately 20,584 eligible schools (the universe list), and an area frame developed by the Census Bureau, consisting of 923 schools identified in 123 sampled geographic areas (Primary Sampling Units or PSUs). The list frame was stratified by level of school (elementary, secondary, combined, other, and unknown) and religious orientation (Catholic, other religious, and nonsectarian); within strata, schools were further sorted by Census region and by student membership size within region. Each school in the sorted frame was assigned a sampling measure of size equal to the square root of student membership.

The area frame is constructed from a sample survey designed to capture those schools not included in the universe list. The 923 schools identified in the sampled areas are weighted to a national estimate of the number of private schools not included in the universe list. This weighted number is then added to the universe count to produce an estimate of the total number of private schools in the United States. For the early estimate, the area frame was stratified by level of school (elementary, secondary, and other) and religious orientation (Catholic, other religious, and nonsectarian). Within strata, schools were further sorted by FIPS (Federal Information Processing Standards) state code, by FIPS county code within states, and by student membership within counties. Samples were selected with probabilities proportionate to size from each stratum. The measure of size used for this purpose was the square root of student membership multiplied by the inverse of the probability of selection of the PSU in which the school is located.

A new estimation procedure was used to produce the 1990 private school early estimates. This procedure used the estimates obtained from the entire universe of private schools in the Private School Survey of 1989 and adjusted these estimates for the change reflected in the 1990 early estimates data collections. The steps of this procedure were: (1) obtain Private School Survey (PSS) universe estimates for the data elements desired; (2) adjust PSS estimates for partial and total nonresponse; (3) collect 1990 early estimates data for the data elements; (4) weight the early estimate sample to reflect the sampling rates (probability of selection) and to adjust for total nonresponse separately by the sampling strata and by enrollment; (5) measure the change for these data elements between the PSS and the early estimates data collection for those schools that were in the early estimates sample and had the appropriate data for both 1989 and 1990; and (6) apply the change calculated in step 5 to the data from all of the schools in the PSS universe. Numbers in the tables and text have been rounded. Ratios have been calculated on the actual estimates rather than the rounded values. The 1990 early estimates were adjusted to account for both total and partial nonresponses.

Sample survey data, such as the private school estimates data, are subject to error due to variations in sampling. The standard error is a measure of the variability due to sampling when estimating a statistic. Estimates of standard errors were computed using a variance estimation procedure for complex sample survey data known as balanced repeated replication. The standard errors for private school early estimates for school years 1989–90 and 1990–91 are shown in the table below.

Students (1990–91)	Teachers (1990–91)	Graduates (1989–90)
96,270.9	7,341.5	15,850.2

Survey estimates are also subject to errors of reporting and errors made in the collection and processing of the data. These errors, called nonsampling errors, can sometimes bias the data. Nonsampling errors may include such things as differences in the respondents' interpretations of the meaning to the questions, differences related to the particular time the survey was conducted, or errors in data preparation. The survey instrument used in the 1990–91 private school early estimates data collection was revised as a result of the experiences of the 1989–90 private school early estimates data collection. The content of the survey was developed in consultation with representatives of private school associations attending NCES meetings for users of private school data. The questionnaire and instructions were reviewed extensively by NCES staff. Manual and machine editing of the questionnaires was conducted to check the data for accuracy and consistency. Data were keyed with 100-percent verification.

Undercoverage in the list and area frames is another possible source of nonsampling error. The area frame was used to complement the list frame through the identification of schools missing from the list frame. As the Private School Early Estimates System and the Private School Survey (the universe data collection) system develop, both the list and area frames will be updated periodically.

Questions concerning the Private School Early Estimates System can be directed to:

Sharon A. Bobbitt
Elementary/Secondary Education Statistics Division
National Center for Education Statistics
555 New Jersey Avenue NW
Washington, DC 20208

Private School Early Estimates System: 1991–92. Early in September 1991, questionnaires were mailed to a national probability sample of 1,163 private elementary and secondary schools. Telephone collection of the data began in early October and was completed in mid-October. The overall response rate was 96.5 percent: 1,064 of the 1,103 eligible schools. Some 60 of the original 1,163 schools in the sample were determined to be out of scope. After adjusting for out-of-scope schools, the weighted estimate of private schools is 24,284.

The sampling frame used for the Private School Early Estimates Survey was the 1989–1990 NCES Private School Survey (PSS). This survey collected information on the number of teachers and students in private schools, by school religious orientation and level as well as actual and projected counts of high school graduates. The PSS, and therefore the early estimates survey, uses two nonoverlapping frames: the list frame of approximately 21,515 eligible schools (the universe list), and an area frame developed by the Census Bureau, consisting of 933 schools identified in 124 sampled geographic areas (Primary Sampling Units or PSUs). The area frame is constructed from a sample survey designed to capture those schools not included in the universe list and is repeated every 2 years. The 933 schools identified in the sampled areas are weighted to a national estimate of the number of private schools not included in the universe list. This weighted number is then added to the universe count to produce an estimate of the total number of private schools in the United States.

For the early estimates, the list frame was stratified by level of school (elementary, secondary, combined, other, and unknown) and religious orientation (Catholic, other religious, and nonsectarian); within strata, schools were further sorted by Census region and by student membership size within region. Each school in the sorted frame was assigned a sampling measure of size equal to the square root of student membership.

The area frame was stratified by level of school (elementary, secondary, and other) and religious orientation (Catholic, other religious, and nonsectarian). Within strata, schools were further sorted by FIPS (Federal Information Processing Standards) state code, by FIPS county code within states, and by student membership within counties. Samples were selected with probabilities proportionate to size from each stratum. The measure of size used for this purpose was the square root of student membership multiplied by the inverse of the probability of selection of the PSU in which the school is located.

The list and area samples for the 1991 early estimates were the same as the 1990 early estimate samples.

The estimation procedure used the estimates obtained from the NCES frame of private schools (1989 Private School Survey) and adjusted those estimates for the change reflected in the 1991 early estimates data collections. The steps of this procedure were: 1) obtain Private School Survey (PSS) frame estimates for the data elements desired, adjusting for both partial and total nonresponse; 2) collect 1991 early estimates data for the data elements; 3) weight the early estimate sample to reflect the sampling rates (probability of selection), adjusting for total nonresponse separately by the sampling strata and by enrollment; 4) for each of the data elements, compute the weighted ratio of the 1991 early estimates data and the 1989 PSS data for those schools that reported for both time periods (the change from 1989 to 1991); and 5) multiply the change calculated in step 4 by the appropriate PSS estimate in step 1. Numbers in the tables and text have been rounded. Ratios have been calculated on the actual estimates rather than the rounded values. The 1990 early estimates were adjusted to account for both total and partial nonresponse.

Sample survey data, such as the private school estimates data, are subject to error due to variations in sampling. The standard error is a measure of the variability due to sampling when estimating a statistic. Estimates of standard errors were computed using a variance estimation procedure for complex sample survey data known as balanced repeated replication. The standard errors for private school early estimates for school years 1990–91 and 1991–92 are shown in the table below.

Students (1991–92)	Teachers (1991–92)	Graduates (1990–91)
80,031.0	8,320.1	13,062.3

Estimates of standard errors were computed using a variance estimation procedure for complex sample survey data known as balanced repeated replication (BRR)—a technique that splits the sample into several different half-samples. Weight adjusted estimates are computed from the half-samples. Finally, the standard error of the half-sample estimates is used as an approximation for the full-sample standard error.

Survey estimates are also subject to errors of reporting and errors made in the collection and processing of the data. These errors, called nonsampling errors, can sometimes bias the data. While general sampling theory can be used to estimate the sampling variability of an estimate, nonsampling errors are not easy to measure and usually require either an experiment to be conducted as part of the data collection procedure or use of data external to the study.

Nonsampling errors may include such things as differences in the respondents' interpretation of the meaning of the questions, differences related to the particular time the survey was conducted, or errors in data preparation. The content of the survey was developed in consultation with representatives of private school associations attending NCES meetings for users of private school data. The questionnaire and instructions were reviewed extensively by NCES staff. Manual and machine editing of the questionnaires was conducted to check the data for accuracy and consistency. Data were keyed with 100-percent verification.

Undercoverage in the list and area frames is another possible source of nonsampling error. The area frame was used to complement the list frame through the identification of schools missing from the list frame. The area frame represents approximately 20 percent of the total number of private schools. The estimates in this report do not take into account newly opened private schools. As a result, the estimates of students, teachers, and graduates may be biased and lower than the actual numbers. The 1991–92 list and area frame updates to the PSS will be reflected in next year's early estimates, and so new schools will be included in those new estimates. As the Private School Early Estimates System and the Private School Survey (the universe data collection) system develop, both the list and area frames will be updated periodically.

Questions concerning the Private School Early Estimates System can be directed to:

Sharon A. Bobbitt
Elementary/Secondary Education Statistics Division
National Center for Education Statistics
555 New Jersey Avenue NW
Washington, DC 20208

Private School Early Estimates System: 1992–93. Early in September 1992, advance questionnaires were mailed to a national probability sample of 1,167 private elementary and secondary schools. Telephone collection of the data began in early October and was completed in mid-October. The telephone data collection used Computer Assisted Telephone Interviewing (CATI) technology to collect the data and perform preliminary edits. The overall response rate was 93.31 percent: 1,045 of the 1,120 eligible schools. Some 47 of the original 1,167 schools in the sample were determined to be out-of-scope. After adjusting for out-of-scope schools, the weighted estimate of private schools is 26,011.

The sampling frame used for the Private School Early Estimates Survey was the 1991–92 NCES Private School Survey (PSS). This survey collected information on the number of teachers and students in private schools, by school religious orientation and level as well as actual and projected counts of high school graduates. The PSS, and therefore the early estimates survey, uses two nonoverlapping frames: the list frame of approximately 24,000 eligible schools (the universe list), and an area frame developed by the Census Bureau, consisting of 355 schools identified in 124 sampled geographic areas (Primary Sampling Units or PSUs). The area frame is constructed from a sample survey designed to capture those schools not included in the universe list and is repeated every 2 years. The 355 schools identified in the sampled areas are weighted to a national estimate of the number of private schools not included in the universe list. This weighted number is then added to the universe count to produce an estimate of the total number of private schools in the United States.

For the early estimates, the list frame was stratified by level of school (elementary, secondary, and combined) and religious orientation (Catholic, other religious, and nonsectarian). Within strata, schools were further sorted by Census region (Northeast, Midwest, South, and West), by urbanicity (urban, suburban, and rural) within region, and by student membership size within urbanicity. Each school in the sorted frame was assigned a sampling measure of size equal to the square root of student membership.

The area frame was stratified by level of school (elementary, secondary, and combined) and religious orientation (Catholic, other religious, and nonsectarian). Within strata, schools were further sorted by FIPS (Federal Information Processing Standards) state code, by PSU within state, and by student membership within PSU. Samples were selected with probabilities proportionate to size from each stratum. The measure of size used for this purpose was the square root of student membership multiplied by the inverse of the probability of selection of the PSU in which the school is located.

The estimation procedure is a two-step process. The first step is to produce estimates based on the NCES frame for private schools (1991–92 Private School Survey). These estimates are adjusted for total school nonresponse, as well as item nonresponse. The second step is to update the PSS based estimates, using the data collected in the 1992 Early Estimates Survey (EES). This EES update is a ratio estimate of the 1992 estimate from EES divided by the 1991 estimate based on the 1991 PSS data for the EES sample. The estimates in the tables are the PSS based estimates time the EES update. The early estimates in this report incorporate the relevant estimates from the PSS and update then using data collected in the EES.

The private school early estimates are based on a sample; these estimates may differ somewhat from figures that would have been obtained if a complete census of private schools had been taken using the same questionnaire and procedures. The standard error indicates the magnitude of the sampling error, the variability due to sampling when estimating a statistic. It indicates how much variance there is in the population of possible estimates of a parameter for a given sample size. Standard errors can be used as a measure of the precision expected from a particular sample. If all possible samples were surveyed under similar conditions, intervals of 1.96 standard errors below to 1.96 standard errors above a particular statistic would include the true population parameter being estimated in about 95 percent of the samples. This is a 95 percent confidence interval. For example, for the ratio of private school pupils to private school teachers in 1992–93, the estimate for all private schools is 14.9 and the standard error is 0.2. The 95 percent confidence interval for this statistic extends from 14.9 - (0.2 times 1.96) to 14.9 + (0.2 times 1.96) or from 14.5 to 15.3. The standard error for the 4,964,258 students in private schools is 116,612. The 95 percent confidence interval for this statistic extends from 4,735,698 to 5,192,818.

Estimates of standard errors were computed using a variance estimation procedure for complex sample survey data known as balanced repeated replication (BRR)—a technique that splits the sample into several different half-samples. Weight adjusted estimates are computed from the half-samples. Finally, the standard error of the half-sample estimates is used as an approximation for the full-sample standard error. The standard errors for private school early estimates for school years 1991–92 and 1992–93 are shown in the table below.

Students (1992–93)	Teachers (1992–93)	Graduates (1991–92)
116,612.2	8,714.8	6,071.4

Survey estimates are also subject to errors of reporting and errors made in the collection and processing of the data. These errors, called nonsampling errors, can sometimes bias the data. While general sampling theory can be used to estimate the sampling variability of an estimate, nonsampling errors are not easy to measure and usually require either an experiment conducted as part of the data collection procedure or use of data external to the study.

Nonsampling errors may include such things as differences in the respondents' interpretation of the meaning of the questions, differences related to the particular time the survey was conducted, or errors in data preparation. The content of the survey was developed in consultation with representatives of private school associations attending NCES meetings for users of private school data. The questionnaire and instructions were reviewed extensively by NCES staff. The CATI instrument provided on-line internal consistency checks (i.e., totals equal sum of parts) as well as consistency checks with 1991 data for the sample school. Interviewers resolved discrepancies with the school during the course of the interview. Machine editing of the questionnaires was conducted to check the data for accuracy and consistency. Data inputs into the CATI system were transferred directly to processing, avoiding potential keying errors.

Undercoverage in the list and area frames is another possible source of nonsampling error. The area frame was used to complement the list frame through the identification of schools missing from the list frame. The area frame represents approximately 10 percent of the total number of private schools. The 1991–92 list and area frame updates to the PSS were reflected in this year's early estimates, and so schools newly opened since 1989 are included in those new estimates.

Questions concerning the Private School Early Estimates System can be directed to:

Sharon A. Bobbitt
Frank H. Johnson
Mary A. Rochon
Elementary/Secondary Education Statistics Division
National Center for Education Statistics
555 New Jersey Avenue NW
Washington, DC 20208

Integrated Postsecondary Education Data System

The Integrated Postsecondary Education Data System (IPEDS) surveys all postsecondary institutions, including universities and colleges, as well as institutions offering technical and vocational education beyond the high school level. This survey, which began in 1986, replaces and supplements the Higher Education General Information Survey (HEGIS).

The IPEDS consists of several integrated components that obtain information on who provides postsecondary education (institutions), who participates in it and completes it (students), what programs are offered and what programs are completed, and both the human and financial resources involved in the provision of institutionally based postsecondary education. Specifically, these components include: "Institutional Characteristics," including institutional activity; fall enrollment, including age and residence; fall enrollment in occupationally specific programs; completions; finance; staff; salaries of full-time instructional faculty; and academic libraries.

The higher education portion of this survey is a census of accredited 2- and 4-year colleges, while data from the technical and vocational institutions are collected through a sample survey. Thus, some portions of the data will be subject to sampling and nonsampling errors, while some portions will be subject only to nonsampling errors.

Prior to the establishment of IPEDS in 1986, HEGIS acquired and maintained statistical data on the characteristics and operations of institutions of higher education. Implemented in 1966, HEGIS was an annual universe survey of institutions listed in the latest **NCES Education Directory, Colleges and Universities**.

The information presented in this report draws on IPEDS surveys that solicited information concerning institutional characteristics, enrollment, degrees, and finances. The higher education portion of this system is a census of accredited 2- and 4-year colleges. Since these surveys cover all institutions in the universe, the data are not subject to sampling error.

However, they are subject to nonsampling error, the sources of which vary with the survey instrument. Each survey will therefore be discussed separately. Information concerning the nonsampling error of the enrollment and degrees surveys is drawn extensively from the HEGIS Post-Survey Validation Study conducted in 1979.

Institutional Characteristics. This survey provided the basis for the universe of institutions presented in the *Education Directory, Colleges and Universities*. The universe comprised institutions that met certain accreditation criteria and offered at least a 1-year program of college-level studies leading toward a degree. All of these institutions were certified as eligible by the U.S. Department of Education's Division of Eligibility and Agency Evaluation. Each fall, institutions listed in the previous year's *Directory* were asked to update a computer printout of their information.

Fall Enrollment. This survey has been part of the IPEDS or HEGIS series since 1966. The enrollment survey response rate was relatively high; the 1991 response rate was 86.6 percent. Major sources of nonsampling error for this survey were classification problems, the unavailability of needed data, interpretation of definitions, the survey due date, and operational errors. Of these, the classification of students appears to have been the main source of error. Institutions had problems in correctly classifying first-time freshmen, other first-time students, and unclassified students for both full-time and part-time categories. These problems occurred most often at 2-year institutions (private and public) and private 4-year institutions. In the 1977–78 HEGIS validation studies, the classification problem led to an estimated overcount of 11,000 full-time students and an undercount of 19,000 part-time students. Although the ratio of error to the grand total was quite small (less than 1 percent), the percentage of errors was as high as 5 percent for detailed student levels and even higher at certain aggregation levels.

Beginning with fall 1986, the survey system was redesigned with the introduction of the Integrated Postsecondary Education (IPEDS) (see above). The new survey system comprises all postsecondary institutions, but also maintains comparability with earlier surveys by allowing HEGIS institutions to be tabulated separately. The new system also provides for preliminary and revised data releases. This allows the Center flexibility to release early data sets while still maintaining a more accurate final data base.

Completions. This survey was part of the HEGIS series throughout its existence. However, the degree classification taxonomy was revised in 1970–71 and 1982–83. Collection of degree data has been maintained through the IPEDS system.

Though information from survey years 1970–71 through 1981–82 is directly comparable, care must be taken if information before or after that period is included in any comparison. Degrees-conferred trend tables arranged by the 1982-83 classification were added to *Projections of Education Statistics* to provide consistent data from 1970–71 to 1988–89. Data in this edition on associate degrees are not comparable with figures for earlier years. The nonresponse rate did not appear to be a significant source of nonsampling error for this survey. The return rate over the years was high, with the response rate for the 1989–90 survey at 92.3 percent. Because of the high return rate, nonsampling error caused by imputation was also minimal.

The major sources of nonsampling error for this survey were differences between the NCES program taxonomy and taxonomies used by the colleges, classification of double majors and double degrees, operational problems, and survey timing. In the 1979 HEGIS validation study, these sources of nonsampling were found to contribute to an error rate of 0.3 percent overreporting of bachelor's degrees and 1.3 percent overreporting of master's degrees. The differences, however, varied greatly among fields. Over 50 percent of the fields selected for the validation study had no errors identified. Categories of fields that had large differences were business and management, education, engineering, letters, and psychology. It was also shown that differences in proportion to the published figures were less than 1 percent for most of the selected fields that had some errors. Exceptions to these were: master's and Ph.D. programs in labor and industrial relations (20 percent and 8 percent); bachelor's and master's programs in art education (3 percent and 4 percent); bachelor's and Ph.D. programs in business and commerce, and in distributive education (5 percent and 9 percent); master's programs in philosophy (8 percent); and Ph.D. programs in psychology (11 percent).

Financial Statistics. This survey was part of the HEGIS series and has been continued under the IPEDS system. Changes were made in the financial survey instruments in fiscal years (FY) 1976, 1982, and 1987. The FY 76 survey instrument contained numerous revisions to earlier survey forms and made direct comparisons of line items very difficult. Beginning in FY 82, Pell Grant data were collected in Federal restricted grants and contracts revenues and restricted scholarships and fellowships expenditures. The introduction of the Integrated Postsecondary Education Data System (IPEDS) in the FY 87 survey included several important changes to the survey instrument and data processing procedures. While these changes were significant, considerable effort has been made to present only comparable information on trends in this report and to note inconsistencies. Finance tables for this publication have been adjusted by subtracting the largely duplicative Pell Grant amounts from the later data to maintain comparability with pre-FY 82 data.

Possible sources of nonsampling error in the financial statistics include nonresponse, imputation, and misclassification. The response rate has been about 85 to 90 percent for most of the years reported. The response rate for the FY 1989 survey was 83.5 percent.

Two general methods of imputation were used in HEGIS. If the prior years' data were available for a nonresponding institution, these data were inflated using the Higher Education Price Index and adjusted according to changes in enrollments. If there were no data for the previous four years, current data were used from Peer institutions selected for location (state or region), control, level, and enrollment size of institution. In most cases, estimates for nonreporting institutions in IPEDS were made using data from peer institutions.

Beginning with FY 87, the new system (IPEDS) comprises all postsecondary institutions, but also maintains comparability with earlier surveys by allowing 2- and 4-year HEGIS institutions to be tabulated separately. The finance data tabulated for this publication reflect totals for the HEGIS or higher education institutions only.

To reduce reporting error, NCES used national standards for reporting finance statistics. These standards are contained in *Financial Accounting and Reporting Manual for Higher Education* published in 1990 by the National Association of College and University Business Officers. Definitions and formats in the survey, wherever possible, are consistent with those in this text.

Questions concerning the surveys used as data sources for this report or other questions concerning HEGIS can be directed to:

Postsecondary Education Statistics Division
National Center for Education Statistics
555 New Jersey Avenue NW
Washington, DC 20208

Bureau of the Census

Current Population Survey

Current estimates of school enrollment, as well as social and economic characteristics of students, are based on data collected in the Census Bureau's monthly survey of about 60,000 households. The monthly Current Population Survey (CPS) sample consists of 729 areas comprising 1,973 counties, independent cities, and minor civil divisions throughout the 50 states and the District of Columbia. The sample was initially selected from the 1980 census files and is periodically updated to reflect new housing construction.

The monthly CPS deals primarily with labor force data for the civilian noninstitutional population (i.e., excluding military personnel and their families living on post and inmates of institutions). In addition, on October of each year, supplemental questions are asked about highest grade completed, level of current enrollment, attendance status, number and types of courses, degree or certificate objective, and type of organization offering instruction for each member of the household.

The estimation procedure used for the monthly CPS data involves inflating weighted sample results to independent estimates of characteristics of the civilian noninstitutional population in the United States by age, sex, and race. These independent estimates are based on statistics from decennial censuses that include statistics on births, deaths, immigration, and emigration and statistics on the population in the armed services. Generalized standard error tables are in the *Current Population Reports*. The data are subject to both nonsampling and sampling errors.

More information is available in the *Current Population Reports*, Series P-20, or by contacting:

Education and Social Stratification Branch
Bureau of the Census
U.S. Department of Commerce
Washington, DC 20233

School Enrollment. Each October, the Current Population Survey (CPS) includes supplemental questions on the enrollment status of the population 3 years old and over. The main sources of nonsampling variability in the responses to the supplement are those inherent in the survey instrument. The question concerning educational attainment may be sensitive for some respondents who may not want to acknowledge their lack of a high school diploma. The question of current enrollment may not be answered accurately for various reasons. Some respondents may not know current grade information for every student in the household, a problem especially prevalent for households with members in college or in nursery school. Confusion over college credits or hours taken by a student may make it difficult to determine the year in which the student is enrolled. Problems may occur with the definition of nursery school (a group or class organized to provide educational experiences for children) where respondents' interpretations of "educational experiences" vary.

Questions concerning the CPS "School Enrollment" survey may be directed to:

Education and Social Stratification Branch
Bureau of the Census
U.S. Department of Commerce
Washington, DC 20233

Other Sources

National Education Association

Estimates of School Statistics

The National Education Association (NEA) reports teacher, revenue, and expenditure data in its annual publication, *Estimates of School Statistics*. Each year, NEA prepares regression-based estimates of financial and other education statistics and submits them to the states for verification. Generally, about 30 states adjust these estimates based on their own data. These preliminary data are published by NEA along with revised data from previous years. States are asked to revise previously submitted

data as final figures become available. The most recent publication contains all changes reported to the NEA.

Some expenditure projections use revised estimates of financial data prepared by NEA because this organization was the most current source. Since expenditure data reported to NCES must be certified for use in Department of Education formula grant programs (such as Chapter I of the Education Consolidation and Improvement Act), NCES data are not available as soon as NEA estimates.

Further information on NEA surveys can be obtained from:

National Education Association—Research
1201 16th Street NW
Washington, DC 20036

DRI/McGraw-Hill

DRI/McGraw-Hill provides an information system that includes more than 125 databases: simulation and planning models; regular publications and special studies; data retrieval and management systems; and access to experts on economic, financial, industrial, and market activities. One service is the DRI U.S. Annual Model Forecast Data Bank, which contains annual projections of the U.S. economic and financial conditions, including forecasts for the federal government, incomes, population, prices and wages, and state and local government, over a long-term (10 to 25-year) forecast period.

Additional information is available from:

DRI/McGraw-Hill
24 Hartwell Avenue
Lexington, MA 02173

Appendix D

Glossary

Data Terms

Associate degree: A degree granted for the successful completion of a subbaccalaureate program of studies, usually requiring at least 2 years (or the equivalent) of full-time college-level study. This term includes degrees granted in a cooperative or work–study program.

Average daily attendance (ADA): The aggregate attendance of a school during a reporting period (normally a school year) divided by the number of days school is in session during this period. Only days on which the pupils are under the guidance and direction of teachers should be considered days in session.

Average daily membership (ADM): The aggregate membership of a school during a reporting period (normally a school year) divided by the number of days school is in session during this period. Only days on which the pupils are under the guidance and direction of teachers should be considered as days in session. The average daily membership for groups of schools having varying lengths of terms is the average of the average daily memberships obtained for the individual schools.

Bachelor's degree: A degree granted for the successful completion of a baccalaureate program of studies, usually requiring at least 4 years (or the equivalent) of full-time college-level study. This term includes degrees granted in a cooperative or work–study program.

Classroom teacher: A staff member assigned the professional activities of instructing pupils in self-contained classes or courses, or in classroom situations. Usually expressed in full-time equivalents.

Class size: The membership of a class at a given date.

Cohort: A group of individuals that have a statistical factor in common, for example, year of birth.

College: A postsecondary school that offers a general or liberal arts education, usually leading to an associate, bachelor's, master's, doctor's, or first-professional degree. Junior colleges and community colleges are included in this term.

Constant dollars: Dollar amounts that have been adjusted by means of price and cost indexes to eliminate inflationary factors and allow direct comparison across years.

Consumer Price Index (CPI): This price index measures the average change in the cost of a fixed market basket of goods and services purchased by consumers.

Current dollars: Dollar amounts that have not been adjusted to compensate for inflation.

Current expenditures (elementary/secondary): The expenditures for operating local public schools, excluding capital outlay and interest on school debt. These expenditures include such items as salaries for school personnel, fixed charges, student transportation, school books and materials, and energy costs.

Current expenditures per pupil in average daily attendance: Current expenditures for the regular school term divided by the average daily attendance of full-time pupils (or full-time-equivalency of pupils) during the term. See also *current expenditures* and *average daily attendance*.

Current-fund expenditures (higher education): Money spent to meet current operating costs, including salaries, wages, utilities, student services, public services, research libraries, scholarships and fellowships, auxiliary enterprises, hospitals, and independent operations. Excludes loans, capital expenditures, and investments.

Current Population Survey: See Appendix C, Data Sources.

Disposable income: Current income received by persons less their contributions for social insurance, personal tax, and nontax payments. It is the income available to persons for spending and saving. Nontax payments include passport fees, fines and penalties, donations, and tuitions and fees paid to schools and hospitals operated mainly by the government. See also *personal income*.

Doctor's degree: An earned degree carrying the title of doctor. The Doctor of Philosophy degree (Ph.D.) is the highest academic degree and requires mastery within a field of knowledge and demonstrated ability to perform scholarly research. Other doctorates are awarded for fulfilling specialized requirements in professional fields, such as education (Ed.D.), musical arts (D.M.A.), business administration (D.B.A.), and engineering (D.Eng. or D.E.S.). Many doctor's degrees in both academic and professional fields require an earned master's degree as a prerequisite. First-professional degrees, such as M.D. and D.D.S., are not included under this heading.

Educational and general expenditures: The sum of current funds expenditures on instruction, research, public service, academic support, student services, institutional support, operation and maintenance of plant, and awards from restricted and unrestricted funds.

Elementary school: A school classified as elementary by state and local practice and composed of any span of grades not above grade 8. A preschool or kindergarten school is included under this heading only if it is an integral part of an elementary school or a regularly established school system.

Elementary and secondary schools: As used in this publication, includes only regular schools, that is, schools that are part of state and local school systems and also most not-for-profit private elementary and secondary schools, both religiously affiliated and nonsectarian. Schools not included in this term are subcollegiate departments of institutions of higher education, American residential schools for exceptional children, federal schools for Indians, and federal schools on military posts and other federal installations.

Enrollment: The number of students registered in a given school unit at a given time, generally in the fall of a year.

Expenditures: Charges incurred, whether paid or unpaid, that are presumed to benefit the current fiscal year. For elementary and secondary schools, these include all charges for current outlays plus capital outlays and interest on school debt. For institutions of higher education, these include current outlays plus capital outlays. For government, these include charges net of recoveries and other correcting transactions other than for retirement of debt, investment in securities, or extension of credit. Government expenditures include only external transactions, such as the provision of perquisites or other payments in kind. Aggregates for groups of governments exclude intergovernmental transactions.

Expenditures per pupil: Charges incurred for a particular period of time divided by a student unit of measure, such as average daily attendance or average daily membership.

First-professional degree: A degree that signifies both completion of the academic requirements for beginning practice in a given profession and a level of professional skill beyond that normally required for a bachelor's degree. This degree usually is based on a program requiring at least 2 academic years of work before entrance and a

total of at least 6 academic years of work to complete the degree program, including both prior required college work and the professional program itself. By NCES definition, first-professional degrees are awarded in the fields of dentistry (D.D.S or D.M.D.), medicine (M.D.), optometry (O.D.), osteopathic medicine (D.O.), pharmacy (D.Phar.), podiatric medicine (D.P.M.), veterinary medicine (D.V.M.), chiropractic (D.C. or D.C.M.), law (LL.B. or J.D.), and theological professions (M.Div. or M.H.L.).

First-professional enrollment: The number of students enrolled in a professional school or program that requires at least 2 years of academic college work for entrance and a total of at least 6 years for a degree. By NCES definition, first-professional enrollment includes only students in certain programs. (See *first-professional degree* for a list of programs.)

Full-time enrollment: The number of students enrolled in higher education courses with total credit load equal to at least 75 percent of the normal full-time course load.

Full-time-equivalent (FTE) enrollment: For institutions of higher education, enrollment of full-time students, plus the full-time equivalent of part-time students as reported by institutions. In the absence of an equivalent reported by an institution, the FTE enrollment is estimated by adding one-third of part-time enrollment to full-time enrollment.

Full-time worker: In educational institutions, an employee whose position requires being on the job on school days throughout the school year at least the number of hours the schools are in session; for higher education, a member of an educational institution's staff who is employed full time.

Graduate: An individual who has received formal recognition for the successful completion of a prescribed program of studies.

Graduate enrollment: The number of students who hold the bachelor's or first-professional degree, or the equivalent, and who are working toward a master's or doctor's degree. First-professional students are counted separately. These enrollment data measure those students who are registered at a particular time during the fall. At some institutions, graduate enrollment also includes students who are in postbaccalaureate classes but not in degree programs.

High school: A secondary school offering the final years of high school work necessary for graduation, usually including grades 10, 11, and 12 (in a 6-3-3 plan), or grades 9, 10, 11, and 12 (in a 6-2-4 plan).

Higher education: Study beyond secondary school at an institution that offers programs terminating in an associate, baccalaureate, or higher degree.

Higher education institutions (traditional classifications):

4-year institution: An institution legally authorized to offer and offering at least a 4-year program of college-level studies wholly or principally creditable toward a bachelor's degree. A university is a postsecondary institution that typically includes one or more graduate professional schools.

2-year institution: An institution legally authorized to offer and offering at least a 2-year program of college-level studies that terminates in an associate degree or is principally creditable toward a baccalaureate.

Higher Education Price Index: A price index which measures average changes in the prices of goods and services purchased by colleges and universities through current-fund education and general expenditures (excluding expenditures for sponsored research and auxiliary enterprises).

Instructional staff: Full-time-equivalent number of positions, not the number of individuals occupying the positions during the school year. In local schools, it includes all public elementary and secondary (junior and senior high) day-school positions that are in the nature of teaching or the improvement of the teaching–learning situation. Includes consultants or supervisors of instruction, principals, teachers, guidance personnel, librarians, psychological personnel, and other instructional staff. Excludes administrative staff, attendance personnel, clerical personnel, and junior college staff.

Master's degree: A degree awarded for successful completion of a program generally requiring 1 or 2 years of full-time college-level study beyond the bachelor's degree. One type of master's degree, including the Master of Arts degree (M.A.) and the Master of Science degree (M.S.) is awarded in the liberal arts and sciences for advanced scholarship in a subject field or discipline and demonstrated ability to perform scholarly research. A second type of master's degree is awarded for the completion of a professionally oriented program, for example, an M.Ed. in education, an M.B.A. in business administration, an M.F.A. in fine arts, an M.M. in music, an M.S.W. in social work, or an M.P.A. in public administration. A third type of master's degree is awarded in professional fields for study beyond the first-professional degree, for example, the Master of Laws (LL.M.) and Master of Science in various medical specializations.

Part-time enrollment: The number of students enrolled in higher education courses with a total credit load of less than 75 percent of the normal full-time credit load.

Personal income: Current income received by persons from all sources minus their personal contributions for social insurance. Classified as "persons" are individuals (including owners of unincorporated firms), nonprofit institutions serving individuals, private trust funds, and private noninsured welfare funds. Personal income includes transfers (payments not resulting from current production) from government and business such as social security benefits, military pensions, and so forth, but excludes transfers among persons.

Postbaccalaureate enrollment: The number of graduate and first-professional students working toward advanced degrees and students enrolled in graduate-level classes but not enrolled in degree programs. See also *graduate enrollment* and *first-professional enrollment*.

Private institution: A school or institution that is controlled by an individual or agency other than a state, a subdivision of a state, or the federal government; that is usually supported primarily by other than public funds; and the operation of whose program rests with other than publicly elected or appointed officials.

Property tax: The sum of money collected from a tax levied against the value of property.

Public school or institution: A school or institution controlled and operated by publicly elected or appointed officials and deriving its primary support from public funds.

Pupil–teacher ratio: The enrollment of pupils at a given period of time, divided by the full-time-equivalent number of classroom teachers serving these pupils during the same period.

Revenues: All funds received from external sources, net of refunds and correcting transactions. Noncash transactions such as receipt of services, commodities, or other receipts "in kind" are excluded, as are funds received from the issuance of debt, liquidation of investments, or nonroutine sale of property.

Revenues receipts: Additions to assets that do not incur an obligation that must be met at some future date and do not represent exchanges of property for money. Assets must be available for expenditures.

Salary: The total amount regularly paid or stipulated to be paid to an individual, before deductions, for personal services rendered while on the payroll of a business or organization.

School: A division of the school system consisting of students in one or more grades or other identifiable groups and organized to give instruction of a defined type. One school may share a building with another school or one school may be housed in several buildings.

Secondary instructional level: The general level of instruction provided for pupils in secondary schools (generally covering grades 7 through 12 or 9 through 12) and any instruction of a comparable nature and difficulty provided for adults and youth beyond the age of compulsory school attendance.

Secondary school: A school including any span of grades beginning with the next grade following an elementary or middle school (usually 7, 8, or 9) and ending with or below grade 12. Both junior high schools and senior high schools are included.

Senior high school: A secondary school offering the final years of high school work necessary for graduation.

Student: An individual for whom instruction is provided in an educational program under the jurisdiction of a school, school system, or other educational institution. No distinction is made between the terms ''student'' and ''pupil,'' although ''student'' may refer to one receiving instruction at any level while ''pupil'' refers only to one attending school at the elementary or secondary level. The term ''student'' is used to include individuals at all instructional levels. A student may receive instruction in a school facility or in another location, such as at home or in a hospital. Instruction may be provided by direct student-teacher interaction or by some other approved medium, such as television, radio, telephone, or correspondence.

Tax base: The collective value of objects, assets, and income components against which a tax is levied.

Total expenditure per pupil in average daily attendance: Includes all expenditures allocable to per pupil costs divided by average daily attendance. These allocable expenditures include current expenditures for regular school programs, interest on school debt, and capital outlay. Beginning in 1980-81, expenditures for administration by state governments are excluded and expenditures for other programs (summer schools, community colleges, and private schools) are included.

Unclassified students: Students who are not candidates for a degree or other formal award, although they are taking higher education courses for credit in regular classes with other students.

Undergraduate students: Students registered at an institution of higher education who are working in a program leading to a baccalaureate or other formal award below the baccalaureate, such as an associate degree.

Statistical Terms

Auto-Correlation: Correlation of the error terms from different observations of the same variable. Also called *serial correlation.*

Degrees of freedom: The number of free or linearly independent sample observations used in the calculation of a statistic.

Dependent variable: A mathematical variable whose value is determined by that of one or more other variables in a function. In regression analysis, when a random variable, y, is expressed as a function of variables x_1, x_2,..., plus a stochastic term, the y is known as the "dependent variable."

Double exponential smoothing: A method that takes a single smoothed average component of demand and smoothes it a second time to allow for estimation of a trend effect.

Durbin-Watson statistic: A statistic testing the independence of errors in least squares regression against the alternative of first-order serial correlation. The statistic is a simple linear transformation of the first-order serial correlation of residuals and, although its distribution is unknown, it is tested by bounding statistics that follow R. L. Anderson's distribution.

Econometrics: The quantitative examination of economic trends and relationships using statistical techniques, and the development, examination, and refinement of those techniques.

Estimate: A numerical value obtained from a statistical sample and assigned to a population parameter. The particular value yielded by an estimator in a given set of circumstances or the rule by which such particular values are calculated.

Estimating equation: An equation involving observed quantities and an unknown that serves to estimate the latter.

Estimation: Estimation is concerned with inference about the numerical value of unknown population values from incomplete data, such as a sample. If a single figure is calculated for each unknown parameter, the process is called point estimation. If an interval is calculated within which the parameter is likely, in some sense, to lie, the process is called interval estimation.

Exogenous variable: Variables for which the values are determined outside the model but which influence the model.

Exponential smoothing: A method used in time series to smooth or to predict a series. There are various forms, but all are based on the supposition that more remote history has less importance than more recent history.

Ex-Ante forecast: When forecasting a dependent variable for some time period t using a model with at least one independent variable, the forecast of the dependent variable is an ex-ante forecast if the values for the independent variables for time period t are themselves not known.

Ex-Post forecast: When forecasting a dependent variable for some time period t using a model with at least one independent variable, the forecast of the dependent variable is an ex-post forecast if the values for the independent variables for time period t are the actual values. Ex-post forecasts are often used in forecast evaluation.

First-Order serial correlation: When errors in one time period are correlated directly with errors in the ensuing time period. Also called *auto-correlation.*

Forecast: An estimate of the future based on rational study and analysis of available pertinent data, as opposed to subjective prediction.

Forecasting: Assessing the magnitude which a quantity will assume at some future point in time: as distinct from "estimation," which attempts to assess the magnitude of an already existent quantity.

Forecast horizon: The number of time periods into the future which are forecasted. Forecasts for next year are said to have a 1-year forecast horizon.

Function: A mathematical correspondence that assigns exactly one element of one set to each element of the same or another set. A variable that depends on and varies with another.

Functional form: A mathematical statement of the relationship among the variables in a model.

Independent variable: In regression analysis, when a random variable, y, is expressed as a function of variables x_1, x_2,..., plus a stochastic term, the x's are known as "independent variables."

Lag: An event occurring at time $t + k$ $(k > 0)$ is said to lag behind an event occurring at time t, the extent of the lag being k. An event occurring k time periods before another may be regarded as having a negative lag.

Maximum likelihood estimation: A method of estimating a parameter or parameters of a population by that value (or values) that maximizes (or maximize) the likelihood of a sample.

Mean absolute percentage error (MAPE): The average value of the absolute value of errors expressed in percentage terms.

Model: A system of postulates, data, and inferences presented as a mathematical description of a phenomenon such as an actual system or process. The actual phenomenon is represented by the model in order to explain it, to predict it, and to control it.

Ordinary least squares (OLS): The estimator that minimizes the sum of squared residuals.

Parameter: A quantity that describes a statistical population.

Projection: In relation to a time series, an estimate of future values based on a current trend.

R^2: The coefficient of determination; the square of the correlation coefficient between the dependent variable and its OLS estimate.

$\bar{R}^2$ (also called the adjusted R^2): The coefficient of determination adjusted for the degrees of freedom.

Regression analysis: A statistical technique for investigating and modeling the relationship between variables.

Rho: A measure of the correlation coefficient between errors in time period t and time period t minus 1.

Serial correlation: Correlation of the error terms from different observations. Also called *auto-correlation*.

Standard error of estimate: An expression for the standard deviation of the observed values about a regression line. An estimate of the variation likely to be encountered in making predictions from the regression equation.

Time series: A set of ordered observations on a quantitative characteristic of an individual or collective phenomenon taken at different points in time. Usually the observations are successive and equally spaced in time.

Time series analysis: The branch of quantitative forecasting in which data for one variable are examined for patterns of trend, seasonality, and cycle.

Variable: A quantity that may assume any one of a set of values.

ISBN 0-16-042091-1